# DR. NORBORNE BERKELEY POWELL

*Presented by the Citizens of the City of Macon to N B Powell Representative of Talbot County in the Senate of the State of Georgia for his manly firmness and political independence in protecting the interests of said City in the State Legislature Dec 1836*

*This book is for all who have interest in the Powell family history and are living that ongoing history. The effort to publish this history is for current and future generations who may never meet one another. The focus is on the direct lineage of NORBORNE BERKELEY POWELL. A tradition transferred to the oldest living male descendant an engraved silver pitcher, given to N.B. Powell in 1836 by the citizens of Macon, Georgia, in appreciation for his efforts on behalf of their interests. His story is in this book.*

# The POWELL Tradition

Compiled and written
by James B. Powell II

Grateful Steps
Asheville North Carolina

Grateful Steps Foundation
Crest Mountain
30 Ben Lippen School Road #107
Asheville, North Carolina 28806

Copyright © 2019 by James B. Powell II

Powell, James B. II
*The Powell Tradition*

Photographs are from the personal collection of family
unless otherwise indicated in a caption.
Gemealogy information on pages 120-122, 126, 131 are modified from
the Internet Presentation of the Barritt family, http://tree.barrittfamily.net/
ISBN 978-1-945714-32-0 Paperback

Printed in the United States of America
at Lightning Source

FIRST EDITION

All rights reserved. No part of this book
may be reproduced in any manner whatsoever
without written permission from the author.

www.gratefulsteps.org

Dedication:

TO ALL THE LADIES WHO MARRIED POWELLS
AND TO OUR DAUGHTERS

Norborne Berkeley Powell     Elizabeth Ann Rebecca Holmes

# Contents

| | |
|---|---|
| Introduction | ix |
| Genealogy | 7 |
| History | 15 |
|   Macon, Georgia | 18 |
|     Wesleyan College | 19, 26 |
|     Banking laws | 19 |
|     Medical licensure | 19 |
|   Chunnenuggee Ridge Community | 28 |
|     Family Homestead | 51 |
|     Garden Club | 57 |
|     Last Will of Norborne Berkeley Powell | 67 |
| Events | 75 |
|   "Keyhole" Reunion | 76 |
|   Cousins Reunions | 96 |
|     Cousins Reunion I | 99 |
|     Cousins Reunion II | 101 |
|     Cousins Reunion III | 105 |
| Appendix | 111 |
|   First Generations | 112 |
|   Lineages | |
|     Richard Holmes Powell | 137 |
|     Benjamin Philip Powell | 159 |
|     Floyd Berkeley Powell | 218 |

# INTRODUCTION

Greetings to all who are Powells or have interest in the Powell family history and are living that ongoing history. The effort to publish this history for us now and for future generations who may never meet one another came to me as the oldest male Powell in direct lineage to NORBORNE BERKELEY POWELL. By tradition, I am in possession of the SILVER PITCHER given to him in 1836 by the citizens of Macon, Georgia, in appreciation for his efforts on behalf of their interests. His story is in this book.

I have known my grandfather, Benjamin Philip Powell and two of his brothers, Richard Holmes Powell and Floyd Berkeley Powell. James Blackmon Powell (my namesake and my father's namesake) died unmarried as a young man, and a fifth brother died in infancy. Three were Sigma Nu fraternity members, two at the University of Alabama, and my namesake, at Auburn (see photos with Sigma Nu pins).

Benjamin Philip Powell

James Blackmon Powell

Richard Holmes Powell

Floyd Berkeley Powell

In my lifetime, the possessors of THE PITCHER were Richard Holmes Powell Jr., Dick and Page's father; James B. Powell, my father; Dr. N.B. Powell, Berkeley's father (also Sigma Nu at the University of Alabama, as were my father, my brother and I); and Key Powell. Key Powell should have been the author and publisher of this effort—he was capable, witty and charming, loving life and his roles in it. But we lost him to cancer too soon.

Preceding my possession of THE PITCHER, historical accounts were all "word of mouth." Prior possessers all knew one another, saw one another at least occasionally and knew the history of the tradition. I worry that our tradition could be lost if not preserved in a more sustainable form. Originally, I wanted a scrapbook—much of which is contained in this book—but the shortcoming was that only the possessor of THE PITCHER would have the information, and thus eventually, the tradition could be lost.

So . . . why do this? Short answer is to attempt to maintain family contact (as each of us may choose or not) and to provide enough copies for each of you for two or three generations, after which a revision and update may be required.

This effort is partly from memory, partly from many sources duly recognized and partly from many bags and folders of letters and articles passed down. All living male Powells were asked to participate, not only in providing information from their *memories,* including their collection of articles and photos, but also of their *current* family and its history. Because of varying sources from varying times, there is an inevitable varying interpretation of happenings and events. This variance is a form of intrigue that invites current participation, which should bring us living Powells more closely connected.

This is a wonderful story of a proud family; its generations of Southern traditions; and its spouses, brothers, sisters and cousins—a history spanning over two hundred years from the Antebellum South; through the War Between the States with its Post-War Reconstruction; the Great Depression; two World Wars, all affecting hardship, pain and loss; to the present.

The twenty-first-century Powells face the same or similar issues that confronted the nineteenth- and twentieth-century Powells, issues that continue to divide us and our country. Knowledge of our past history should provide some confidence in addressing those issues, to wit Senator Powell's address to the Georgia Senate, which is in this book, verbatim.

Cousin Berkeley, a student of this history, is the namesake of our Renaissance Man—the first Dr.

N.B. Powell—and is a gifted photographer and writer whose efforts helped make this book, with all Powells contributing memories, a resounding success.

Only by working with a dedicated local publisher and friend, Micki Cabaniss, was I able to bring this book to fruition. I have asked each Powell to participate by:

• Providing a bio about himself, where he is, what he does, his family and any historical articles or photographs, and anecdotes about the Powell lineage (weddings, reunions).

• Providing a current address (both Email and USPS and phone numbers).

• Providing a full name, nicknames, birthdays and the same information for the children and grandchildren, including preceding generations, i.e. father and grandfather.

A master genealogy chart depicts the male lineage. The Appendix has the information as provided.

Why did our successful forebearer leave all his achievements in Macon and Georgia and move his family to what essentially was a "new frontier" on Chunnenuggee Ridge in Alabama? We do not know. Perhaps his wife's health, perhaps new challenges, or perhaps economic opportunities. Perhaps his son's marriage to Mary Ann Blackmon of an established Alabama family. With the signing of The Treaty of

Cusseta in 1832, the Creek Indian wars ended, enabling Dr. N.B. Powell to purchase more than four thousand acres of Indians' allotments.

The settlement on Chunnenuggee Ridge grew and prospered as an antebellum community. Dr. Powell started a horticultural society and the first Garden Club in the USA. He became renowned when his likeness was etched by lightning on his study's window pane. He continued his medical practice and successful farming. The original home, "Old Field House," still exists and is owned currently by the Smith family. An added brick façade and porch is on the current house, but inside, the main house is as it was in the 1840s. Photos of that time are on the walls. Below the ridge and behind the house is the family burial site. Photos and available accounts are included in this book.

I know first-hand this history and these sites, having grown up in Union Springs, Alabama. The B.P. Powell clan and all my first cousins who visited their grandparents in Union Springs also share these memories. Four recent reunions revived these memories and are included in a special section of the book.

*James B. Powell II*

# GENEALOGY

# The Powell Family Genealogy

The first Powell of early English records was William Powell, who was descended from the royal family of Wales, acknowledged early in the reign of Queen Elizabeth with their "seat" as Castle Madoc in Brecknoch County, Wales. William Powell is credited with rebuilding the castle in the late 1500s. The current representative of the family in England is Nathaniel Powell, Esq. of Buckhurst Hall, Essex County.

From this lineage, Powells emigrated to Virginia. The land upon which Williamsburg, Virginia, was built was first deeded to Benjamin Powell by the king of England. Nathaniel Powell came to Jamestown in 1607. He wrote much of John Smith's *History of Virginia* and made the first map of Virginia, which today is preserved in the British Museum. Powells were among the earliest and wealthiest shipowners and planters in the Colonies, owning much of what is now York County, Virginia.

The Indian Massacre of 1622 took the lives of 342 men, women and children, living in plantations up and down the river from Jamestown Fort. But all at the fort except five survived due to the military planning of Captain William Powell. He was murdered by the Indians later in 1623.

According to these early English records, it is from these Welsh Powie/Powells that we are all descended.

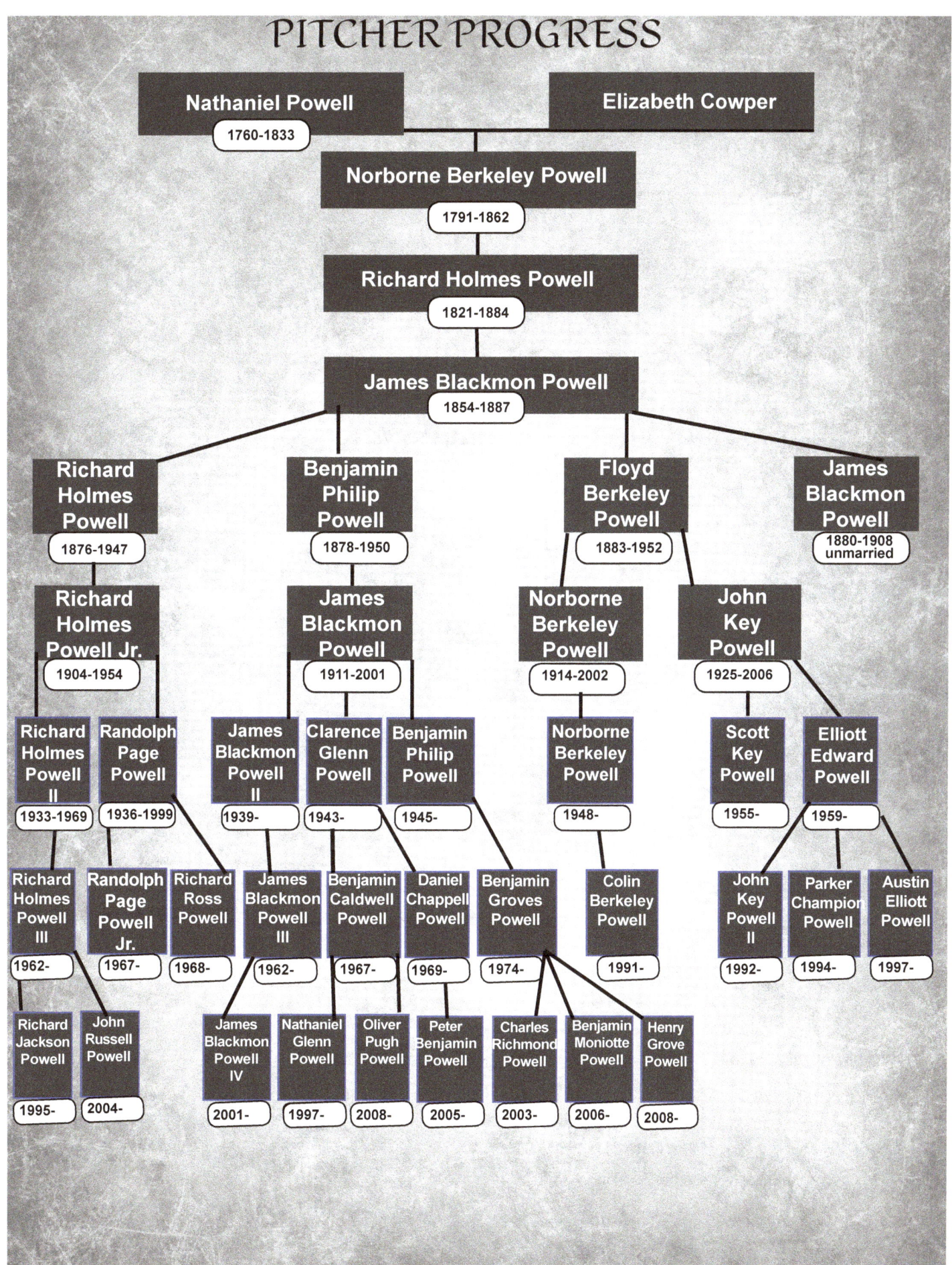

**Editor's Note:** The following narrative is a summary captured by Berkeley from discussions at the Keyhole Reunion:

**N. BERKELEY POWELL, M.D.**
PLASTIC AND RECONSTRUCTIVE SURGERY

713/960-9422

1224 TWELVE OAKS TOWER
4126 SOUTHWEST FREEWAY
HOUSTON, TEXAS 77027

```
          POWELL GENEOLOGICAL NARRATIVE, JANUARY 1984
                     BY JAMES BLACKMON POWELL
                       UNION SPRINGS ALABAMA
```

DR. NATHANIEL POWELL and his brother, WILLIAM POWELL, are said to have come to Virginia with Capt. John Smith. Dr. Nathanial Powell and his whole family were masacered by Indians. His brother, William Powell, gathered together a force of men and avenged his death.

(Several generations are missing)

LUCAS POWELL, descendant of WILLIAM POWELL, was born about 1722. He was a member of the Committee of Safety in Amherst, Virginia in 1775 & 1776. He was elected "one of the 21 most fit, able, and discrete men" of the county to form the county committee "to review the men to be enlisted, etc., and to pay the recruits as soon as enlistment." Lucas Powell first married ELIZABETH EDWARDS in 1754 and they had seven (7) children. She died 20 years later in 1774, whereupon Lucas married a widow, ELIZABETH ROE COWPER, who had 5 daughters and 2 sons by her previous marriage.

NATHANIEL POWELL, born in 1760, the 5th child and son of Lucas Powell and Elizabeth Edwards, married his step-sister, ELIZABETH COWPER, who was the eldest daughter of Elizabeth Roe Cowper. Nathaniel Powell enlisted in the Ninth Virginia Regiment, served through the war, and was present at the siege of Yorktown when he was only 21. He was one of the victorious witnesses of Cornwallis' surrender at Yorktown. In 1827, at the age of 67, Nathaniel and his wife moved to Tennessee from Nelson County, Virginia (formerly Amherst County). Less than 6 years later he died near Lebanon, Tennessee on January 8, 1833, at about the age of 72. There is a monument to his memory in the town of Lebanon, Tenn.

DR. NORBORNE BERKELEY POWELL was born in 1791, the 7th child of Elizabeth Cowper and 31 year old Nathaniel Powell. He was born in Nelson County, Virginia and was educated at Cabell's School in that county and later at the University of Pennsylvania Medical College. He moved to Georgia where he opened an office in Monticello, Georgia in 1816. There he met and married ELIZA HOLMES, the daughter of Rev. Richard Holmes. Still later, while living in Talbatton, Ga., he was elected to the Georgia State Senate from 1835 through 1837. While there he introduced three pieces of legislation:

1) A bill to establish the first State Bank in Georgia
2) A bill which mandated that every physician in Georgia go before a medical board for examination in order to eliminate charlatans and quacks. (This would be the establishment of the State Board of Medical Examiners).
3) Led the fight to keep Weslyan College (the first women's college) in Macon, Georgia. Some say he introduced the bill which founded Weslyan College; but the inscription on a silver pitcher

POWELL GENEOLOGY                                                              PAGE 2

> given to him by the grateful city of Macon suggests that he led
> the fight to keep the college there.

As of February, 1984, the silver pitcher is in the possession of James
Blackmon Powell of Union Springs, Alabama, who is the great-great-
grandson of Dr. N. B. Powell. By tradition, the pitcher is to be
handed down to the oldest living male Powell in the direct lineage.
The inscription on the pitcher reads:

> "Presented by the citizens of the City of Macon to N B Powell
> Representative of Talbot County in the Senate of the State of
> Georgia for his manly firmness and political independence in
> protecting the interests of said city in the State Legislature.
> Dec. 1836"

You could write a book about Dr. N. B. Powell, but just to list a few
of the things he did: He built his home on top of the Chunnenuggee
Ridge (now in the state of Alabama) where it was discovered that
lightning had photographed or etched his picture on a pane of window
glass. Mrs. Augusta Evans Wilson, his niece, used this fact in her
only 'detective novel' entitled "At the Mercy of Tiberius". She wrote
several best sellers before and after the War Between the States.
He started a horticultural society in 1847 and prizes were awarded for
the best horticultural plots, best flower arrangements, etc. Mrs.
Lucile Cary Lowery (a granddaughter of Dr. N. B. Powell) proved by
documentary evidence that his horticultural society became the
Chunnenuggee (Alabama) Garden Club and was the first such club in
America.
Dr. N. B. Powell is buried in a family cemetery in back of his old home
on Chunnenuggee Ridge. (J. B. Powell told me that he hadn't been to
the plot in about 8 years but, even at that time, the place had largely
been reclaimed by the enlarging tree trunks and roots and that many of
the tombstones were already broken and difficult to read. He also said
that he had at his house a list of the headstone inscriptions from the
cemetery. -NBP)

RICHARD HOLMES POWELL was the second of seven children born to Dr.
Norborne Berkeley Powell and Eliza Holmes Powell and was his oldest
son. He married MARY ANN BLACKMON. Colonel Richard Holmes Powell was
wounded at the battle of "Seven Pines" near Richman (sic) during the
War Between the States. (J. B. Powell told me that Dr. N. B. Powell
supposedly went to Richmond to bring his wounded son home and care for
him. In doing so he probably saved Richard's life. -NBP)
The Colonel built his home, "Della Rosa", in Union Springs, Alabama in
1857 and I can remember when Callie and Virginia ("Gee Gee"), two of
his granddaughters, had an open house tea to celebrate it's 100th
birthday.
The same year (1857) he also started the first Sunday School
(Methodist) in Union Springs which met in his own parlor. Between 1859
- 1860 the first Methodist church was built. When it was being
dedicated in 1861, Bishop George Pierce asked if the building had any
indebtedness. When it was reported that $1,600.00 was still due, Dr.
N. B. Powell stood and said, "I will assume $500 of the debt and my
son, Richard Holmes Powell, who is now with General Lee in the Virginia
army will take $500." Seconds later the entire balance of the debt was
raised.

POWELL GENEOLOGY

JAMES BLACKMON POWELL was born in 1854 and married ALMYRA HINSON BROWN.  He was the youngest of the 6 children of Richard Holmes Powell and Mary Ann Blackmon.  He was my grandfather for whom I am named.  He and his wife both died very young. (Dad has said that they had tuberculosis ("consumption"). -NBP)  They had 5 sons:
1) RICHARD HOLMES POWELL
2) JAMES BLACKMON POWELL
3) BENJAMIN PHILIP POWELL
4) FLOYD BERKELEY POWELL
5) ALTO (Died in infancy)

When their parents died, the four boys went to live at "Della Rosa" with their paternal aunt, Virginia Eliza Powell, who married Captain A. H. Pickett.  The Picketts had seven daughters, so with the Powell boys they had a full house, especially at meal times.  My Pop said "When the Powell boys passed their plates for seconds, Captain Pickett would say, 'Try the gravy, boys: the meat is all gone.'"
The Powell boys were not destitute because their parents left an estate to take care of them.  I have a letter written by James Blackmon Powell (one of the four brothers) in 1874 to his step-father when he was beginning his last year in school in Virginia.  It is very interesting and informative.

From James Blackmon Powell and Almyra Hinson Brown, the grandparents of James B., Richard H., Norborne B., and J. Key Powell, I will try to draw a family tree as follows:

```
              Male Descendants Only!
      JAMES BLACKMON POWELL ----- ALMYRA HINSON BROWN
                            !
                            !
 ---------------------------------------------------------------
 !              !                 !              !              !
RICHARD HOLMES  JAMES BLACKMON    BENJAMIN PHILIP FLOYD BERKELEY ALTO
 !              (Died unmarried)  !              !             (Infant
 !                                !              !              death)
 !                                !              !
RICHARD HOLMES         JAMES BLACKMON   NORBORNE BERKELEY  JOHN KEY
 !                         !                   !              !
 ----------------          ----------------   -------------
 !        !                !     !      !     !        !     !
RICHARD  PAGE            JAMES GLENN  BEN  N. BERKELEY SCOTT ELLIOTT
```

12

# Early Genealogy

Editor's Note:
A September 23, 2019, Bloomberg news article was serendipitously noted when the opening paragraph stated:

"Of the roughly 5 million acres in Virginia granted to the Fairfax family by the kings of England in the 17th century, just a sliver—merely 600 acres or so—ended up in the hands of the Powell family by 1827. Politicians and gentleman merchants, the Powells built a lovely mansion they called Llangollen, which then passed from one illustrious owner to the next.

Llangollen is the Welsh derivative of "Church of St. Gall."

With its illustrious history, the current property is listed for sale at $34M. The property is protected by the Virginia Department of Historic Resources, Commonwealth of Virginia, National Register of Historic Places. The original house was a modest 20x15-feet, built in 1795, probably never lived in but built to protect the title. The Loyalist Fairfax family was forced to sell, and the purchaser was Levin (Leven) Powell in a speculation deal in 1807.

It is likely that this Powell is the fifth son of William Powell and one of his three wives. There were five brothers—Lucas Powell, being in our lineage, was the grandfather of Dr. Norborne Berkeley Powell (see diagram on page 14).

# The Lineage of William Powell

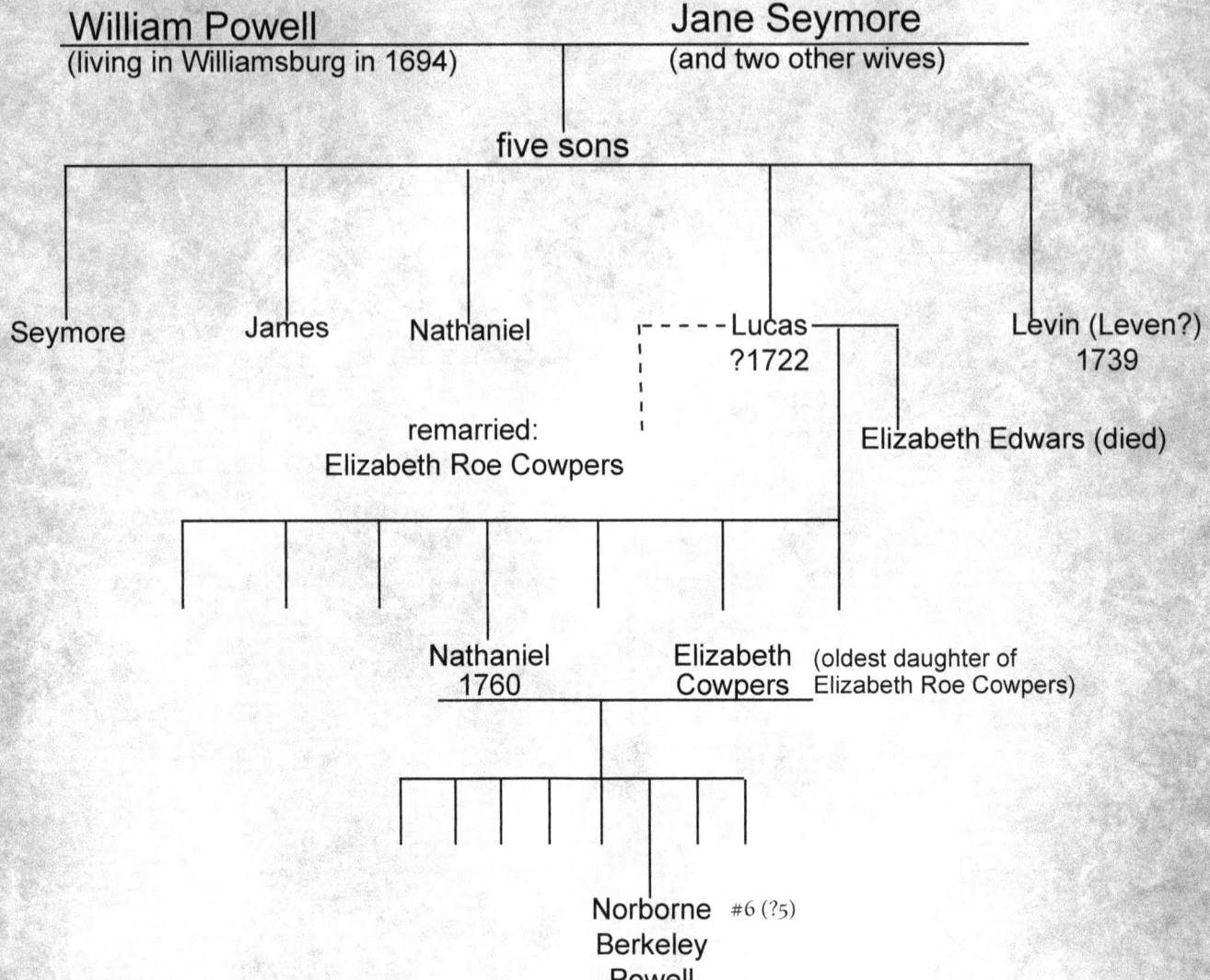

## References for Future Study:

1. Tarmy, James. *Bloomburg News.* "A Gilded Age Playboy's 1,100 Acre Polo Estate is Up for Sale" September 23, 2019.
2. "Llangollen." *National Register of Historic Places.* https://www.dhr.virginia.gov/historic-registers/053-0408/
2. Ball, Rosalie Nolan. *Powell Family History* – Rosalie Nolan Ball, 1938. (written in her own hand.)
3. *The Powell Family in America – Rootswed*, a maintained website: http://freepages.rootsweb.com/~eaglesnest/genealogy/Histories/powell.html.
4. Lucas, S. Emmett. *The Powell Families of Virginia and the South.* Southern Historical Press. 1969, (1977 revision, Greenville.) Note: The editor/publisher did not include our lineage of the eight he researched. There are only minor references to the William Powell lineage, as he states in the third page of the Foreword. There are multiple William Powells in Virginia from 1600–1800.

# HISTORY

Dr. Norborne Berkeley Powell's extensive interests in medicine and horticulture—including plantation crops, forests and fruit-bearing trees, gardens and their presentations and flowers of all seasons—drew people with similar interests to his efforts in organizing annual events. His business and finance acumen, his passion for education and his willingness to serve the public's interests were seen in his Macon life and repeated in his Chunnenuggee Ridge life. Examples of his universal interests and dedication to them are:

- Retrieving his wounded son, Richard Holmes, from Richmond during the War Between the States.
- Continuing his medical practice.
- Donating the land and money to build the Methodist church in Union Springs on the corner of Powell and Blackmon Streets.
- Accepting the first Trustee appointment (in 1856) to the new East Alabama Male College affiliated with the Methodist-Episcopal Church South—which became Auburn University.

The following histories included in this book detail from others' perspectives Dr. Powell's interests:

- *The Wesleyan Alumnae,* February 12, 1925, by his great-grandson, Floyd Berkeley Powell.
- *The Founding of Wesleyan,* the early history with Senator Powell's address to the Senate of the State of Georgia, an article by Marion Napier Smith.
- *Chunnenuggee: A Short History,* compiled by Mrs. Annie Mae Turner, teacher, writer, historian and down-the-street Chunnennuggee friend and neighbor.

# Macon, Georgia

## Wesleyan College
## Banking Laws
## Medical Licensure

# THE WESLEYAN ALUMNAE

NOVEMBER, FEBRUARY, MAY, AUGUST

Subscription Price, $1.00 per year

Entered as second-class matter February 12, 1925 at the Post Office at Macon, Georgia

under the Act of March 3, 1879.

Volume XVIII  
Editor: Eunice Thomson
Member American Alumni Council
Number 1

## WESLEYAN FOUNDER

In the Georgia Legislature in 1836, at the time of Wesleyan's charter was Dr. Norborne Berkeley Powell, a man of high principles and deep insight. It was he who introduced the bill for the charter, and he was presented by the citizens of Macon a silver pitcher and dipper in appreciation for his services on behalf of the people of the city.

In possession of the silver today is his great-grandson, Floyd Berkeley Powell of Tuskegee, Alabama. At our request he graciously consented to write an article about his distinguished ancestor for the magazine, and to send us a picture of himself with the silver pitcher.

### DR. NORBORNE BERKELEY POWELL
#### By Floyd Berkeley Powell

Born September 13, 1791, Nelson County, Virginia

Died October 4, 1862, Union Springs, Ala.

Educated Cabells School, Nelson County, Va. and the University of Pennsylvania Medical College, Philadelphia.

Settled in Georgia at Talbotton in 1816, and practiced medicine in a large area; was elected to the Georgia Senate in 1835, serving in 1835, 1836, and 1837.

During his term in the State Senate, he introduced three outstanding pieces of legislation: (1) the bill which established the first state bank in Georgia, (2) the bill which founded Wesleyan College, first college chartered for women, (3) the bill which made it obligatory that every doctor practicing medicine in Georgia go before a medical board for examination in order to eliminate charlatans and quacks . . . . These far-sighted statutory laws did much to make Georgia famous

Floyd Berkeley Powell

*with the pitcher given to his great-grandfather.*

throughout the nation and the banking law and the medical board law have been copied by many states.

Dr. Powell was an influential figure in Georgia; he had a well rounded education not alone in medicine but in agriculture, horticulture, banking, and the business world; he also was an orator and was amongst the first to speak out for prohibition and made speeches throughout the country for a number of years. He was a great Methodist, and many times served as a lay-preacher; but aside from medicine his real interest was in the field of education. He was a deep student of medicine, and from such studies made heroic efforts to educate people along lines of sanitation, health care and the building of barriers to thwart many common diseases of that time. In 1619 the House of Burgesses was founded in Virginia, and in 1624 Virginia became a royal province. The Powells came over from England in the 1630 period, and two of the Powells are named as Burgesses on the monument standing today in the Jamestown-Williamsburg vicinity. There were related Powells up and down the James River; Dr. Powell was the son of Nathaniel Powell and grandson of William Powell, both of whom left imprints on the early days of Virginia.

Dr. Powell, thinking the climate of the high ridge country of Chunnenuggee near Union Springs, would improve his wife's health, moved to that section of Alabama in December 1838. He bought several thousands of acres of land from the Indians of Macon County, Alabama, and these deeds were signed by President Martin Van Buren in 1841 and by President John Tyler in 1843. The Government being guardian of Indians, the President had to approve the sale of all Indian lands and affix his signature to all conveyances. Several of these old land grants are in the possession of Floyd Berkeley Powell of Tuskegee, and some have been given to the Alabama Archives of History.

Dr. Powell built a home on the top of Chunnenuggee Ridge; he soon had a dozen or more Virginia-Georgia families located there. It was one of the most cultural and interesting of the old settlements of Alabama. One of his first acts was to build a college at Chunnenuggee for the people of that community, and the President of that school was Dr. Ellison, at one time the President of Wesleyan College. Dr. Powell was interested in all types of agriculture and horticulture; he gave to the women of the community five acres of land, and offered silver cups, waiters and bowls for the best garden. There was founded the first garden club of America in 1848 and the plot of land set apart for this horticultural display is owned now by the Garden Club of Union Springs, Alabama, and appropriately marked.

Some years ago, it was claimed by a Boston Garden Club that it had the distinction of being the FIRST Garden Club in America. Mrs. Lucile Cary Lowry of Dallas refuted this claim by documentary evidence in Alabama newspapers which plainly proved that the Chunnenuggee (Alabama) Garden Club was the first such club established in America. From the said club there grew the Alabama Horticultural Society, and Dr. Norborne Berkeley Powell was its first president, founded about 1850 at Montgomery, Alabama's capital. Dr. Powell was a big land-owner and had many slaves; these slaves remained in the Powell family and, even after they were freed, working as share-croppers as late as 1890, and today some of the grandchildren of these slaves remain on the same land. This fact spoke well of the treatment they received.

At the old Powell home on Chunnenuggee Ridge it was discovered that lighting had photographed or etched Dr. Powell's picture on the window glass. Mrs. Augusta Evans Wilson, who was a frequent visitor at this old home, got her idea here for solving the murder in the story "At The Mercy Of Tiberius," and it makes a sensational story. This old window glass is in the Archives of History at our state capitol.

Dr. Powell presents a picture of a great thinker, a great scholar and a true sourthern gentleman. He believed in education, but he was devout in wishing that education do something for future generations. This is shown by the three bills he introduced in one session of the Georgia Legislature back in 1836; establishment of the First State Bank in Georgia; a law requiring medical practitioners to go before a medical board for the purpose of qualifying as good doctors, and eliminating charlatans and quacks; and his bill which established Wesleyan College for Women.

Mrs. Robert M. Smith
254 Buford Pl.
Macon, GA 31204

Editor's note: Mrs. Robert M. Smith, nee Marion Napier, was the daughter of Vida Ross Napier, a Wesleyan alumnus, Class of 1901, who has the distinction of being the first woman to argue a case before the Georgia Supreme Court. This is an edited version of her 1997 "The Founding of Wesleyan." In her research, Mrs. Smith and her brother, Hendley V. Napier, an attorney in Macon, visited my father, James B. Powell, in Union Springs in October 1995 to see and hear firsthand the history of Dr. N.B. Powell and the Chunnenuggee community.

## THE FOUNDING OF WESLEYAN

Wesleyan College was the first college in the world to award degrees to women. The story of how a female college was founded in Macon begins in a community divided. Macon was chartered by the Georgia Legislature in 1823. In the next ten or twelve years, the little town grew rapidly. As new families moved in, small private schools were the only means of educating the children. These schools were not equipped to offer higher education. Boys were sent to distant American colleges, or to Europe, but girls had no opportunity.

Plantation owners needed financing for their large cotton crops; houses and commercial buildings were needed; the real estate and building businesses needed financial support. Shipping on the Ocmulgee River from Macon to Darien and Savannah increased so fast that a business building barges was started to handle the freight. All this activity meant that the small banking institutions of Macon needed help from the State to finance the business community. It was necessary for large business transactions to be handled through banks in the older, larger towns of Savannah and Charleston, leaving the business community in Macon to stagnate while the older cities reaped the benefits of Macon's growing economy.

In 1835 there was ongoing discussion in Macon about the need for education for females. The ability of women to absorb higher education was heatedly debated. Did females need to be educated? Could they learn higher mathematics, psychology and the sciences? Should the city spend the money for something that probably would not work? People were very outspoken, writing letters to the local paper but not signing their names or using fictitious names.

As the town grew, the need for schools became apparent. Several small private schools were sponsored by the local citizens. The largest for females was fifteen miles out of Macon in Clinton, which at the time was larger than Macon. After a City Meeting, the Methodist Church offered to sponsor a female college though sectarian feelings attracted other denominations to sponsor. Debated were reasons why the school would be a benefit to the city and how the benefits would offset the $75,000.00, which the community needed to raise.

A meeting of the citizens of Macon was convened at the Methodist church for the purpose of discussing the claims of the contemplated college for the education of females. Civic leaders and educators were called upon to present their views on the subject. Small private schools could prepare students for higher education, but higher education for girls was not considered necessary. They were not capable of comprehending more than reading, writing a little arithmetic and embroidery. A girl was expected to look pretty, run her husband's home, and have and raise children. But it was becoming apparent that this was faulty reasoning. Girls needed to be educated as much as boys. However, not everyone agreed.

Several groups worked to get pledges of seed money but had not raised enough to make the college a reality. A group of Macon men interested in funding the Ocmulgee bank offered to contribute $25.000.00 if the legislature would authorize more capital so they could make larger loans and take advantage of the shipping on the Ocmulgee River and the rapid business expansion in the growing town.

The Georgia Conference of the Methodist Episcopal Church, by a unanimous vote, took sponsorship of the proposed college under its fostering care and appointed Trustees.

The legislature was in session at the capitol of Georgia, then in 1836 in Milledgeville, when the Bill was introduced to incorporate the Ocmulgee Bank. If passed, the bank stockholders' pledge of $25,000 would begin funding the proposed Female College. The fate of the Bill was in doubt until the last day of the Senate session. Intense interest fostered passionate speeches by both proponents and opponents as the debate progressed to the the Senate vote.

As reported by a lobbyist who observed the debate and wrote:

> Just at this time when all seemed to be lost, and gloom and dismay pressed heavily upon the advocates of the Bill, the honorable Senator from Talbot stepped forth with all the pith-force and talent for which he was so justly admired, and gave a turn to the debate, and saved the Bill in the very throes of death. Yes, my dear sir, the liberal, high-minded, dignified, and honest course of legislation pursued by Mr. Powell of Talbot, has won for himself the admiration of his political opponents, and he stands doubly endeared by his political friends. Citizens of Columbus, inhabitants of Macon, the honorable Senator from Talbot have stood by you in evil as well as good report, and defended you nobly from the foul aspersions that have been so repeatedly and wantonly thrown upon their citizens.

Mr. Powell of Talbot rose and said:

> I feel constrained as a humble advocate of the measure to again ask the indulgence of the Senate, to notice a few of the remarks of the honorable senators who opposed the bill. The senator of Newton spoke of our being fettered and yoked by these banking institutions and objected to the amount of capital stock required and said he would prefer granting those privileges to smaller companies, in order that those companies might be more generally enjoyed. Now, Mr. President, as the gentleman seems to have such awful apprehension about this ruin that will be brought upon the people by the failure of banks and banking and banking incorporations, his mode to remedy the existing and anticipated evils surely must be the most absurd imaginable: for he purposes to augment the number of banking associations without increasing the liability on stockholders or throwing any additional safeguards around the community in which those institutions are located; and, sir, after yielding to the gentleman's propositions and scaling down the amount down, they still continue their strike and exert all their powers of argument and ingenuity to defeat a measure that I regard as being vastly important to the best interest of this country. I confess, Mr. President, my surprise at the course the gentlemen have taken in relation to this Bill: and, sir, the dangers and disasters so eloquently depicted and powerfully portrayed by the senators from Early and Chatham, I confess are enough to alarm and deter the advocates of this Bill. But, Mr. President, I regard these wrought pictures as the offspring of a deluded imagination. It is nothing new, sir, to have politicians become prophets when they fail to carry their projects. We learned a lesson upon that subject from our great politicians in the national legislature. One mighty scene of ruin was to cover the land when the deposits were changed. But, happy for the country, no such predictions were verified: the people continued prosperous and happy.

> In reply to the honorable senator from Chatham, with whom it is my misfortune to differ widely upon this subject, I can assure him that I am as far from being influenced by bonuses or bribes as he or any other man, and was really surprised to hear such motives attributed to those who support this Bill. That honorable gentleman, hereto, in all his legislation has displayed liberality and forecast so characteristic of an able statesman, that he might well be called the defender and champion of internal improvement. But why, Mr. President, this veering about? This comes under the honorable gentlemen's rate. He has told us in the most emphatic and eloquent terms that he would support all and every measure and would tend to increase the commercial facilities and supply the want of banking capitol and more especially if a portion of that capital should be applied to improve the condition of the country. It is far from my purpose to charge any with inconsistency. Yet, Mr. President, how can gentlemen reconcile their conduct after having been the leaders in all the grand schemes of splendid banking and railroad projects. We have shown, Mr. President, that the city of Macon, with her great and growing commerce, receiving eighty thousand bales of cotton annually, amounting to between six and eight millions of dollars, operating upon a banking capital of two hundred thousand dollars! And, sir, what has been the result of such parsimonious legislation? It has been the means of quartering upon our citizens amd foreign agencies, and driving her enterprising merchants, who purchase the produce of the country, to your distant cities and towns more liberally supplied, to obtain the necessary means to carry on her ordinary commercial operations.
>
> In conclusion, Mr. President, permit me to allude to that part of this proposition which has for its object the endowment of a female college. Can the boasted friend of science object to the Bill on this ground? Surely not. And certainly, Mr. President, all must admit that the diffusion of knowledge tends more to ameliorate the condition of man, to elevate his moral character than anything else. I regard the proposition of bestowing a part of the profit of the incorporation upon the female college of Macon, as being a liberal one, and highly creditable to those who conceived the project; and, sir, let others regard it as they may, knowing the source from whence it emanated, its object and design, it affords me heart-felt pleasure to yield it my support. I disregard the idea of any improper means being used to effect the passage of this bill. I have the pleasure of knowing the individuals who are applying to you for these privileges; and I am proud to say that they are enlightened, high minded honorable men, whose responsibility and integrity guarantee the safety of the community. I call upon honorable senators to pause for a moment before they record their vote against a measure so vitally important. The age in which we live requires that we should do something to elevate the female character. Establish liberally endowed seminaries of learning among us, and our soil will be fruitful in genius as profits in female talents as any portion of the inhabitable globe. I trust, Mr. President, the day begins to dawn when we too may boast of ourfemale authors, to women who will look as the ornaments and pride of our glorious republic. To such females we may look with confidence, for our future statesmen and heroes. This subject, sir, is near to my heart. The interest and welfare of my offspring are interwoven with its fibres. The senate, I trust will pardon me for this trespassing upon their time and patience at this late hour.

After the speech by Senator Norborne Berkely Powell, the Bill was passed.

On January 2, 1837, the *Macon Telegraph* referred to the passage of the Bill as follows:

> We mentioned a week or two ago that the citizens of Macon had presented a "silver pitcher" to the Honorable Norborne B. Powell, Senator from Talbot County, for his liberal, enlightened and patriotic course in the legislature, in aid of their local interests and the interests of the State generally. It gratifies us this morning to be able to lay the correspondence on the subject before our readers.

TO THE HONORABLE NORBORNE B. POWELL;
Macon, 28th December 1836

Respected Sir—The enlightened, manly and liberal course pursued by you as a member of the Senate in our state Legislature for the past two years in all questions relating the City of Macon, having convinced us that your friendship for her citizens and decided interest in her interests are firm and undeviating, the undersigned citizens of Macon are desirous to signify to you their approbation of your conduct in some manner entirely unequivocal, not merely on account of the benefit that has accrued to their city by reason of your elevated policy, but to render their homage to the statesmanship spirit that actuated it, have provided for you a Silver Pitcher, of which they crave your acceptance.

Hoping that your useful life may be long be spared to your country, we subscribe ourselves.

Your obliged fellow citizens

Letter received from Norborne Berkeley Powell as follows:
Liberty, Talbot County, 4 Jan. 1837.

Gentlemen—Your communication of the 28th ult. I had the honor to receive by yesterday's mail, and I avail myself of the earliest opportunity of responding. The flattering terms in which you were pleased to allude to my public course during the brief period of my legislative career could not fail to excite in my bosom the liveliest of emotion. To merit the confidence of so an enlightened a portion of my fellow-citizens is to me a source of the highest gratifications. That your young and prosperous city, daily growing in importance, with a population not surpassed for enterprise, intelligence, and patriotism, should be entitled to the fostering care of the legislature, seemed to me altogether reasonable. Having a knowledge of the pecuniary wants and the consequent commercial embarrassments under which your people labored, it afforded me great pleasure to co-operate with the patriotic delegation from your county in effecting the passage of such laws as I deemed important to your prosperity and welfare.

That your petitions for legislative enactments should have met with such violent opposition was to me a matter of deep regret, and charity toward those whom we had to encounter would induce the belief they were in want of correct information relative of the situation in which you were placed.

I am sensible that so distinguished an honor as you propose is more than commensurate with any merit of mine—one so wholly unknown to fame, so little versed in political science, and so recently from the humble walks of private life. In accepting your valuable present, I do so with mingled feelings pride and gratification, and suffer me to assure you gentlemen, I will treasure it as an invaluable memento of your esteem and friendship. Accept for yourselves, the best wishes of my heart and your future prosperity and happiness.

Your friend and fellow citizen,
N.B. Powell

Chartered on December 23, 1836, The Georgia Female College Board of Trustees advised the public that classes would begin on the first Monday in January and conclude on the second Wednesday in July. The first class is said to have been 90 students. In December 1842, the name of the college was changed to Wesleyan Female College, shortened to Wesleyan College in 1917. It is the birthplace of the first sororities in the United States, Alpha Delta Pi in 1851 and Phi Mu in 1852. Wesleyan has the world's oldest alumni association, begun in 1859.

Marion Napier Smith
7/26/1997

# WESLEYAN COLLEGE THRIVES TODAY

As evidenced by the college website https://www.wesleyancollege.edu/:

Wesleyan College is committed to women's education and helping every student find a unique voice and purpose. As the first college in the world chartered to grant degrees to women and shaped by Methodist values, Wesleyan provides students an academically challenging and relevant liberal arts education. Our diverse, inclusive community encourages creativity, innovation, and leadership so all graduates are prepared to thrive in a complex world.

In 2018 the Wesleyan College board of trustees approved a new mission statement that affirms the College's commitment to the undergraduate education of women and the graduate education of women and men. Guiding principles describe a community that is academically challenging, purposeful, inclusive, and connected. Using the slogan "One Wesleyan. Many Voices. Find Yours.," the three-year strategic plan, focuses on recruiting and retaining students and securing the long-term financial health of the institution.

Academic buildings are located around our large, open, central quadrangle. Our beautiful 200-acre wooded campus, along with historically significant Georgian style buildings, is listed in the National Register of Historic Places.

Due to the efforts of the Wesleyan College Alumnae Association, the entire Wesleyan campus is listed in the National Register of Historic Places as the Wesleyan College Historic District. The designation was approved for Wesleyan in 2004 because the campus meets four areas of significance—architecture, landscape architecture, community planning and development and education. The Wesleyan College Historic District includes the entire 200-acre campus and consists of approximately thirty buildings, the majority of which are Georgian Revival-style and historically significant.

# Chunnenuggee Ridge Community

## Family Homestead Garden Club

# CHUNNENUGGEE

## A SHORT HISTORY

> THIS TABLET
> MARKS THE LOCATION OF
> CHUNNENUGGEE PUBLIC GARDEN
> ESTABLISHED MARCH, 1847
> HONORS ITS FOUNDERS
> COMMEMORATES THEIR CIVIC PRIDE
> AND GRATEFULLY RECOGNIZES
> THE SURVIVAL OF THEIR INTERESTS
> IN THE
> IMMORTAL BEAUTIES OF NATURE
>
> HERE EMPLACED MARCH 1947
> BY THE CHUNNENUGGEE PUBLIC GARDEN CLUB
> OF UNION SPRINGS, ALABAMA

## CHUNNENUGGEE
## PUBLIC GARDEN CLUB

FIRST GARDEN CLUB OF AMERICA

UNION SPRINGS, ALABAMA

# CHUNNENUGGEE

Chunnenuggee is an Anglicized Indian word meaning "high bluff" or "up and down." The Indian word is TCHA-NA-NAGHI which means "high long ridge." Sometimes the term used is CHUNNENUGGEE RIDGE, and it refers to the "high long ridge" which early settlers quickly recognized as fertile ground, both the rich prairie land below the bluff and the sandy soil interspersed with rich dark loam on the uplands.

In <u>A History of Bullock County, 1866-1906</u>, written by local historian John Rumph and published in 1955, the following description is given:

"Bullock County presents an interesting geological history in the variety and beauty of its landscape and the nature and variety of its soils. The most outstanding characteristic of the county is the Chunnenuggee Ridge, known locally as 'The Ridge.'

"The Ridge divides the county into two parts and forms the watershed of three river systems: the Pea, the Conecuh, and the Tallapoosa. This ridge is the continuation

-1-

of the high ground that enters the state near West Point, Georgia. The ridge runs southwestwardly across the county, separating the prairie region and the sandy hill region. North of the ridge is a belt of low hills and irregular ridges with a network of V-shaped valleys and wet weather streams known as the 'hill prairie country.' High Ridge in the southwestern section of the county marks the highest elevation. The lowest point is five miles north of Fitzpatrick where Line Creek leaves the county. The western portion of the county is very hilly and rough except in the extreme northern part where the land is fairly level. The roughest terrain is found along the escarpment of Chunnenuggee in the northeastern section."

The ridge is quite evident in the vicinity of Union Springs where the land is marked by a rather abrupt ascent of several hundred feet in height. All deeds to this property along the ridge, between the town of Union Springs and a station called Peachburg, describe the land as being "bounded on the north by the meandering of the bluff." The surface soil here, unlike the prairie land

-2-

below, is sandy and looks as if it had been left there centuries ago by the receding waters of the Gulf of Mexico. However, beneath this layer of sand there is apparently a soil rich enough to nourish the large native trees, shrubs, and flowers which still flourish in it.

After the Creek Indians left this area in 1832, white settlers came from Virginia, Georgia, and other states to develop the virgin soil. Like the patriarchs of old, they brought with them their families, their flocks, and their slaves. They settled first on the low prairie lands, building their houses from logs hewn from native trees. Some of these new plantations contained several thousand acres of land. However, winter rains and bad roads combined to deny the settlers the pleasures of visiting from one plantation to another. Many of the planters left their fields to the supervision of overseers who with slave labor continued cultivating the land. The owners themselves moved to higher ground and built their homes, many of them on the Chunnenuggee Ridge.

One of these early pioneers was a Virginian, Dr. Norborne Berkley Powell who moved to the Chunnenuggee Ridge in 1838. A noted physician, banker, and businessman, he purchased from the Indians several thousand acres of land in what was then Macon County. The deeds to the property were signed by President Martin Van Buren in 1841 and President John Tyler in 1843.

On the site of the Indian War Council Lodge, Dr. Powell built his home on a five acre tract of land and called it "Old Field." The magnificent trees of nearby forests provided the timber and Dr. Powell's own carpenters, bricklayers, and other artisans furnished the labor that produced the beautiful country home of a plantation czar. An architect was evidently available as the home is considered to be a fine example of Greek Revival architecture which flourished between 1820 and 1860. The columns support a full entablature, and the rectangular transom over the door, flanked by side lights, was another popular characteristic of this particular architectural style. The shouldered architrave trim is widely used for the doors and windows. The one-story house has two exterior chimneys. Although the home has been extensively renovated, it remains today structurally very much as it was originally.

And originally it was a comfortable home for the master and his family, the house and grounds alone requiring the work of twenty slaves, each a specialist in his line, to keep it running smoothly.

At the back of the house, beneath the bluff, flowed a cool and abundant spring which furnished all the water needed for home consumption and for the herds of cattle. A primitive but effective refrigeration system, known as a Spring House, kept dairy products, vegetables, and fruits cool and palatable.

This historic home on the Chunnenuggee Ridge is presently owned by Grady and Virginia Smith who have on occasion opened it for visitors on tour.

Lightening photography, an intriguing phenomen guaranteed to whet the interest, is entrenched as a part of the house's

-5-

tradition. During a heavy storm the likeness of Dr. Powell was photographed by lightening as he stood before a window at the rear of the house. The pane of glass, discovered later by a servant, is now preserved in the Alabama State Archives building in Montgomery. The incident was dramatized in a novel by Agusta Wilson called <u>At the Mercy of Tiberius</u>. The story uses lightening photography to untangle a mystery.

Like many southern plantation owners of his time, Dr. Powell loved the flowers and shrubs that grew profusely on the land, and he began to develop his own cultivated flower gardens. The delicious fragrance of wild honeysuckle and the stately beauty of oaks, chestnuts and other native trees soon mingled with the many varieties of carefully nourished shrubs and flowers grown in his home gardens along with the specimen strawberries and other fruits and vegetables. It was natural that Dr. Powell's knowledge of and interest in horticulture would encourage the establishment of an horticultural society in the Chunnenuggee community. The women, too, were interested in gardening and landscaping.

So it was that history records a group of men and women living on the Chunnenuggee Ridge meeting together on the evening of March 6, 1847, for the purpose of organizing a Horticultural Society. The intention was to have monthly exhibits of flowers, fruits, and vegetables in season. Thus was born the Chunnenuggee Horticultural Society which claims to be the first Garden Club in America. The first annual Chunnenuggee Fair was held that year.

Once the "Public Garden" site was secured, the ground was cleared by trained slave gardeners and a special committee was appointed to supervise other committees who worked diligently to develop a perfect garden, giving meticulous care to the time and type of planting.

Minutes of the Chunnenuggee Ridge Horticultural Society reflect the tremendous growth and widespread popularity of this band of ardent gardeners. Persons from nearby Southern cities were brought into the membership. Among the honorary members were nurserymen from as far away as New York and from the neighbor state of Georgia---Augusta, Columbus, and elsewhere.

The monthly exhibits grew into social events with entertainments and suppers. Handsome prizes encouraged the showing of many varieties of flowers artistically arranged. It is noted from the records that dahlia bulbs were often ordered in quantity. It is also noted that the Society decided that anything shown for premium should be grown in the home garden and not be procured elsewhere. By a

-8-

vote of the Society, a small area was set aside in the Public Garden for growing strawberries and cotton, the proceeds to be used for buying premiums for the flower show.

So the Horticultural Society and the Public Garden grew, and it was soon determined that an Annual Fair would be held around the first of May when the flowers were at their best. Known as the Chunnenuggee May Fair, this gala event attracted visitors from near and far. Some arrived by stage coach and the old stage coach inn still stands and has been the home in recent years of the Anderson family.

Following is one account of an early Fair:

"The visitors to the elaborate Chunnenuggee May Fair arrived by way of bright omnibuses drawn by four horses and to the flourish of a clear winding bugle.

"Also following the little road along the edge of the forest to the broad pavilions and rose-covered summer houses in the public gardens, which were the pride of Chunnenuggee Ridge, were many distinguished visitors from afar who came in phaetons and

-9-

barouches and Jinny Lind wagons which were piled high with carpet bags and ladies bonnet boxes."

Though the original layout of the gardens is not known, it is established that a pavillion with a central supporting column surrounded by seats was constructed in 1851. The gardens were enclosed with post and plank fence and were well planted with shrubbery. There were also a number of arbors and a "Lover's Knot" maze.

Evidently rooms were added to the garden house because a later description speaks of "an exhibition house as commodious as a modern club in the Public Garden." It contains "a large salon where concerts were given, a dining room, a hall, and an open pavillion."

The salon, always beautifully decorated for the occasion with a lavish use of cut flowers, was the gathering place for members and the guests for the first evening of the Fair. An excerpt from an old letter indicates how well the Fairs were attended. The letter writer says, "Among the distinguished guests were the top of the pot socially from Columbus, Mobile, and Montgomery as well as many from the Carolinas."

In another account of the May Fair in the early 1850s, R. H. Powell is mentioned as calling the meeting to order. He acted as president since "ladies were not then accustomed to speaking in public." The account continues, "After an introduction by Rev. Williams Henderson, the president's address followed. It was replete with good sense, historical research, classical illusions, and poetic beauty.

"Immediately following this address, the guests repaired to the dining hall where a sumptious feast had been prepared. During this repast soft music floated out from a decorated bower where a small group of Negro players sat. They were probably slaves belonging to Col. Luther Walker who had been trained to play at the entertainments of his beautiful and accomplished daughters. We read that the dessert consisted of ice cream, strawberries, and plain cake, as well as pyramids of beautifully embossed cakes. Since there were no caterers at this time, these cakes were decorated with the skillful fingers of the ladies of the Society."

On one evening of the Fair there was a grand concert given by the young ladies of

-11-

the Ridge in the large salon in the exhibition house, and we read that "the young ladies were charming in their flowered dresden silks as they sat at the harp and piano." And "following the concert an elegant collation was served." After a visit to this most delightful Fair, a young man wrote as follows:

"Flora and Pomona, hand in hand, awakened in me a high admiration for the Chunnenuggee ladies in particular and for horticulture in general, and I made a resolve to forsake bachelorhood and get unto myself a wife, a home and a garden."

History does not record the young man's name nor the details of what might have followed his strong resolve. However, Mrs. Lowery's description of the Public Garden gives us some insight into the romantic possibilities.

"Throughout the grounds of this Public Garden there were summer houses covered with honeysuckle and roses, mingling their perfume with hundreds of blossoms to be inhaled by the young men and women who rested in seats within these flowery retreats to chat or stroll leisurely on the green stretches of lawn beyond. The LOVER'S KNOT was also an intriguing place to wander in such an intricate design that it created a maze with its one concealed entrance, and once within its confines the young ladies and gentlemen were hopelessly lost. The only authoritative statement extant is the admission that it took the 'young lovers at the Chunnenuggee May Fair a remarkable long time to solve the difficulties of escaping from the confines of the tall flowering shrubbery of the Lover's Knot.'"

Since this was strictly an agricultural area, no Fair was complete without specimens of everything grown in the soil as well as samples of the culinary arts of the housewife.

Premiums were awarded and excitement mounted as the time came for the announcement of the coveted awards. In the news accounts of one of the Fairs special mention was made of a Della Robia wreath cleverly designed of strawberries and flowers by Mrs. E. J. Lowery for which she was awarded a prize. In a publication called AMERICAN COTTON PLANTER, we find in the July 1856 issue that a premium for the best essay on horticulture was given to Mrs. Homer Blackmon. Prizes were also given to the women

-13-

skilled in equestrienship, promoted by the young gentlemen of the Ridge. Horseback riding was a universal accomplishment at Chunnenuggee, making for animated contests with skillful and daring riding. An account of this event reads:

"The young ladies wore sweeping riding habits and carried gold topped riding crops, splendidly mounted on spirited horses. It was a thrilling moment when each took the course. . . ."

Mrs. Lowery included in her address a reference to an article written by a visitor to Chunnenuggee in the early fifties and published in the ALABAMA JOURNAL:

"The reputation of this pleasant section, so well known, is by no means exaggerated, either in respect to its floral production, the beauty and accomplishment of the ladies, or the general high culture of its people. I left this pleasant section leaving my kindest thoughts for the genial and refined hospitality that greeted me at every step. Now, my dear Junior, as you are, I suspect, a marrying man, do not in your celebate wanderings forget to visit this garden spot of loveliness and pleasure and you will not wish to go

-14-

further.

"Nowhere will you find more finished beauty, more heightened, refined and ladylike breeding, combined with all that is admirable in household virtues, than in this flower gem among the hills of Macon County.

(Note: this region later became a part of a new county called Bullock)

"On the last night of the Fair, tableaus were given by the young ladies and gentlemen. One particularly effective tableau was the flower filled barge of Elaine. A golden haired Miss Cotton was breath-takingly lovely as the white clad recumbent Elaine, with lilies at her breast, while a young West Point Officer, with his sword at his side, was a handsome, if unrepentant Lancelot."

There is much more to the history of this thriving section of what is now in Bullock COunty. Before the Civil War it was an active community, the center of culture, education, and social life as well a place where horticulture was promoted to the highest degree. Many prominent families lived and worked and entertained on the Ridge, and their stories are worth the telling and perhaps will be at some future date. But none is more thrilling and spectacular than the accounts that have been preserved about the Public Garden and the Chunnenuggee Horticultural Society.

On April 30, 1938, the Annual Convention of the Garden Club of Alabama was in session in Selma, Alabama. Mrs. N. D. Denson of Opelika had been assigned to escort the speaker to the platform. She introduced Mrs. Lucille Cary Lowery, the granddaughter of Dr. Norborne Berkley Powell, the man who donated the land for the First Public Garden at Chunnenuggee.

Mrs. Lowery's address has been preserved in a publication printed and distribted by the Chunnenuggee Public Garden Club of Union Springs. Edited by Mrs. T. M. Francis, then Conservation Chairman of the Garden Club of Alabama, the booklet is called HOME IDEAS, GARDENING, AND CRAFTS BOOK. This book is now out of print and only a few copies remain with members of the Club. The information for this little booklet came primarily from Mrs. Lowery's address. Parts were paraphrased and others quoted directly. Other sources used in the preparation of this brief history are old issues of the Union Springs HERALD, John Rumph's HISTORY OF BULLOCK COUNTY, 1866-1906, MACON REPUBLIC, Tuskegee newspaper of April 18, 1850, MEMORIAL RECORD of ALABAMA published in 1880, old issues of the ALABAMA JOURNAL, and HISTORIC ASSETS OF BULLOCK COUNTY, a publication of the South Central Alabama Development Commission.

    Through the years the Chunnenuggee Public Garden Club has maintained the portion of land preserved as a small replica of the original Public Gardens. The spot is located across the road from the old Powell home which is now the residene of Virginia and Grady Smith. This spot was given to the Garden Club by Mrs. Janice Ikenberry, the former Janice Turnipseed who is the fourth generation heir to the property. In 1976 she gave a large portion of land, including some 250 acres of pecan trees, to Auburn University where she and her husband Dr. Ernest Ikenberry were professor during their distinguished teaching careers. The land is managed by the Auburn Agricultural Experiment Station.

Largely through the efforts of Mrs. H. T. Wood, current president of the Chunnenuggee Public Garden Club, Auburn University has now agreed to contribute to the club the original five acres identified as the location of the first Public Garden.

In 1948 a marker was placed on the site of the Garden and the spot has been cared for through the years by the members of the Chunnenuggee Public Garden Club.

The following account was written by Mrs. Walton Orr and printed in the Union Springs HERALD June 10, 1948.

### UNVEILING OF MARKER HISTORICAL EVENT

*Under the same avenue of stately oaks, where members of the first Garden Club in America often met, and across a road from the original five-acre garden, the members of the Chunnenuggee Public Garden Club and friends met on Tuesday afternoon, June 8, 1948, for an auspicious occasion.*

*A bronze marker was unveiled commemorating the organization of the Chunnenuggee Horticultural Society in 1847. This marker was given by Mrs. Lucille Cary Lowery of Dallas, Texas, a descendant of Dr. N. B. Powell, who gave the land on which the*

-18-

first garden was established. Miss Mittie Wilson, a granddaughter of Col. W. W. Battle, an original member, pulled the cord, as Miss Irene Wilson Orr, a member of the fifth generation of Col. Battle and Capt. William Joseph Lee, paid tribute to those whose memory was honored. The marker is placed in a small garden, surrounded by flowers and shrubbery, on a part of the original garden.

Preceding the unveiling, a most enjoyable program was given, under the beautiful trees leading to the Powell home, now the residence of Mrs. C. R. Barksdale. (NOTE: the home is now, in 1985, the residence of Grady and Virginia Smith) Chairs were grouped near where tables displayed many handsome premiums, now family heirlooms. Mrs. J. T. Wood, president of the present club, presided in a gracious manner.

Miss Mary Cowper Pittman, also a Powell descendant, gave the address of the day in an informal and charming manner. She paid a beautiful tribute to all of the families who settled this community many years ago. They first established culture and then began a beautifucation and constructive program for the advancement of gracious and bounteous living. Proof of the quality of the people of old Chunnenuggee Ridge was given as the speaker read from old records, minutes, and other historical documents. She closed by giving a description of the first Fair held in the

-19-

garden in 1848.

Mrs. F. F. Ravenscroft was introduced and after her interesting remarks, she presented to the present club the handsome silver goblet, a premium won by her grandmother, Mrs. E. A. R. Powell, at the first Fair in 1848, with the date and an appropriate inscription engraved thereon. The goblet was presented to the Garden Club of Alabama at the June 1948 Convention and is now placed in the Alabama State Department of Archives and History.*

Misses Callie Pickett and Mary Ravenscroft, dressed in heirloom dresses, sang sweetly "Long, Long Ago," after which the dedication was held in the little garden, with Rev. C. B. Liddell giving the dedication prayer. After singing "Auld Lang Syne," Rev. H. R. Miller pronounced the benediction.

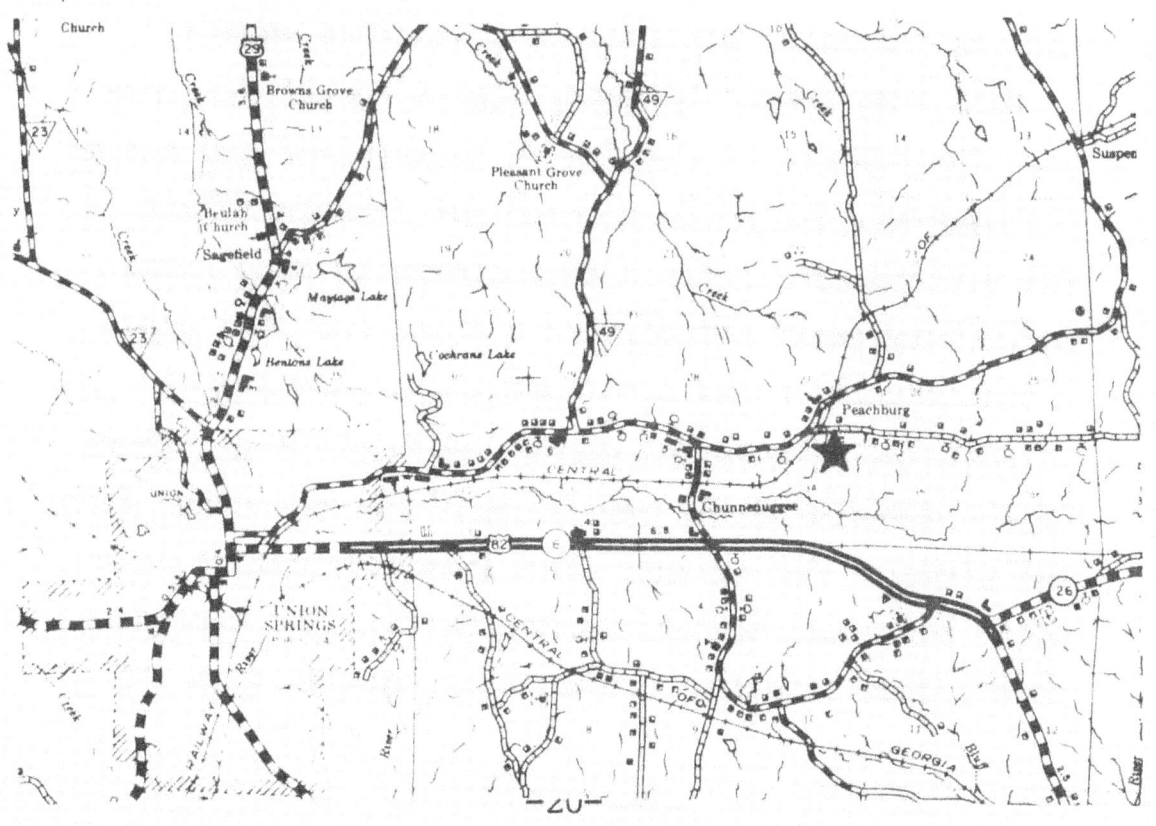

\*     Photo in section "Second Cousins Reunion."

This Publication Is A Product of
TURNER MEDIA STUDIOS
Annie Mae Turner
213 Chunnenuggee Avenue
Union Springs, Alabama 36089

# Family Homestead

The original Powell home, known as "Old Field," is shown on the next page. The picture is as the home appeared in 2014. There is a new brick façade, which hides the original windows that went from the ceiling to the floor and are appreciated only from inside the house. Dr. Norborne Berkeley Powell, who deeded the land for the Garden for $1.00, came from Virginia to Georgia and then to Alabama in 1838. He bought several thousand acres originally occupied by Creek Indians who called the area "TCHA-NA-NAGHI," meaning "long, high ridge." Slave carpenters and bricklayers from his plantation built his home from natural resources in the area. In 1844 the Greek Revival home was completed on the site of a former Indian war council lodge. Dr. Powell's likeness was imprinted on a window pane by lightning during a storm. Author Augusta Wilson dramatized this event in a novel entitled *At the Mercy of Tiberius*, where lightning photography solved a mystery. The glass pane is preserved in the Alabama Department of Archives & History in Montgomery.

Text is modified from the original description
from the Alabama Department of Archives and History:
2006:Co. Rd. 40 east of Union Springs 32.15872N 85.63852W.

The two photos above are displayed in the hallway of the house
by the current owners, the Smiths. The photos are circa 1850.

Home site of Norborne Berkeley Powell
as it appears today

## "OLD FIELD HOUSE"

February, 1978—Page

# THE FACE IN THE WINDOWPANE

by Donnie McCotter

Once upon a time high atop Chunnenuggee Ridge in Bullock County where the Appalachian Mountains begin to fade into the ground, an old doctor stepped to his back door and called across the night to the cook in the back yard. Just at that moment lightning struck so hard a tree cracked and the sky flammed up like daylight.

The doctor went on with his evening activities and thought no more about the great bolt of lightning. But the next morning when the cook came to the main house from the kitchen that was set off like all old kitchens from the house, she was startled by a shadow in the windowpane by the back door. There like a portrait was the old doctor's face in the glass.

And it remains today—a picture struck by lightning, etched forever in a pane of glass.

People came to the old house for years to see that picture in the glass, both to marvel at the mystery of it all and, perhaps, to wonder if such a thing were not befitting a doctor who was famous to that section of Alabama, untamed when Dr. Norborne Berkeley Powell arrived in the 1830s.

Now more than a hundred years later that windowpane has circled through parts of America and, it is said, Europe, too. Long ago it was replaced by a new pane, for the wonder of it all was too great to be contained on Chunnenuggee Ridge near Union Springs.

There are no Doubting Thomases, for the face stares toward the edge of the pane with stern honesty, and one has but to see a picture of the old doctor to know that it is he.

Like a delicate piece of Alabama history it is lovingly handled and almost secretly guarded today in the library of the Alabama Archives and History in Montgomery. Go there, and someone will carefully unwrap a moderate-size piece of glass for you. Slowly, as light begins to focus on the pane, the sharply defined profile of Dr. Powell will come to life.

Something may happen to you at that moment as it did to writer Augusta Evans Wilson, who was so inspired by what she saw, she wrote "At the Mercy of Tiberius". Her story of a murderer who's identity was established from his image with upraised dagger burned into the glass by a timely flash of lightning, is one of many stories and legends that had its beginning at the Powell house on Chunnenuggee Ridge.

Tales come and go about the etching in the glass. Some say it is a man's hand and declare they've seen pictures of the windowpane. Some say that they've heard the story but don't know where the house is located in Alabama. Strangely enough, no one seems to doubt that there is such a picture in glass.

Dr. Norborne Powell does not roam the house that still stands on Peachburg Road like a ghost may do. His spirit seems content to remain in reverent history and in the hearts of family members who still visit the Powell cemetery behind the house built about 1840.

Though the house itself is an inviting-looking one, the people inside make it a warm home, as though to continue a century-and-more tradition.

Virginia and Grady Smith bought the house in 1969 for their five children and themselves. One night when she first moved into the house and all other members of the family were away, Virginia looked into a pane of glass by the back door and saw an etching—just for a moment.

She does not see an etching now, and nor does one notice anything when looking into matching windowpanes at the front of the house. But the camera caught a cloud, or a figure, or an etching that yet nestles inside a windowpane at Dr. Powell's beloved "Old Field House" on Chunnenuggee Ridge, just as though the old doctor doesn't want to leave.

June 22, 1966

Information below is from Mr. and Mrs. R. Jay Lawrence, Union Springs, Alabama.

Dr. Edward Henry Cary, great-grandson of Colonel R. H. Powell, who was born and reared in Bullock County, carried the window pane to Dallas, Texas, and it was their understanding that he later gave it to the Alabama Department of Archives and History where it is currently stored.

Mr. Lawrence remembered seeing it in the house when was a boy. He remembered the family talking about the window pane.

Information below is from Peter A. Brannon, Alabama Archives Curator. Location: Cabinet 27, Drawer 5.

Portrait of Dr. N.B. Powell, taken by lightning in 1850s during a heavy thunderstorm on Chunnenuggee Ridge out from Union Springs, Alabama. House later owned by the C.S. Barkdales.

# Family Burial Site

On a knoll beneath the Chunnenuggee Ridge, about one-forth of a mile behind the Old Field House home, are grave stones of Dr. Powell, his wife and other immediate family members.

James B. Powell, my father at age 88, at the burial site, April 1999.

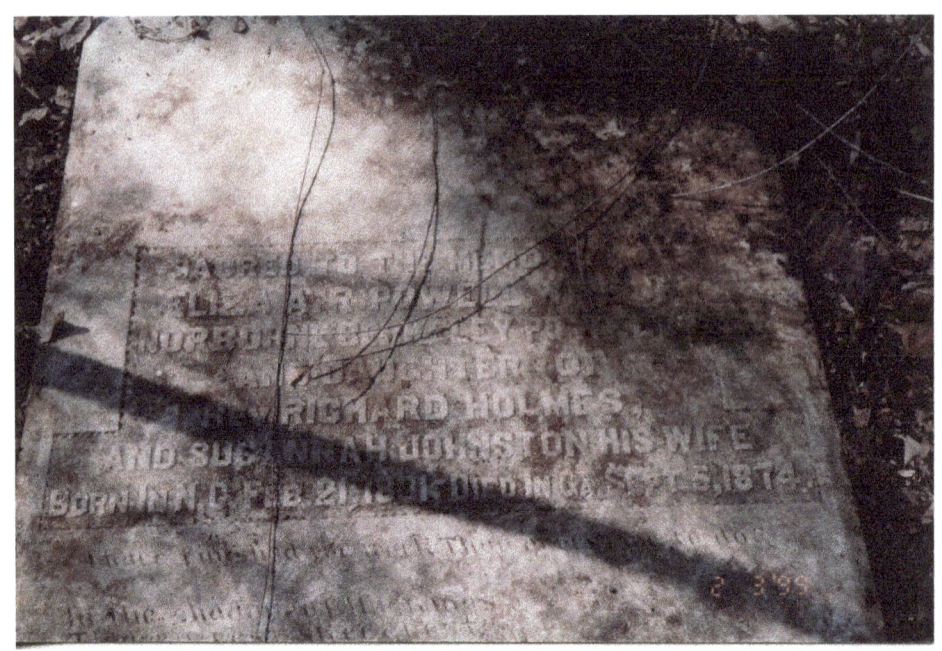

In Memoriam
SACRED
in the memory of
NORBORNE BERKELEY POWELL, M.D.
Born in Nelson, Va. 1790
Died at Chunnenuggee, Al.
Oct. 4, 1862
in the full assurance of a blissful eternity

Eliz. A.R. Powell, wife of
NORBORNE BERKELEY POWELL
and daughter of
Rev. Richard Holmes
and Savannah Johnston, his wife
Born in N.C. Feb. 27, 1801
Died in Ga. Sept. 6, 1874

# Chunnenuggee Public Garden
## 1847

As listed on the Alabama Register of Landmarks and Heritage on March 5, 1976:

The entrance gate to the Chunnenuggee Public Garden was located within this 90-X 120-foot strip. The Chunnenuggee Ridge Horticultural Society, organized on March 6, 1847, established the Garden in the same year. Now known as the Chunnenuggee Public Garden Club, it lays claim to being the oldest continuously existing garden club in the nation. The Society held an annual Chunnenuggee May Fair between 1848 and 1860, when the War Between the States interrupted the event. The circular garden house, summer houses and a "Lover's Knot" (a maze of tall flowering shrubbery) once were part of the five acres planted with rare fruits, flowers and shrubberies, which attracted visitors throughout the South to the Fair. The Fair was revived as the Chunnenuggee Fair in Union Springs in 1980 by the Bullock County Historical Society.

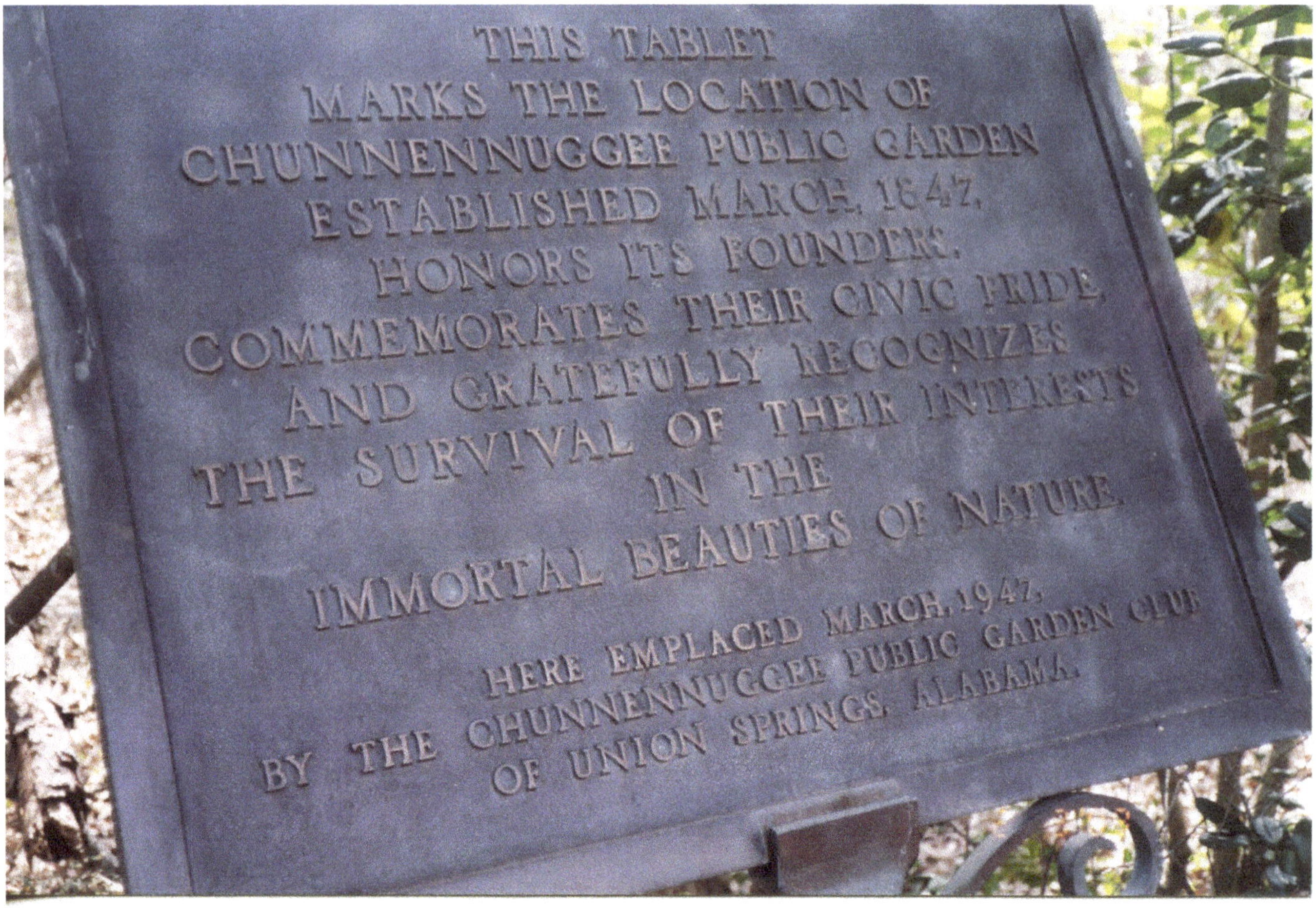

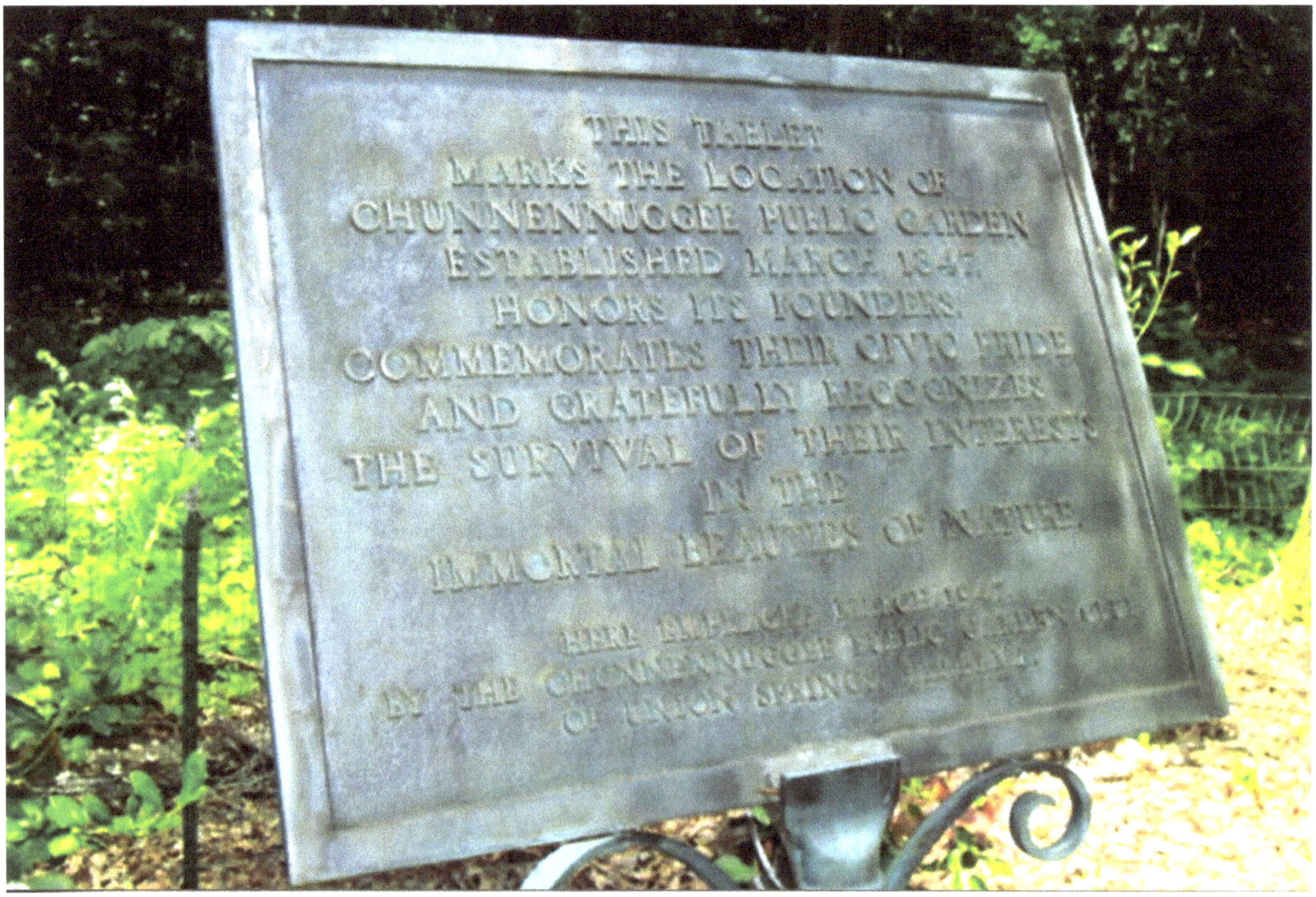

THIS TABLET
MARKS THE LOCATION OF
CHUNNENNUGGEE PUBLIC GARDEN
ESTABLISHED MARCH, 1847,
HONORS ITS FOUNDERS,
COMMEMORATES THEIR CIVIC PRIDE,
AND GRATEFULLY RECOGNIZES
THE SURVIVAL OF THEIR INTERESTS
IN THE
IMMORTAL BEAUTIES OF NATURE.

HERE EMPLACED MARCH, 1947,
BY THE CHUNNENNUGGEE PUBLIC GARDEN CLUB
OF UNION SPRINGS, ALABAMA.

# Chunnenuggee Ridge Public Gardens

As to the claims of where and when the first garden club in America was established, the address by Mrs. Lucille Cary Lowery (the granddaughter of Dr. N.B. Powell) given in 1938 in Selma, Alabama, at the annual meeting of the Garden Club of Alabama, documented the founding and history of the Chunnenuggee Horticultural Society and the Public Garden Club from 1846–1862. This address is contained in records at the Alabama Department of Archives and History as noted in the Section: History, Chunnenuggee Ridge Community.

Twenty-nine years later, in 1891, the first chapter of Garden Clubs of America was established in Athens, Georgia.

Form 10-300
(July 1969)

UNITED STATES DEPARTMENT OF THE INTERIOR
NATIONAL PARK SERVICE

NATIONAL REGISTER OF HISTORIC PLACES
INVENTORY – NOMINATION FORM

*(Type all entries – complete applicable sections)*

STATE: ALABAMA
COUNTY: Bullock
FOR NPS USE ONLY
ENTRY NUMBER | DATE

## 1. NAME

COMMON: Chunnenugee Ridge

AND/OR HISTORIC: Chunnenugee Public Gardens

## 2. LOCATION

STREET AND NUMBER: Union Springs Vicinity

CITY OR TOWN: NE ¼ of NE ¼ of S.33, T 14, R-24

STATE: Alabama  CODE: 01  COUNTY: Bullock  CODE: 011

## 3. CLASSIFICATION

CATEGORY (Check One):
- [ ] District
- [X] Site
- [ ] Building
- [ ] Structure
- [ ] Object

OWNERSHIP:
- [ ] Public
- [X] Private
- [ ] Both

Public Acquisition:
- [ ] In Process
- [ ] Being Considered

STATUS:
- [ ] Occupied
- [X] Unoccupied
- [ ] Preservation work in progress

ACCESSIBLE TO THE PUBLIC:
Yes:
- [ ] Restricted
- [X] Unrestricted
- [ ] No

PRESENT USE (Check One or More as Appropriate):
- [ ] Agricultural
- [ ] Commercial
- [ ] Educational
- [ ] Entertainment
- [ ] Government
- [ ] Industrial
- [ ] Military
- [ ] Museum
- [ ] Park
- [ ] Private Residence
- [ ] Religious
- [ ] Scientific
- [ ] Transportation
- [X] Other (Specify) woods
- [ ] Comments

## 4. OWNER OF PROPERTY

OWNER'S NAME: Mrs. W.O. Turnipseed

STREET AND NUMBER: 201 Chunnenugee Ridge Avenue

CITY OR TOWN: Union Springs  STATE: Alabama  CODE: 01

## 5. LOCATION OF LEGAL DESCRIPTION

COURTHOUSE, REGISTRY OF DEEDS, ETC: Bullock County Courthouse

STREET AND NUMBER:

CITY OR TOWN: Union Springs  STATE: Alabama  CODE: 01

## 6. REPRESENTATION IN EXISTING SURVEYS

TITLE OF SURVEY:

DATE OF SURVEY:  [ ] Federal  [ ] State  [ ] County  [ ] Local

DEPOSITORY FOR SURVEY RECORDS:

STREET AND NUMBER:

CITY OR TOWN:  STATE:  CODE:

# 7. DESCRIPTION

| CONDITION | (Check One) | | | | | |
|---|---|---|---|---|---|---|
| | ☐ Excellent | ☐ Good | ☐ Fair | ☐ Deteriorated | ☒ Ruins | ☐ Unexposed |
| | (Check One) | | | (Check One) | | |
| | ☒ Altered | | ☐ Unaltered | ☐ Moved | ☒ Original Site | |

DESCRIBE THE PRESENT AND ORIGINAL (if known) PHYSICAL APPEARANCE

    The Chunnenuggee Ridge Public Garden consisted of a five acre tract of land located on the Peachburg Road across from the residence of Dr. N.B. Powell. The original layout of the rather elaborate garden is not known, but it was enclosed with a post and plank fence, was well planted with shrubery and contained a latticed pavillion. This pavillion was constructed in 1851, and had a central column encircled with seats. In addition there were arbors and a 'Lover's Knot' maze.

    The area is now planted with pecan trees but a small (90 foot by 120 foot) plot has been made into a garden.

Form 10-300a  
(July 1969)

UNITED STATES DEPARTMENT OF THE INTERIOR  
NATIONAL PARK SERVICE

NATIONAL REGISTER OF HISTORIC PLACES  
INVENTORY - NOMINATION FORM

*(Continuation Sheet)*

STATE: ALABAMA  
COUNTY: Bullock

(Number all entries)

(Significance Continued)

A small section of the original gardens has been acquired by the Chunnenuggee Horticultural Society, which was organized in 1938, and has been planted as a garden.

Received OCT 22 1974 NATIONAL REGISTER

## 8. SIGNIFICANCE

**PERIOD** (Check One or More as Appropriate)
- ☐ Pre-Columbian
- ☐ 15th Century
- ☐ 16th Century
- ☐ 17th Century
- ☐ 18th Century
- ☒ 19th Century
- ☐ 20th Century

**SPECIFIC DATE(S)** (If Applicable and Known)

**AREAS OF SIGNIFICANCE** (Check One or More as Appropriate)

- Aboriginal
  - ☐ Prehistoric
  - ☐ Historic
- ☒ Agriculture
- ☐ Architecture
- ☐ Art
- ☐ Commerce
- ☐ Communications
- ☐ Conservation
- ☐ Education
- ☐ Engineering
- ☐ Industry
- ☐ Invention
- ☐ Landscape Architecture
- ☐ Literature
- ☐ Military
- ☐ Music
- ☐ Political
- ☐ Religion/Philosophy
- ☐ Science
- ☐ Sculpture
- ☐ Social/Humanitarian
- ☐ Theater
- ☐ Transportation
- ☐ Urban Planning
- ☐ Other (Specify)

**STATEMENT OF SIGNIFICANCE**

The Chunnenuggee Ridge Public Garden was Alabama's first public garden and was designed and developed by the first horticultural society in the state and one of the South's earlier botanical organizations.

In the 1840's a number of planters with lands in the area surrounding Chunnenuggee Ridge moved their homes to this higher land, leaving their plantations under the supervision of overseers. By the early 1850's, the community was well established and two colleges and several churches were built.

On the evening of March 6, 1847, a group of men and women met for the purpose of organizing a horticultural society with the intention of having monthly exhibits of flowers and, in season, fruits and vegetables.

At the third meeting of the society in late March, it was resolved that the society would lay out and build a public garden and a committee was appointed to select and acquire a suitable site. As this same meeting A.J. Downing was elected an honorary member.

Later the society decided to hold a public fair on the second of May. The fair, which was very successful, became an annual event known as the Chunnenuggee May Fair and attracted crowds from nearby cities.

By November of 1847, the property committee had acquired by donation a tract of land belonging to Dr. N.B. Powell with the stipulation that the property revert to him should it cease to be used as a public pleasure ground.

The site was cleared and the garden laid out by the slaves of the society members. A section of the garden was set aside for growing cotton and strawberries which were sold to defray the cost of prizes for the flower shows.

Several buildings were constructed in the garden and the annual fairs continued until shortly before the Civil War. During the war the gardens fell to ruins and the property was acquired in the 1920's by the present owner.

## 9. MAJOR BIBLIOGRAPHICAL REFERENCES

Garden Club of Alabama - Year Book Number Five, 1938-1939

Minutes of the Chunnenuggee Horticultural Society, in files of Archives and History.

## 10. GEOGRAPHICAL DATA

LATITUDE AND LONGITUDE COORDINATES DEFINING THE CENTER POINT OF A PROPERTY OF LESS THAN TEN ACRES

Latitude: 32° 09' 23"
Longitude: 85° 38' 11"

APPROXIMATE ACREAGE OF NOMINATED PROPERTY: 5

## 11. FORM PREPARED BY

NAME AND TITLE: W. Warner Floyd

ORGANIZATION: Alabama Historical Commission

DATE: Oct. 10, 1974

STREET AND NUMBER: 725 Monroe St.

CITY OR TOWN: Montgomery

STATE: Alabama  CODE: 01

## 12. STATE LIAISON OFFICER CERTIFICATION

As the designated State Liaison Officer for the National Historic Preservation Act of 1966 (Public Law 89-665), I hereby nominate this property for inclusion in the National Register and certify that it has been evaluated according to the criteria and procedures set forth by the National Park Service. The recommended level of significance of this nomination is:

National ☐  State ☒  Local ☐

Name: Mils B. Howard Jr.

Title: SHPO Ala.

Date: Oct. 14, 1974

### NATIONAL REGISTER VERIFICATION

I hereby certify that this property is included in the National Register.

Chief, Office of Archeology and Historic Preservation

Date _____
ATTEST:

Keeper of The National Register

Date _____

Form No. 10-301  
Rev. 7-72

UNITED STATES DEPARTMENT OF THE INTERIOR  
NATIONAL PARK SERVICE

# NATIONAL REGISTER OF HISTORIC PLACES
## PROPERTY MAP FORM

*(Type all entries - attach to or enclose with map)*

STATE: ALABAMA  
COUNTY: BULLOCK  
FOR NPS USE ONLY  
ENTRY NUMBER | DATE

### 1. NAME
COMMON: Chunnenuggee Ridge  
AND/OR HISTORIC: Chunnenuggee Public Gardens

### 2. LOCATION
STREET AND NUMBER: Union Springs Vicinity  
CITY OR TOWN: NE ¼ of NE ¼ of S 33, T 14, R 24  
STATE: Alabama | CODE: 01 | COUNTY: Bullock | CODE: 011

### 3. MAP REFERENCE
SOURCE: Alabama State Highway Department, Bureau of Planning & Programming General Highway Map Bullock County  
SCALE: 1 inch equals 2 miles  
DATE: 1967

### 4. REQUIREMENTS
TO BE INCLUDED ON ALL MAPS
1. Property broundaries where required.
2. North arrow.
3. Latitude and longitude reference.

RECEIVED OCT 22 1974 NATIONAL REGISTER

☆ U.S. GOVERNMENT PRINTING OFFICE : 1973-729-148/1441 3-1

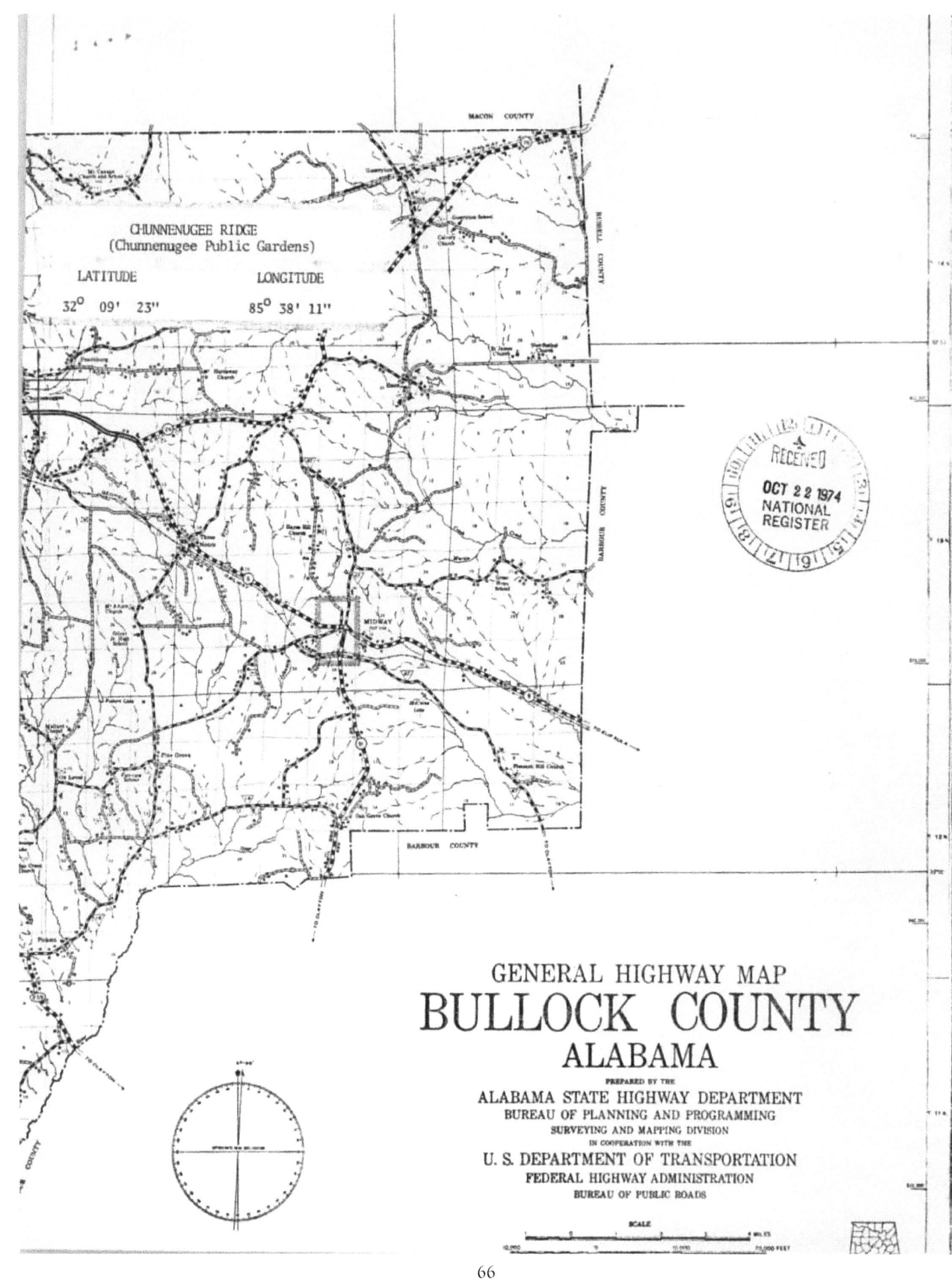

# Norborne Berkeley Powell
## Last Will and Testament
## September 3, 1862

WILL OF N.B. POWELL

Chunnynuggee
Macon County Alabama

In the name of God I, Norborne B. Powell of the county & state aforesaid being sound in mind & knowing the uncertainty of Human Life declare this my Last will & Testament hereby revoking & making void all former wills by me at any time heretofore made in name & form as follows

Item 1st

I give & bequeath to my beloved wife Eliza A. B. Powell my homestead composed of several tracks of land viz. a large portion of section 33 & the 1/2 of section 34 of same range & Township also 70 acres adjoining W. W. Baker & J. F. Couuch with all the houses thereon, improvements of all kinds stock furniture &c&c also the plantation known as the Cole place with all the stock plantation utensils & supplies for one year &c comprising several tracks of land making from six to eight hundred acres also carriage, carriages & horses & buggy & harness also the following negroes. Ben Haines & family Tom Jackson Henry Ogletree, Gracie & Mary Henry, Hamilton the carpenter, Minta daughter of Lucy which said Minta after death of my wife goes to J. F. Carter for the use & benefit of his daughter Mary)— Johnny & his wife Jane & their children Maria & her children Horace & his wife, Hannah & Dora Eli & his wife Lucy Jane & their children. Except

Amos Joe son of Martha, Columbus & his wife Judy & their children, Sarah & her two John Stewart & Clu Ephraim & Phillis, uncle Jerry & aunt Judy aunt Patience Ambrose & Rose & mill Andrew — all the above property and Eli's six mules, wagon & harness, to hold during her natural life & at her death to be equally divided among my lawful heirs & representatives.

Item 2d

To my beloved daughter, Lucy L Powell, I give & bequeath the following negro slaves — Andrew & his wife Celia & their children except John Henry, Nash Pitt, Alexander son of Ann; Anna & her children Meredith Ellen, Big Jerry & his wife Julianna & their children, Perry & Margarett & their children & five thousand dollars.

Item 3rd

To Doct. James M. Foster for the use & benefit of his children Fortune D. & Mary Cowper, children of my beloved daughter Anna I give & bequeath the following negro slaves in addition to those heretofore given Tom Gracy, Jesse, Bill Sussex & his wife Sybey & their children, Cato, James & his wife Cordelia & their children (Except Becky) Wesley & his wife Maria & their children.

Item 4th

I give & bequeath to my beloved daughter Virginia A Blackman the following negro slaves in addition to those heretofore given, Dick Hawkins & his wife Eliza & their children Stanly & his wife Webbe & their children (Except Mary Lane) Simon Robertson & his wife Lucy & their children Except Simon Ann,

When ever Lucy is demanded & five hundred & fifty dollars paid for her & her youngest child by Col R Spencer they are to be given up, Bill Rock, Winny, Jake & Martha & their children Joe.

Item 5th

To my son James L Powell I give & bequeath the following negro slaves in adition to those heretofore given Lewis Essex & David sons of old Lewis Charlotte & her child, Sam Long & his wife Jane & their children except Aaron, Peter, Kentucky, Sam, John Deal & Frank

Item 6th

To L F Carter I give & bequeath the following negro slaves for the use & benefit of my grand daughter Mary Carter. Job & his wife Aggy & their children, Madison & Wash Williams Jack Hicks & his wife & child. Susan Jacob & Emeline Keziah & child, Moses & Elizabeth & their child little Eli & minty Henry at the death of my beloved wife

Item 7th

To my beloved son R. H. Powell I give & bequeath the following negro slaves, viz, Stephen & minty his wife & Levin & his wife Louisa & their children except Levin, Henry Ketch Sandy & Becky & their son Levi, Joe & Rachel his wife, Jessie Hitchcock, John Fogy & Cinthia, Long Ben Ginny & her child. Judge Gabe Henry Mobly, Chillabuck, Tom Salter & an, Honor.

Item 8th

As a faithful steward my beloved brother Seymour has superintended my agricultural affairs for years thus relieving me of nearly all the care of the management of my estate, for these valuable services as well as in consideration of my cordial love for him as an affectionate brother I bequeath him the sum of ten thousand dollars & a certain negro by name John Henry

Item 9th

To my Grand daughter Rebecca Beatrice Blackmon I give & bequeath a negro girl named Lucy daughter of Long Ben.

Item 10th

To my Grand daughter Eugenia H Weems I give & bequeath a negro girl named Mary Jane daughter of Stanly

Item 11th

To my Grand son Nathaniel Powell I give & bequeath a negro boy named Erin son of Zerno

Item 12th

To my Grand daughter Anastasia Blackmon I give & bequeath a negro girl named Simon Ann daughter of Simon Robertson

Item 13th

To my Grand daughter Eliza P Blackmon I give & bequeath a negro girl Becky daughter of Cato Jones.

Item 14th

To my niece Susannah Holmes I bequeath the sum of five hundred dollars for the purchase of a negro girl

Item 15th

To my ~~Nephew~~ Nephew S. G. Powell I give & bequeath a negro boy named Marses son of Ritta

Item 16th

To my friend Capt A Seale I bequeath a good saddle horse

Item 17th

To my friend W H Ellison I bequeath a gold watch

Item 18th

To my Grand son Horborne Bottom Powell son of my son James L. Powell I give and bequeath a negro boy named Aaron son of Malvina

Item 19th

Cherishing a deep sense of gratitude towards Mrs Chaney Pomeroy for kind treatment at her house in deep affliction many years since when I was comparitively a stranger I give & bequeath to her a sum of money sufficient for the purchase of a likely negro girl 12 or 14 years old and at her death said negro to be the property of her daughter Jane Eliza & her heirs.

Item 20th

In relation to my real estate composing my prairie plantation composing section 1 Township 14 Range 22 the 1/2 of section 2 same Range & Township known as the Hinds Tract section 35 Township 15 Range 23 & Section 26 same Range & Township known as the Henry place I direct that it be divided into five tracts of same number of acres, made equal by appraisment and distributed between the following viz, Virginia H Blackmon Richard H Powell James M Fox for the use & benefit of children Horborne P & Mary Cowper, James L Powell & Lucy J Powell. My executors will at such time as they deem proper sell all the perishable property, embracing stock of all kinds corn fodder Cotton Plantation tools &c &c Except such stock & corn & fodder as have been otherwise appropriated & after payings all legal claims against the Estate & the bequests made in the foregoing clauses, divide the proceeds equaly among the six heirs of my Estate

Item 21st

I will & bequeath to William K Harris at this time Judge of Probate Court of Macon County, Alabama & to his successors in office in Trust, four acres of land in Section 28 Township 14 of Range 24 in said County & State as a family Cemetery making the grave of my daughter Mary Carter the centre of said plot also the right of way from the public road to said cemetery by the most acceptable rout, not to interfere with the grave yard enclosures for the joint use of my family & any branches of the same that may desire to use it for the purpose set apart

Item 22nd

My Executors are hereby directed to collect all claims due the Estate dispose of all property real & personal not otherwise definitely appropriated and divide the proceeds equaly among afore mentioned heirs, and I do hereby make & ordain my beloved sons, Richard H & James L Powell my executors of this my last will and testament and it is my especial wish & direction that they be not required to give bond or make returns to the probate or any court, and they are especialy directed to apply to the Legislature for an act authorizing them to carry out the specifications ~~of this will charging such commissions as are customary & right.~~

In testimony whereof I have hereunto set my hand and seal to this my will written on one & a half sheets of paper in the presence of the witnesses this third day of Sept one thousand eight hundred and sixty two.

Signed, delivered & published by the said N B Powell as & for his last will & testament in presence of me & at his request & in his presence & in the presence of each other we have subscribed our names as witnesses there to.

    N B Powell — (L S)

J H Cunningham
J O Hays
D M Phelps

# EVENTS

"Keyhole" Reunion
Cousins Reunion I
Cousins Reunion II
Cousins Reunion III

# "Keyhole" Reunion

The "Keyhole" Reunion of then living Powell males was the culmination of Cousin Key's enthusiasm and persistence. It was held at his Litchfield Beach, South Carolina, beach house in February 1984. He planned the weekend well though the weather was rainy and damp as the "Low Country of South Carolina" can be in February. But after the usual greetings and "Hello" to cousins who had never met, the weekend was highlighted by the multi-generational perspectives of tales, stories and jokes, part of the Powell heritage for years.

Some of the correspondence before and after the gathering is included, as well as candid photos taken by Berkeley.

Not present were :
- NB Powell, urologist from Houston, Berkeley's father, who was recovering from surgery.
- Ben Powell, my brother, who was attending an anesthesiology meeting in Hawaii.

Representing the BP Powell lineage:
- Jim Powell, my father
- JB Powell II, otolaryngologist in Asheville, North Carolina
- Glenn Powell, my brother, lawyer in Tuscaloosa, Alabama

Representing the RH Powell lineage:
- Page Powell, general surgeon in Johnson City, Tennessee

Representing the NP Powell lineage:
- Key Powell, the event organizer, general insurance agent in Columbia, South Carolina
- Elliott and Scott Powell, Key's sons, all of Columbia, South Carolina
- Berkeley Powell, plastic surgeon, in Houston, Texas

LEFT TO RIGHT:
SCOTT, PAGE, JIM, GLENN, KEY, JIM II, ELLIOTT

There were many highlights, the best of which were stories of the current and the past that connected us; jokes from all generations were told, with Glenn and Berkeley competing; and playing Trivial Pursuit, which Berkeley won easily. (He was accused of reading all the cards for weeks before while locked in his "john.") We visited Brookgreen Gardens, a national treasure, renowned for its gardens and sculptures. Everyone had oysters and shrimp in abundance and, of course, an evening of Low Counry BBQ with hush puppies.

As we were packing on Sunday, we discussed with enthusiasm plans for a second male reunion. But, alas, time, promotions, and other priorities were excuses for it not happening.

Family reunions that are not for weddings, funerals or obligatory family gatherings are rare, at least for us. Generational contacts and friendships beyond just immediate family tend not to exceed two generations, which is the case now. My children and grandchildren have not met or known the generations in their lineage or the generations in the other lineages. This book is our way to reconnect.

BERKELEY, GLENN, ELLIOTT, SCOTT, JIM II
PAGE, JIM, KEY

FATHER AND SONS

Fun and Togetherness

**JOHN HANCOCK MUTUAL LIFE INSURANCE COMPANY**
BOSTON, MASSACHUSETTS

To: The Powell Clan   At: _____   Date: _____

Re: 1st Reunion

From: Key Powell   Ans. Letter: _____   Agent or Debit: _____

I'm sorry to be so late in following-up on our First Annual Powerful Powell Clan Reunion. I have been recuperating from my bout with the orthopot's scapel on my left elbow — a 12" scar to retract ~~on my use~~ my ulner nerve. Hopefully, a success. Since I'm left handed, I've been unable to write. Actually, this is my first attempt to combat the written word. Hope this is legible.

We will <u>90%</u> in attendance at the "Key Hole" in North Litchfield Beach, S.C. on Feb. 10-12, '84. Ben, unfortunately, will be in Hawaii during our time together. I tried other dates, but I feel that we should stick

JOHN HANCOCK MUTUAL LIFE INSURANCE COMPANY
BOSTON, MASSACHUSETTS

②

To: _____ At: _____ Date: _____
Re: _____
From: _____ Ans. Letter: _____ Agent or Debit: _____

with what we ~~have~~. Jimmy ~~has~~ promised to fill-in as well as possible for Brother Ben. By the way, there will be a Mini-Powell Reunion on Thanksgiving in Asheville, N.C., when Jimmy and Ben will ~~host~~ Father Jim and Brother Glenn (and families) for the big feast. Take notes and also plan our ~~February~~ agenda.

I shall fill-in all the details in the coming weeks. Prior to ~~our~~ February. This is merely a confirmation of our get-together. We will have with us: Houston — Norborne & Berkeley; Tuscaloosa — Glenn; Union Springs — Jim; Johnson City, Tenn. — Page; Asheville — Jimmy; and, Columbia — Scott, Elliott & yours truly. Also, from Univ. of Va. (maybe) James Blackmon Powell III. Should be a lot of fun. Best regards to all

Key.

**JOHN HANCOCK MUTUAL LIFE INSURANCE COMPANY**
**BOSTON, MASSACHUSETTS**

*I have suggested to Page that he pick you up. He will call you. Will little Jim be there? Key.*

To: ~~Jim~~ Powell's   At: _____   Date: 1/27/84

From: Key Powell   Ans. Letter: Re-Union   Re: ~~Friday~~   Agent or Debit: _____

Dear All —

Please excuse my silence since my original letter. I always have a very hectic end of the year, and this year was no exception. Then on Jan. 4th, Penny and I flew to Hawaii for 11 days. We then returned to La Costa, Calif. for a 4 day Hancock General Agents Meeting. We returned just in time for my Annual Awards Banquet which was Wednesday. I finally chased my out-of-town guests away yesterday at 4:30 pm. So.... I have been busy.

Now for the exciting news! Two weeks from today (hard to believe) we will all gather at the Key Hole at beautiful North Litchfield Beach, S.C. We have ample accommodations (6 B.R. and 5 baths) and I will handle all the groceries and liquid libation supplies. We will eat Saturday breakfast and lunch at the house and go out for the best seafood eating anywhere — on Friday and Saturday nights. Sunday we will eat in again and then head homeward. If Glennie, Bitsie, Caroline, Jayne or Penny want to send something sweet, I won't send it back. ~~However,~~ The food, etc. is my responsibility.

I'm happy to report that 9 out of 10

# JOHN HANCOCK MUTUAL LIFE INSURANCE COMPANY
## BOSTON, MASSACHUSETTS

To:_____ At:_____ Date:_____

Re:_____

From:_____ Ans. Letter:_____ Agent or Debit:_____

— TRULY AMAZING! — OF US WILL BE THERE. ALL BUT BEN IN ~~ASHEVILLE~~, WHO ~~HAD~~ HAD A ~~HAWAII~~ TRIP ALL ARRANGED. HE'S ~~FORGIVEN~~ FORGIVEN.

NORBORNE & BERKELEY ARE FLYING IN ON THURSDAY (9th) BASICALLY TO SEE MOTHER. — 89½ — ~~BIG JIM~~ & GLENN ARE DRIVING FROM TUSCALOOSA AND UNION SPRINGS. IT WOULD BE IDEAL IF THEY COULD DRIVE OVER THURSDAY AND SPEND ~~THURSDAY NIGHT~~ (IF YOU WANT TO). PAGE & ~~JIM~~ DR. JIM WILL EACH DRIVE DOWN. N. LITCHFIELD IS 2 HRS. 40 MIN FROM MY HOUSE — 140 MILES. I'M NOT SURE IF LITTLE JIM (SR. AT U. OF VA.) IS COMING?? SCOTT AND ELLIOTT WILL DRIVE DOWN TOGETHER FROM COLUMBIA. SO,.... WE SHOULD ALL ARRIVE MID ~~AFTERNOON~~ ON FRIDAY. ANY PROBLEM, LET ME KNOW. BEACH HOUSE # 803-237-2839. A MAP & DIRECTIONS ARE ENCLOSED.

NOW: BRING PICTURES OF YOUR FAMILY. I HOPE WE CAN PUT ~~DOWN~~ ON PAPER A FAMILY TREE. NORBORNE, JIM & I — MAYBE PAGE — SHOULD HAVE SOME GOOD ONES TO SHOW OFF. WE WILL WANT EACH OF US TO FILL IN THE "MISSING YEARS" FOR THE REST OF US. HOPEFULLY, WE CAN MAKE THIS AN ANNUAL AFFAIR. ONE DAY, WE MIGHT EVEN INVOLVE THE LADIES. I'M SO GLAD THAT WE ARE HAVING

# JOHN HANCOCK MUTUAL LIFE INSURANCE COMPANY
## BOSTON, MASSACHUSETTS

To:_____ At:_____ Date:_____

Re:_____

From:_____ Ans. Letter:_____ Agent or Debit:_____

THE 9090 ATTENDANCE THIS YEAR.

Any other ideas that you wish to discuss, do, ~~etc.~~ will be ~~eagerly~~ accepted. I'm totally open to all suggestions.

One more thing. No coats, ties. Sweaters and slacks, blue jeans, or totally casual clothing. A walk on the beach is a must, so, sneakers and loafers. No dressing up! My beach maid will clean up when we leave. Come prepared to relax and enjoy. We are gonna have fun.

Any questions, suggestions, or whatever between now and then, call me:

OFFICE: 803-799-9769 PRIVATE *
  "   : 803-799-9604 LEAVE WORD
HOME: 803-788-5086

I would appreciate it if each of you would drop me a short note-card-giving me your travel plans. An envelope is enclosed for your convenience.

Really looking forward to your presence.

Love

DRIVE TO:

LITCHFIELD BEACH
2 MILES NORTH JUST BEYOND
BUZZ'S ROOST YOU WILL SEE
SIGN NORTH LITCHFIELD - TURN RIGHT (BOYLE)
DRIVE TO PARKER STREET (BEACH ROAD)
TURN LEFT (NORTH) FOR EXACTLY
½ MILE. THE "KEY HOLE" IS
ON THE RIGHT. EXETER
LOOP ROAD RUNS INTO
MY DRIVEWAY. MY HOUSE
IS ON "STILTS" AND IS
BROWN WITH WHITE TRIM.

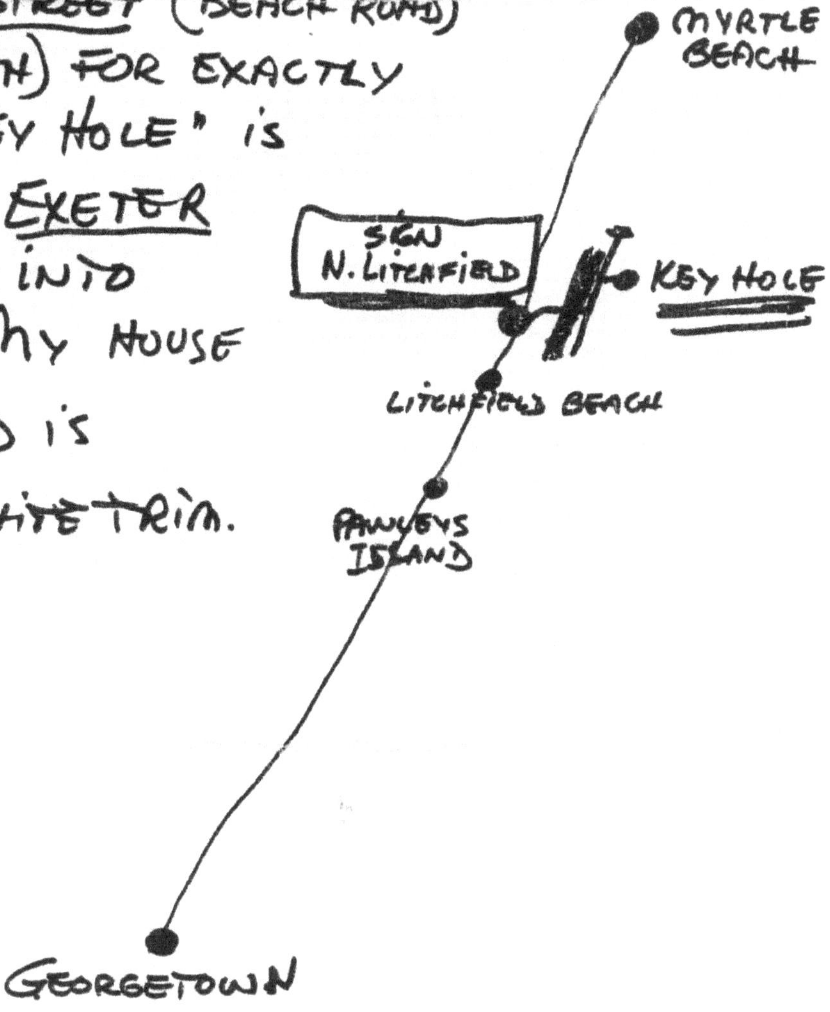

James B. Powell — Glennie
P.O. Box 390 - Union Springs, Ala. 36089    Res. 205-738-2415

Norborne B. Powell, M.D. — Lib    Bus. 713-626-0772
4126 Southwest Freeway #1726 - Houston, Tex. 77027    Res. 713-528-7987

J. Key Powell, CLU — Penny    Bus. 803-799-9769 *
P.O. Box 11428 - Columbia, S.C. 29211    Res. 803-788-5086

James B. Powell, II, M.D. — Bitsy    Bus. 704-254-3517
131 McDowell St. Asheville, N.C. 28801    Res. 704-274-1696

R. Page Powell, M.D. — Jayne    Bus.
403 Princeton - Johnson City, Tenn 37601    Res.

* N. Berkeley Powell, Jr. M.D. — Kimberley    Bus. 713-960-9427
4126 Southwest Freeway #1224 - Houston, Texas 77027    Res. 713-627-022
*

Benjamin P. Powell, M.D — Jeanne    Bus.
421 Vanderbilt Rd. - Asheville, N.C. 28803    Res. 704-274-33

Glenn Powell — Caroline    Res. 205-345-307
Woodridge - 1520 7th Court N.E. Tuscaloosa, Ala. 35406

Scott K. Powell — Kelly    Bus. 803-799-9604
P.O. Box 11428 - Columbia, S.C. 29211    Res. 803-782-5451

Elliott E. Powell —    Bus.-803-782-0
5424 Pinestraw Rd. - Columbia, S.C. 29206    Res. 803-782-4

**N. BERKELEY POWELL, M.D.**
PLASTIC AND RECONSTRUCTIVE SURGERY

713/960-9422

1224 TWELVE OAKS TOWER
4126 SOUTHWEST FREEWAY
HOUSTON, TEXAS 77027

March 20, 1984

Dear Cousin, Jim

Enclosed are a bunch of goodies that are the real reason for this mailing. As promised, each of you is getting an 8 x 10 photo of the collected clan. In addition, I have enclosed to some of you some relevant 3 x 5 prints that I thought you might enjoy.

Also, using my word processor, I re-typed the geneology that Jim was kind enough to put together. It is verbatim except for some small embellishments that Norborne has told me or that Jim told me at Lytchfield but didn't include in the written document. I would also like to make a plea for a moritorium on any more children named Richard Holmes Powell for at least a generation or so. This I do in the name of geneological clarity and plain old sanity.

There is also enclosed an obituary for a Norborne Berkeley Powell who was the (?) grandson of THE Norborne Berkeley Powell, M.D., which I thought might be of interest to everybody. For James B. and Page, I am enclosing some things about Richard Holmes Powell. All these little scraps come from Floyd's scrapbook, which Daddy just recently exhumed from somewhere in his attic. There is more hiding in that same attic, including some original land grant certificates to Dr. N. B. Powell signed by two different presidents, Tyler and (?)Polk, which Dad is still trying to uncover. If he's successful, I'll send xerox copies of those to everyone too.

I can't tell you how much I enjoyed the chance to get to know you all in an unhurried way. If we are supposed to be blessed with friends and stuck with relatives, then I am twice blessed. Glenn was trying to find family similarities but he and I pretty well decided that the strongest familial trait was an excellent, undiluted sense of humor.

Lastly I want to thank Key for his organizational genious, his sheer perseverance in getting the reunion off the ground, and his wonderful hospitality. It was a joy to be able to share such cordial good times. In closing let me say only that coming from a family of characters is a helluva responsibilty. Still, I have every intention of living up to that resonsibility.

With warmest reagrds,

**N. BERKELEY POWELL, M.D.**
PLASTIC AND RECONSTRUCTIVE SURGERY

713/960-9422

1224 TWELVE OAKS TOWER
4126 SOUTHWEST FREEWAY
HOUSTON, TEXAS 77027

September 9, 1984

Dear Cousin:

Once started its hard to stop. I am enclosing some additional information on the Powell family that I thought was worth sharing. This should include (if I don't forget to take it to the office for Xeroxing) a little of the 1820 Census of some of the Tennessee Powells and their slaves.

I hope that any of you who have the itch to send something will include me on the list of targets. Especially since all of you are closer to the heartland of American Powelliana than am I.

Dad celebrated his 70th birthday in good health on July 24th and promptly left town for two weeks in Nova Scotia. Not even that could kill him so he's back and back to practicing medicine between trips. Hope that this finds everyone well. Please pardon the 'Dear All' format of the letter.

Sincerely,

*Berkeley*

N. Berkeley Powell, M.D.

NBP/ms

## <<< THE POWELL FAMILY >>>

The name was originally spelled *Powie*. In the early part of the reign (1558 - 1603) of Queen Elizabeth, the son of Powie, or Powel, of Mindenhall, England, married Agnes, daughter of John Webb, Esq., and it is believed that from this union came the line that became the American family of Powells. The present representative of the family in England is Nathaniel Powell, Esq., of Buckhurst Hall, Essex County.

The Powells in America are descendants of the royal family of Wales, coming from one of the younger sons of one of the old Kings of Wales. Castle Madoc Brecon, in the County of Brechnoc, Wales, was the home of the Virginia branch of the family before emigrating to America. *(There is no present day Welsh county by the name of Brechnoc and I don't think there has ever been. This probably represents a place name, perhaps Brecon, in the County of Powys. In the same Welsh county is a rugged mountain region known as the Brecon Beacons. The castle mentioned must have been in this area. —NBP)*

Three of the family were Judges on the King's Bench in England. One Capt. John Powell was the first Governor (*about 1630*) of the Isle of Barbados under English rule. They were among the earliest and wealthiest ship owners and commanders in the Colonies. One Anthony Powell was military commander of Sir Walter Raleigh's Colonists who first landed in America in 1583 at Roanoke Island, where Fort Raleigh was built. Powells Point on the coast was named in his honor.

Captain Nathaniel Powell, who came to Jamestown, Virginia in 1607, wrote much of John Smith's *History of Virginia*. It was he who made the first map of Virginia. This was sent back to England, where it is now preserved in the British Museum. (See Brown's *Genesis of the United States*, pp 596, 791 ff.)

The land upon which Williamsburg, Virginia was built was first deeded to Benjamin Powell by the King of England.

"Captains William and Nathaniel Powell had large grants of land from the Crown, which they located in the Colony of Virginia. Lyon G. Tyler, who has investigated the subject, says that at one time nearly the whole of York County, Virginia, was owned by the Powells; he gets this from old records. The above-named Captains William and Nathaniel Powell were officers in the English Army. They came with Captain John Smith to the English possessions in America, and settles in Jamestown, Virginia, in 1607, the first permanent English Colony in America. William Powell was one of the Incorporators of the second Virginia Charter in 1607. ( See Brown's *Genesis* )"

"Sir Stephen Powell (a member of the Virginia Company), invested the amount of 37 pounds and 10 shillings and earned one hundred pounds *(an approximately 268% return on investment!)*. He was one of the six clerks of the Chancery, London, and was knighted at Theobalds, July 21, 1604; M.C. for the Virginia Company, 1609; was still living in 1619."

"The name of Captain Nathaniel Powell is one of the most prominent ...( *the text ends here with the end of the typed page* ).

*{ All of the above was sent to my father, Norborne B. Powell, M.D., by an elderly patient here in Houston, named Gladys Norris in 1984. It was typed on lined paper, apparently by a Mrs. N. R. Eckhardt, Jr., and dated Jan. 16, 1966. She credits her source as Pitcher and Allied Families, p. 415. The italicized notes in the text are mine. --- Berkeley Powell }*

**N. BERKELEY POWELL, M.D.**
PLASTIC AND RECONSTRUCTIVE SURGERY

713/960-9422

A WORD ABOUT NAMES
===================

1224 TWELVE OAKS TOWER
4126 SOUTHWEST FREEWAY
HOUSTON, TEXAS 77027

POWELL was listed in one book I consulted as meaning 'son of Po'. This may be misleading. In looking over Welsh place names, the County of Powys is an ancient designation for the region that forms the eastern boundary district where Wales and England meet. The name Powys also appears in the dim beginnings of Welsh history. *Powie* is probably an English corruption of this name or an alternate spelling. Powyll or Powell, means 'son of Powys' probably in the sense that the family was from this Welsh district. The description of the Powells quoted in *Genesis of the United States* seems to support the original location of the family in this area. This makes sense for other reasons, since it helps tie in the name BERKELEY.

BERKELEY: The English county bordering on the southeastern part of Wales is Gloucestershire. Through this county runs the lovely Severn River, which near its mouth flows through the Vale (or Valley) of Berkeley. Berkeley Castle sits near the eastern bank of the Severn, only about 8 miles from the Welsh frontier. This again seems to be a place name.

NORBORNE is a little harder for me to pin down at this point, but it, too, probably is a place name of sorts. The original spelling was probably *Norbourne*, which may already have been a corruption of Northbourne. A *bourne* is a Middle English word for a creek or brook, but such landmarks were frequently used to mark boundaries.

Both before and after the Norman Conquest in 1066, many French words made their way into English. There is a word with the same spelling in Middle French (*bourne*) which meant a boundary or limit. In fact, the two words have a common root in Old French *bodne*. The word 'boundary' itself comes from the same stem. In Gloucestershire the Isbourne (Eastbourne) still flows into the Severn. Westbourne and Southbourne name streams and exist as place names in other parts of England to this day. The name of the Australian city of Melbourne probably has similar origins, meaning 'sweet brook'.

FLOYD and Lloyd are alternate English spellings of the same Welsh name. Welsh, like Irish and Scottish, is one of the old Celtic languages spoken by the earliest inhabitants of the British Isles. The Celts predated the Anglo-Saxons in Britain by at least 2000 years. Many sounds in Celtish do not exist in English, which is at root a Germanic language. These Welsh words confounded the English and lead to many attempts at transliteration of the *ll* (double-l) sound.

-- Berkeley Powell

JIM POWELL

October 3, 1984

Dear Powells (males)

It is time to begin planning for our second Reunion. First if possible, we want a 100% attendance; so will try to pick a date that suits every one. I suggest the last week end in Ferruary 1985 (21 th. thru 23rd.) or the first week end in March (28th. thru 2nd.)

Write me and let me know which of these two date you like and if neither suits you suggest other that do; also any that conflict with your plans. When I hear from every one I'll try to pick a date that suits all.

Since I do not have a Key Hole, and our house will not accomodate all of us; have decided to meet in Tuscaloosa, Ala. We can get Condos (two and three bed rooms) at the North River Golf and Country Club for about $30.00 each per night. More about this later when we pick a date. Glenn will act as our tour director and I am sure will find plenty interesting things for us to do.

Let me hear from you as soon as possible about the dates. Have suggested Thursday-Friday & Saturday nights but if some cant get there until Friday is O. K. We will meet anyone in Birmingham that wishes to fly since it is hard to get flights into Tuscaloosa

Best regards to all of you,

Jim

Jimmy - Have not heard from you in so long !! need to get one of those "still alive cards" Hope one of these dates will suit you and of course we want Jimbo.

Love
Daddy

Jan. 10, 1985

Dear Members of the Clan
(Dr. N. B. Powell Clan)

Based on the reponse from my letter of Oct. 3, 1984, I believe the majority of you feel like we should wait a while before trying to have another reunion.

So be it!! We will just put the matter of reunion on the back burner for a while.

If any of you are in our part of the country anytime be sure to come to see us — we have plenty of room.

as ever,
Jim

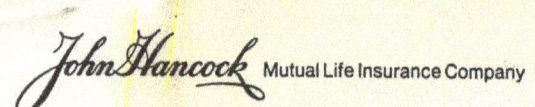 

**J. Key Powell, CLU**
General Agent

1332 Main Street, Capitol Center
P.O. Box 11428
Columbia, South Carolina 29211
Business: (803) 799-9604

September 20, 1985

To: Powell Clan Reunionites
From: J. Key Powell

Here's hoping that everyone is having a good year and that the last three and a half months of eighty-five will be to your liking. This is letter is twofold, so let's get on with it.

First, Barbara Key Powell, Norborne's daughter, who is an attorney for the F. D. I. C. in Oklahoma City, ran across some Powell heritage information which I thought I would share with each of you. She sent it to me and I've had it duplicated and you'll find this material enclosed. I think it skips our side of the family a little bit, but when you think of the numbers of Powell's that preceded us, it's interesting to see how many they did cover and that they came from Virginia, South Carolina and Georgia. I think you will enjoy this information.

Second, in order that we can reconvene our Powell Family Reunion. I thought we should start the planning process now.

I would like to recommend that we return to the "Key-Hole" at beautiful Litchfield Beach, South Carolina for our next get-together. I would like to recommend that we pick a weekend that we can all attend perhaps at the end of March, or the first part of April of 1986. Easter Sunday in '86 is on March 30, so obviously that weekend is out. Why don't we consider then the following weekends: March 7, 8, 9, - 14, 15, 16, - April 4, 5, 6, - 11, 12, 13, - 18, 19, 20.

Send me back-by return mail please - your first, second and third preference of these dates. Also show a date that would be impossible if that is the case. We do want to have 100% attendance. If possible we could even start including grown children this year such as Jim's oldest son who goes to the University of Virginia, and Page, Jr. who goes to the University of Alabama.

Let me hear from you what your thinking is about this. I do think we should get back together while we are all able to do so.

With Much Love,

Key

John Hancock Mutual Life Insurance Company

The Carolinas General Agency

200 Arbor Lake Drive
Suite 100
Columbia, South Carolina 29223
1122 Lady Street
Suite 800
Columbia, South Carolina 29211
(803) 799-9769
Fax: (803) 799-3772

**J. Key Powell, CLU**
General Agent Emeritus

4/30/97

Jimbo —

I had four (100 yrs. old) pictures of the Powell boys enlarged and they look pretty good. I have sent sets to you; your Dad; Norborne; Berkeley; and Elliott. I had negatives made if any more are wanted. Show them to Ben. I just had a long talk with your Dad and he bragged about a great granddaughter. "She's adorable!"

The next time he comes to Asheville, please let Penny and me know. We want to be with you all. Norborne is still a computer recluse. Ugh!

Love to Bitsy

Key.

# Cousins Reunions I, II and III

Ben (Pop) and Asenath (Mom) Powell
Circa 1927.

Senie, Pop, Myra, Mary, Jim
Parents of the cousins with their father.

## "The Cousins"

The cousins are all grandchildren of B.P. "Pop" Powell and Asenath "Mom" Powell by their four children, Myra, Mary, Jim and Asenath. All grew up in Union Springs, Alabama, and returned with their families for many visits. Their children, eleven first cousins, were like extended brothers and sisters, having spent many summers together in Union Springs with other visits to their homes in Ozark, Alabama; Tallahassee and Leesburg, Florida.

The first photo included is circa 1948–49 in the parlor room of Mom and Pop's home. Absent is Jessica Dooley, the youngest of the eleven, who was not yet born! The second photo, the last time we were all together, was in Charlotte, North Carolina, in 1998 for the wedding of Mary Lou and Roger's daughter.

Rowena (Dooley)  Virginia (Anderson)  Sarah (Dooley)  Mary (Carroll)  Mary Lou (Dooley)
Marvin (Carroll)  Jimmy (Powell)  Ben (Powell)  Glenn (Powell)  Ben (Carroll)

Circa 1948–1949
"Mom and Pop's Parlor"

1st Cousins
Grandchildren of Ben and Aseneth Powell

FRONT
Jessica Dooley Kretzchmar, Mary Lou Dooley Clark, Sarah Dooley Araque, Benjamin Philip Powell II
MIDDLE
Rowena Dooley Larsen, John Marvin Carroll, Virginia Anderson Simpson, Mary Carroll Dominey, Benjamin Sam Carroll
BACK
Clarence Glenn Powell, James Blackmon Powell II

JUNE 1998

# Cousins Reunion I

After several years of enthusiastic dialogue, the first reunion, in 2012, was hosted by Ben, Jeanne, Jim and Bitsy in Asheville, North Carolina, with the first two days at Lake Logan, an Episcopal retreat near Asheville. We stayed in cabins around the lake with a central gathering place at the "Sit and Whittle" cabin. Photos, memorabilia, and memories were all shared. Cousins from the N.B. Powell lineage were invited, but Scott's daughter's wedding conflicted. The culmination of the reunion was in Asheville with a magical evening together on the terrace of our country club.

Roger     Ben     Jim     Sarah   Glenn   Marvin     Dick     Ben
Mary Lou   Pat     Bitsy             Georgia   Jessica   Jeanne

Of interest, but not of "Powell" lineage, is our grandmother Sarah Asenath (Smith) Powell who was born in 1883 in Prattville, Alabama. The original land and home, which burned, was rebuilt and restored in the late 1890s, still has her descendants living there and actively farming cotton—McQueen Smith Farms. Mom's brother, Will Howard, married Louise Maytag, sister of L.B. Maytag of "washing machine" fame. Pop (B.P. Powell) assisted his brother in law, L.B. Maytag in acquiring in the 1930s, twelve thousand acres of contiguous land mostly in Bullock County (Union Springs) for a quail hunting preserve. This changed Union Springs forever. An annual hunting field dog trial event in February is recognized as the National Amateur Free-for-All and National Shooting Dog Championship. This two- to three-week event fills Union Springs with guests and participants from all walks of life and importance, The High Social Season! The property remained intact for many years in the Maytag family. The event continues today despite many fewer birds, the cause of which is multifactorial.

The death of James "Jim" B. Powell in 2001 tolled the end of the Powells in Bullock County/Union Springs/Chunnenuggee since Dr. N.B. Powell arrived in 1838.

# Cousins Reunion II

The second cousin reunion was planned and hosted by Marvin and Georgia Carroll of Montgomery and Marvin's fraternal-twin brother Ben and his wife, Pat of Birmingham.

Marvin   Georgia   Pat   Ben

At Union Springs, we were hosted at a hunting club with visits to all the sites and homes—Mom and Pop's home, our former homes, the churches, the Oak Hill Cemetery and most importantly, the original home of Dr. N.B. Powell on Chunnenuggee Ridge. The owners were gracious in hosting us with a tour of the house (including photos seen on the first floor from the antebellum time), the family burial site and the public marker commemorating these sites and the original Garden Club site.

Pat, an artist of renown in Birmingham, created for each cousin a painting, which each is holding as a perfect memory of the event.

Mary Lou, Jessica, Marvin, Sarah, Jim II, Rowena, Susan (daughter of Virginia, deceased, oldest of the eleven cousins), Pat, Glenn

In Montgomery, we were hosted at the Alabama Museum/ Department of Archives and History (next to the Capital Building) by a curator who displayed for us the window pane with the lightning etching of Dr. N.B. Powell. In the main museum were other items from antebellum and reconstruction times, among which was a goblet given to Mrs. N.B. Powell for the "best half-acre of cotton grown" (photo included on page 104). At its pre-war height, the Chunnenuggee community was a vibrant, prosperous settlement of several hundred people.

Ben, Glenn, Jim, Benjamin (Glenn's son), Curator with the windowpane and pitcher.

Pat, Rowena, Sarah, Glenn, Curator

Trophy Cup Inscription:
"Premium awarded to Mrs. GAR Powell by the Chunnenuggee Horticultural Society for a half acre of the best cotton in the Public Garden 1848."

# Cousins Reunion III

In the tradition of the cousins' desire to continue to reunite with one another, the "Dooley Girls" hosted the third reunion in their childhood home in Leesburg, Florida. During a fun-filled four days in March 2019, we all enjoyed visiting their childhood environs of Leesburg, Mt Dora, Tavares and the lakes of Lake County. These were well-planned walking, riding and boating excursions with shopping in the picturesque, vibrant town centers; having lunch where the locals do; and seeing and hearing of cousins' haunts, schools they attended and where their parents taught and coached early in their lives.

Their original home (now almost a hundred years old) is on a large, lakefront lot on Lake Harris. Mary (Lou) and Roger now live in this, the home restored by their preserving the original character with its large, screen porch facing the lake. Sunset cocktails, followed by dinner they had planned and prepared, were among the highlights, providing time for recalling the many, many memories we have of one another, our parents and grandparents and the extended families from marriages.

Attending the events of the reunion were the Dooley girls and spouses.

Left to Right: Jim, Bitsy, Glenn, Pat, Roger, Mary Lou, Dan, Sarah, Ben, Rowena, Georgia, Dick, Jessica

Rowena "Row," the oldest of the four, came with her spouse, Dan Larsen, from their retirement home in Muscle Shoals, Alabama. They both had careers of service: Dan with US Army Intelligence, thirty-one years' active duty, and Rowena with CIA, over twenty-one years. They were stationed at and lived in many exotic places and have three children and nine grandchildren.

Mary—"Mary Lou" as we know her—and her husband, Roger, live in "the home place" now. They are retired from the nursing profession and citrus farming, respectively. They have three children and two grandchildren.

Rowena and Dan and Mary Lou and Roger were "sweethearts" in high school! Dan's father was the priest for the Episcopal church in Leesburg. With Dan as tour director, we visited and enjoyed its serene setting.

Sarah, now living only a few blocks from the "home place," is a multitalented music professional. While visiting her sister "Row" and Dan, she met Luis Araque, an Ecuadorian army officer attending a U.S. military school in Panama taught by Dan. Dan introduced Sarah and Luis. Though neither spoke the other's language, they managed to date, fall in love, marry and live their lives in Quito for thirty plus years having two children, now living in U.S. (no grandchildren, yet!). Their romance and resulting marriage reminds us of their mother's meeting their father, Jesse Dooley, when he came to Union Springs with a traveling semi-pro baseball team, met Senie, and dated her much to "Pop's" initial objections. Sarah, after Luis' death, has relocated to Leesburg, where she is again active in her music and home community.

Jessica, the youngest, was to be a boy. Alas, she was the fourth girl but was given her father's name "Jesse." She, as a flight attendant for Piedmont Airlines, met her spouse, Dick Kretzschmar, a pilot for Piedmont. Both have had fantasy careers, are retired in Virginia

Beach, Virginia, and have two children and three grandchildren.

Attending the reunion were: Ben and Pat Carroll of Birmingham, Alabama, retired banker and active artist, respectively; they brought brother Glenn of Tuscaloosa, Alabama, retired lawyer and full-time general counsel for the University of Alabama Board of Trustees for thirteen years; Georgia Carroll, widow of Marvin, whom we lost to cancer since the 2014 reunion in Montgomery; and Jim and Bitsy Powell of Asheville, North Carolina. Regrettably, May Carroll Dominey and Ben and Jeanne Powell could not attend and were missed.

Of our original eleven first cousins, two have been lost but were with us in our memories.

The agenda of activities was well planned and carried out. The local Hampton Inn hosted us and was convenient. Sarah hosted the first and the third evenings at her home. She presented a DVD she had made for us of our Powell and Dooley ancestry. Mary Lou and Roger had the second evening dinner. Roger and Dan were the bar keepers and sommeliers, keeping us all well "spirited." A highlight of the many activities was a pontoon boat excursion on Lake Harris through the Dora Canal to Lake Eutis and return. A special guide was on board to enhance our awareness of the beautiful and abundant fauna in its semitropical flora setting. The Dora Canal, narrow and jungle-like, is the Alpin River flowing from Lake Harris to Lake Eutis. The guide was quite good.

The last evening's repast was at a local plantation's restaurant, which gave us another "feel" for the Dooley Girls' Florida heritage. After this evening's dinner, as we were saying our last goodbyes with hugs and laughs, the Dooley Girls were humming the refrain from *Les Mis*: "One last day!" We all laughed.

# APPENDIX

# First Generations

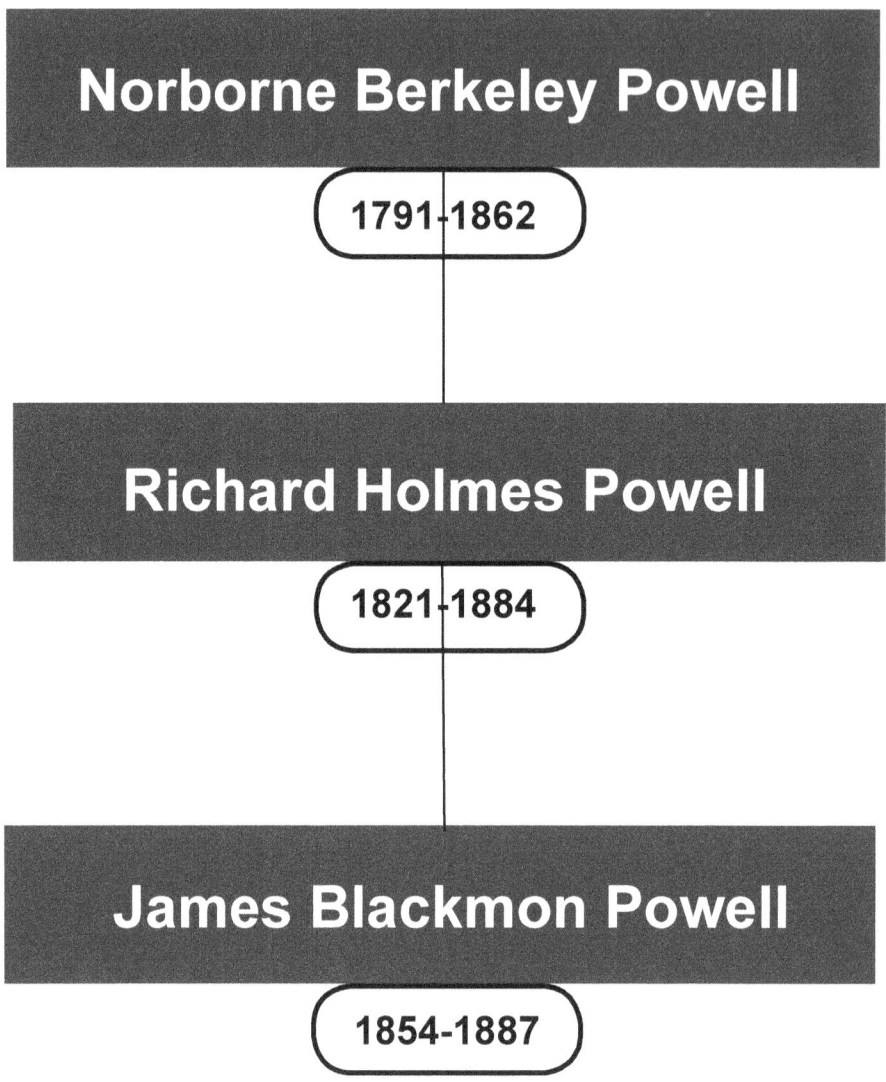

# NORBORNE BERKELEY POWELL
## 1791–1862

# Powell Pitcher article from *Macon Telegraph*, January 1837

(retyped for clarity next page)

WE mentioned a week or two ago that the citizens of Macon had presented a *Silver Pitcher* to the Hon. NORBORNE B. POWELL, Senator from Talbot county, for his liberal, enlightened and patriotic course in the Legislature, in aid of their local interests, and the interests of the State generally. It gratifies us this morning to be able to lay the correspondence on the subject before our readers.

TO THE HON. NORBORNE B. POWELL:

*Macon, 28th December, 1836.*

Respected Sir—The enlightened, manly and liberal course pursued by you as a member of the Senate in our State Legislature for the last two years in all questions relating to the city of Macon, having convinced us that your friendship for her citizens, and decided interest in her welfare are firm and undeviating, the undersigned citizens of Macon are desirous to signify to you their approbation of your conduct in some manner entirely unequivocal, not merely on account of the benefit that has accrued to their city by reason of your elevated policy, but to render their homage to the statesmanlike spirit that actuated it, have provided for you a Silver Pitcher, of which they crave your acceptance.

Hoping that your useful life may be long spared to your country, we subscribe ourselves

Your obliged fellow citizens,

| | |
|---|---|
| Thos R. Lamar, | Henry G. Lamar, |
| James Goddard, | J. Cowles, |
| Robert Collins, | Levi Eckley, |
| Chas J. McDonald, | Washington Poe, |
| Myron Bartlett, | W. Melrose, |
| David Ralston, | Edwd. D. Tracy, |
| Rea & Cotton, | Roger McCall, |
| Frederick Sims, | C. A. Higgins, |
| Wm. Solomons, | J. L. Jones, |
| Jacob Shotwell, | Wm. B. Johnston, |
| F. H. Welman, | Wm. H. Burdsall, |
| E. B. Weed. | Jas A. Nisbet. |

*Liberty, Talbot county, 4th Jan. 1837.*

GENTLEMEN—Your communication of the 28th ult. I had the honor to receive by yesterday's mail, and I avail myself of the earliest opportunity of responding. The flattering terms in which you were pleased to allude to my public course during the brief period of my legislative career could not fail to excite in my bosom the liveliest emotions. To merit the confidence of so enlightened a portion of my fellow-citizens is to me a source of the highest gratification. That your young and prosperous city, daily growing in importance, with a population not surpassed for enterprize, intelligence and patriotism, should be entitled to the fostering care of the Legislature, seemed to me altogether reasonable. Having a knowledge of the pecuniary wants and the consequent commercial embarrassments under which your people labored, it afforded me great pleasure to co-operate with the patriotic delegation from your county in effecting the passage of such laws as I deemed important to your prosperity and welfare.

That your petitions for legislative enactments should have met with such violent opposition was to me a matter of deep regret, and charity towards those whom we had to encounter would induce the belief that they were in want of correct information relative to the situation in which you were placed.

I am sensible that so distinguished an honor as you propose, is more than commensurate with any merit of mine—one so wholly unknown to fame, so little versed in political science, and so recently from the humble walks of private life. In accepting your valuable present, I do so with mingled feelings of pride and gratification, and suffer me to assure you gentlemen, I will treasure it as an invaluable memento of your esteem and friendship. Accept for yourselves individually, the best wishes of my heart for your future prosperity and happiness.

Your friend and fellow citizen,

N. B. POWELL.

To Messrs Henry G. Lamar J. Cowles and others.

## Powell Pitcher article from *Macon Telegraph* January 1837

We mentioned a week or two ago that the citizens of Macon had presented a silver picture to the Honorable Norborne B. Powell, Senator from Talbot county, for his liberal, enlightened and patriotic course in the Legislature, in aid of their local interest, and the interests of the State generally. It gratifies us this morning to be able to lay the correspondence on the subject before our readers.

### To the Honorable Norborne B. Powell:

*Macon, 28th December, 1836*

Respected Sir —

The enlightened, manly and liberal course pursued by you as a member of the Senate in our State Legislature for the last two years in all questions relating to the city of Macon, having convinced us that your friendship for her citizens, and decided interest in her welfare are firm and undeviating, the undersigned citizens of Macon are desirous to signify to you the approbation of your conduct in some manner entirely unequivocal, not merely on account of the benefit that it has accrued to their city by reason of your elevated policy, but to render their homage to the statesman like spirit that actuated it, have provided for you a Silver Pitcher, of which they crave your acceptance.

Hoping that your useful life may be long spared to your country, we subscribe ourselves

Your obliged fellow citizens,

| | |
|---|---|
| *Thomas R. Lamar* | *Henry G. Lamar* |
| *James Goddard* | *J. Cowles* |
| *Robert Collins* | *Levi Eckley* |
| *Charles J. McDonald* | *Washington Poe* |
| *Myron Bartlett* | *W. Melrose* |
| *David Ralston* | *Edward D. Tracy* |
| *Rea X. Cotton* | *Roger McCall* |
| *Frederick Sims* | *C. A. Higgins* |
| *William Solomons* | *J. L. Jones* |
| *Jacob Shotwell* | *William B. Johnston* |
| *F. H. Welman* | *William H. Burdsall* |
| *E. B. Weed* | *James A. Nisbet* |

**Powell Pitcher article from *Macon Telegraph* January 1837**

*Liberty, Talbot County, 4th January 1837*

Gentlemen —

Your communication of the 28th December I had the honor to receive by yesterday's mail, and I avail myself of the earliest opportunity of responding. The flattering terms in which you were pleased to allude to my public course during the brief period of my legislative career could not fail to excite in my bosom the liveliest emotions. To merit the confidence of so enlightened a portion of my fellow citizens is to me a source of the highest gratification. That your young and prosperous city, daily growing in importance, with a population not surpassed for enterprise, intelligence or patriotism, should be entitled to the fostering care of the Legislature, seem to me altogether reasonable. Having a knowledge of the pecuniary wants and the consequent commercial embarrassments under which your people labored, it afforded me great pleasure to co-operate with the patriotic delegation from your county in affecting the passage of such laws as I deemed important to your prosperity and welfare.

That your petitions for legislative enactments should have met with such violent opposition was to me a matter of deep regret, and charity toward those whom we had to encounter would induce the belief that they were in want of correct information relative to the situation in which you were placed.

I am sensible that so distinguished an honor as you propose, is more than commensurate with any merit of mine - one so wholly unknown to fame, so little versed in political science, and so recently from the humble walks of private life. In accepting your valuable present, I do so with mingled feelings of pride and gratification, and suffer me to assure you gentleman, I will treasure it as an invaluable memento of your esteem and friendship. Accept for yourselves individually, the best wishes of my heart for your future prosperity and happiness.

Your friend and fellow citizen,

N. B. Powell

*To Messrs Henry G Lamar, J. Cowles and others.*

*The Birmingham News*, Sunday, October 17, 1982

## A Day in the Life of Alabama

# In 1850s, his tour-to-learn mix of pain, beauty

Dr. Norborne Powell, right, sent his son, James, on journey

By **Clarke Stallworth**
News associate editor

The money was burning a hole in his pocket.

Young James Lucas Powell was touring the Midwest in the spring of 1857, looking for places to invest. His father, a prominent educator from Union Springs, thought travel would broaden his education.

The father, Dr. Norborne Berkley Powell, had been a Georgia educator and legislator, serving in the Georgia State Senate from 1818 to 1838.

In that time, he sponsored the enabling legislation which chartered Wesleyan College in Macon, Ga., which probably was the world's first women's college.

Then Dr. Powell and his family came to Union Springs, then in Macon County, later in Bullock County. His wife needed a change of scene for her health.

The Georgia educator started another college on Chunnanuggee Ridge, then in Macon County, later in Bullock County. The school later moved to Tuskegee, where it became Tuskegee College for Women.

And the same college later was moved to Montgomery, and is today Huntingdon College.

THE WEALTHY educator thought his son ought to travel, to broaden his education. So he gave him $2,150, including some checks from prominent New York banks, and put him on the stage to Columbus, Ga.

From there, the young man took a train to Atlanta and Nashville, where he boarded a steamboat bound for the Midwest.

The young man tried to buy a used steamboat, but failed. On a trip up the Missouri, he bought a lot for $36 in gold in Big Spring, Fillmore County, Minnesota Territory.

Then he met two young men from Tuskegee, and they traveled together, trying to buy land.

Monday the 11th of May — Very cold. Suffered a sore throat today a good deal. Sat by the stove all day.

Tuesday, May 12th — Very white frost and ice this morning. Determined this morning to go to Kansas. Tried to sell a check on New York bank this morning. Failed. Because one man had acted the scoundrel, they take everybody to be scoundrels.

Friday May 15 — Quite cold all day — Passed a piece of beautiful country today, just above Muscatim. The prairie runs into the river's edge for several miles on the Iowa side, and is so lush that you can see cattle grazing at a distance of several miles. The grass is now about two inches high and gives it a beautiful appearance.

Saturday May 16 — Passed Quincy, Illinois, at 10 p.m. While the boat was lying at the wharf taking off freight, four us went ashore and took a view of the City by gas light. We found it to be a very nice and from appearances a very flourishing city.

Sunday, May 17th — Cloudy and very windy and consequently quite cool — Suffered with sore throat the whole of today. Reached St. Louis at 7 p.m. Put up at the Virginia Hotel, a very fine and well constructed house on Main Street.

Monday, May 18th — Tried in vain for two hours this morning to sell my New York checks for want of proper references. Came to the conclusion at 11 a.m. that I had better leave St. Louis as soon as possible and accordingly at 2 p.m. took the cars (railroad) for Jefferson City which place we reached at 8 p.m., making the run (125 miles) in six hours.

Met with Dave Nuckolls and Frank Caldwell from Tuskegee on their way to Kansas. At Jefferson City we took the steamer "Aubry" for Kansas — 250 passengers aboard. About half had to sleep on the floor of the cabin myself among them.

■ See **Powell**, Page 4B

# Powell

**From Page 1B**

Tuesday, May 19th — Awoke this morning feeling rather badly from sleeping uncomfortably. Passed several villages today, to wit, Boonville, Glascow, and the farms are of the prettiest I have seen thus far on the Missouri River. It is about 175 miles above Jefferson City. We had preaching tonight on boat.

Wednesday, May 20 — Ran into a boat about 2 this morning causing a severe crash and considerable excitement among the passengers. The damage to our boat was very slight. Came near sinking the other. We have had 45 Presbyterian ministers aboard until when they got off at Lexington to attend a Conference. I have not felt quite as well as usual — ate too much dinner yesterday.

Friday May 22nd — Walked three miles into the Territory this morning. Beautiful country. Rich lands. Pretty warm work. Neck and throat troubled me smartly today.

Saturday May 23rd — Went to Kansas City today with Nuckolls and after looking about there awhile came to the conclusion that it is destined to become a place of considerable importance. Real estate is enhancing in value very rapidly. Lots are now worth $500 to $5,000.

Returned in the evening very dirty as we had been enveloped in dust all day of which there is more than in any other country it has been my fortune to visit.

Monday May 25th — Rather cool this morning. Tullis and Nuckolls have gone into the Territory this morning on foot to look for claims. Slow rain most of the day. Feel rather lonesome since the boys left.

Tuesday May 26th — Tullis and Nuckolls returned from the Territory today very much pleased with the country but rather doubtful about getting claims.

Thursday May 28th — Left Licompton at 9 a.m. — reached Tecumseh for dinner, where I found Ridley (an acquaintance who is not identified elsewhere in the diary) and lady and Robert White. This is said to be the prettiest location for a town in the Territory. It is situated on the Kansas River 80 miles West of the Missouri line.

It is now in its infancy — Bids fair to be a considerable place — was very much pleased to give Ridley all of my cash to invest and I concluded to go home as soon as possible and get all the money I could raise and send it to him.

Sunday May 31st — Spent the night unpleasantly — feel rather bad this morning — concluded to remain here a day or two. Bowels in rather too lax a condition to travel.

Troubled a good deal until evening when I took some Jacobs Cordial and found great relief and now (7 p.m.) feel almost as well as usual.

Monday June 1st — Feel much better this morning, rested very well last night. Left Westport 6:30 a.m. — reached Kansas City one hour thereafter where I had to wait for a boat until 3 p.m. which I didn't fancy much as there are a few cases of Small Pox in the City.

Got aboard the Steamer W.H. Russell and put out down the river at a pretty brisk rate, she being one of the "fast" boats.

Wednesday, June 3rd — Reached Jefferson City 7 a.m. and at 8:30 took cars (railroad) for St. Louis which place I reach at 3:30 p.m. and without stopping came immediately to the River where found the Steamer Falls City nearly ready to leave and took passage on her, and at 5 p.m. left the levee for Memphis.

Thursday June 4th — Reached Cairo at 9 a.m. Left Cairo at 2 p.m. after taking on 2,100 bushels of coal and considerable freight 8 p.m. Very stormy and quite cool — waves running high — makes the boat rock considerably.

Friday June 5th — Rained most of the last night. Cloudy and cool this morning. The Band gave us some fine music last night. Contributed 25 cents towards remuneration for it. "Pop Goes the Weasil" (sic) was played, which struck my fancy particularly. Reached Memphis 5 p.m. Rainy this evening. Took a walk of an hours length about town.

Saturday June 6th — Left Memphis 6:30 a.m. per Memphis an Charleston Railroad. Passed LaGrange at 9 a.m., a village of 500 or 600 inhabitants, and 48 miles from Memphis — ate dinner at Corinth, 92 miles from Memphis.

Passed Tuscumbia, Decatur, where we crossed the Tennessee River and Huntsville where we supped. Reached Stephenson abo midnight and waiting 2 1/2 hours in the Depot, we took cars for Chattanooga, which place we reached this Sunday morning.

June 7th — At 5:30 a.m., when we took breakfast, and at 7:30 left for Atlanta. Dined at Kingston. Reached Atlanta at 4 p.m. at I left for West Point (Ga.) Supped at Grantsville. Reached West Point 10 p.m. and after waiting an hour, started for Columbus at which I arrived 3 a.m.

Monday June 8th — Put up at Perry house, went to bed and slept till 10 a.m. Knocked about till 2 p.m., took cars for Granny Reached it at 5 p.m. and got aboard Haygood's Stage with five other passengers — reached home at 9:30 p.m. — found all well — took them very much by surprise.

Young Powell went on to serve in the Confederate Army as a lieutenant colonel, and he died in 1867.

(Note: Information for this story came from Powell's travel diary, now owned by his great grandson, George Singleton, 2509 Matzek Road, Birmingham.)

# RICHARD HOLMES POWELL
# 1821–1884

Modified with permission from Internet Presentation:
Barritt Family History Pages

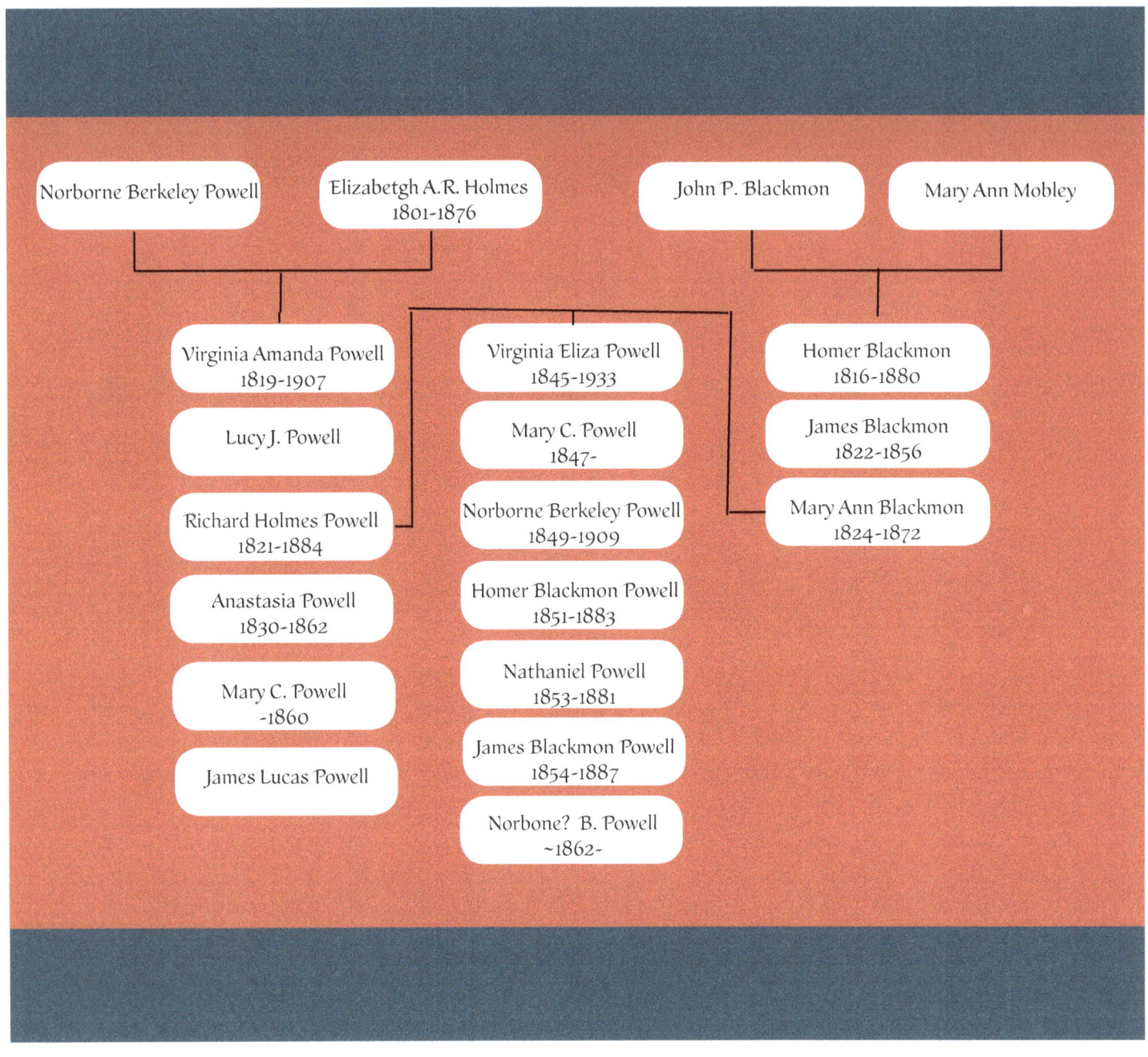

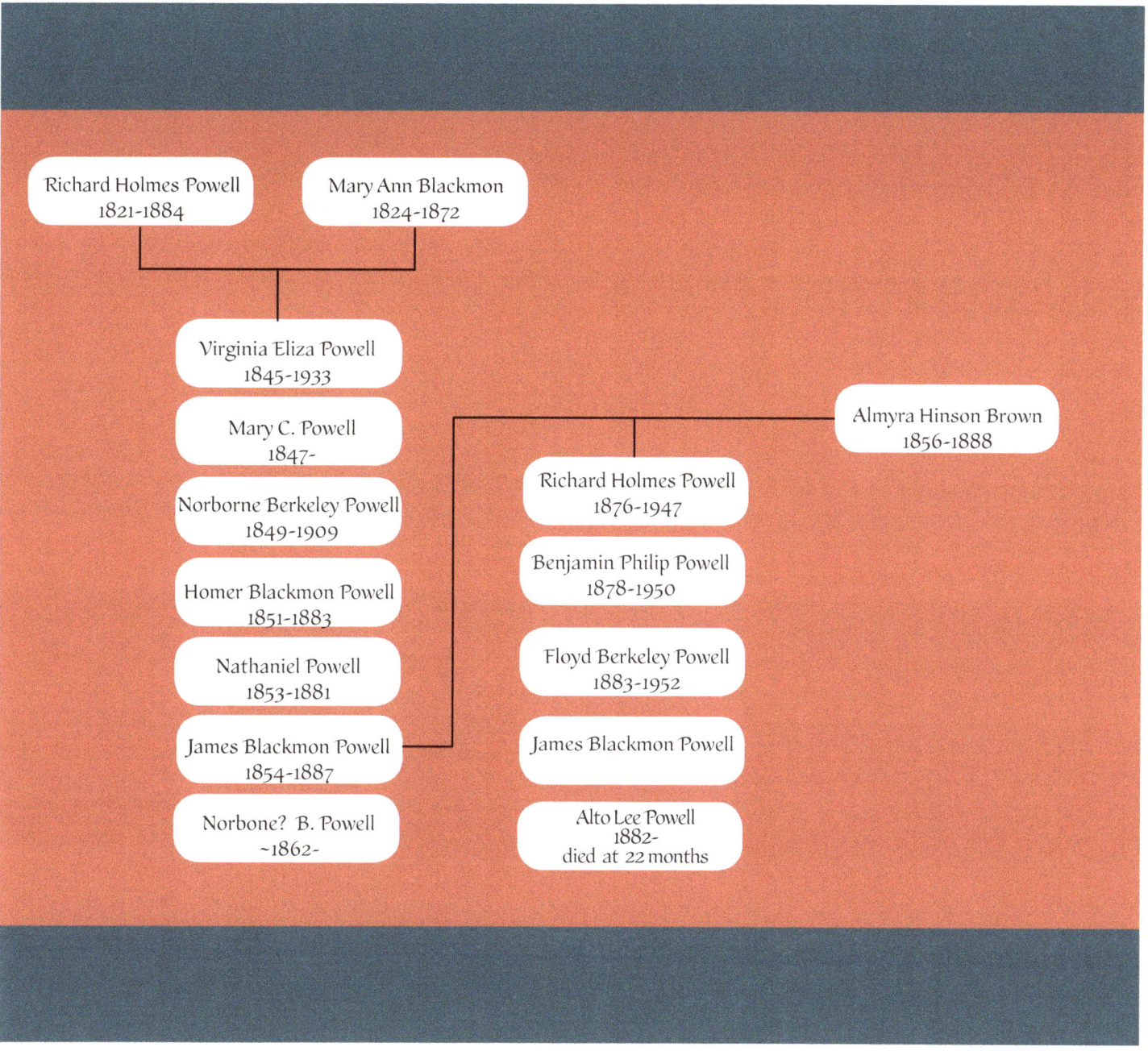

| | |
|---|---|
| Richard Holmes Powell | 11/2/1821 - 10/15/1884 |
| Gravesite | Oak Hill Cemetery, Union Springs, Bullock County, Alabama |
| Parents | Norborne Berkeley Powell<br>Elizabeth A. R. Holmes |
| Wife | Mary Ann Blackmon<br>10/15/1824 - 6/18/1872 |
| Children | Virginia Eliza Powell<br>Mary C. Powell<br>Norborne Berkeley Powell<br>Homer Blackmon Powell<br>Nathaniel Powell<br>James Blackmon Powell<br>Norbone? B. Powell |
| Military Service | Served in the 3d Alabama Infantry Regiment during the Civil War. He served as Captain through the Virginia campaigns, becoming a Major after Gettysburg and later Lieutenant Colonel. He was wounded in 1865 and returned home |
| Community Service | Planter, Journalist, Lawyer, Intendant, Legislator |
| Education | Emory and Randolph-Macon Colleges |

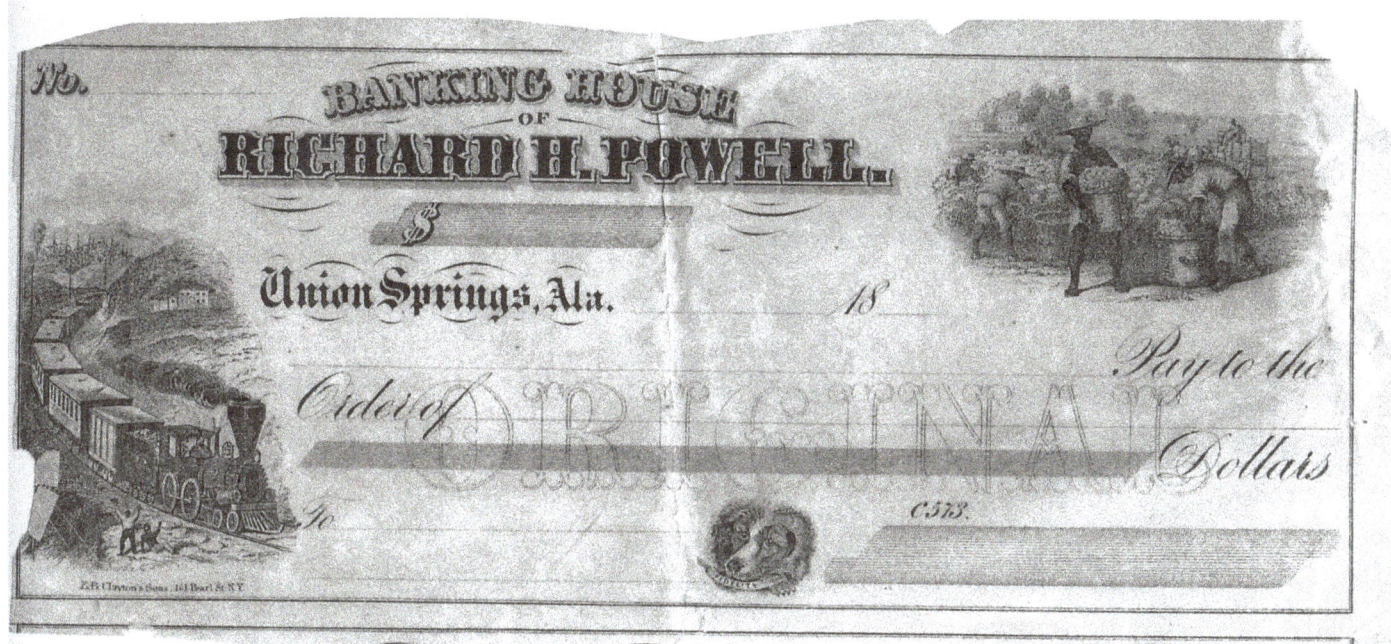

Personal check of Richard H. Powell
during the War Between the States.

According to his obituary in the Montgomery Advertiser, Richard Holmes Powell never shunned public service. Upon returning from the Civil War as a Lieutenant-Colonel, Powell was elected to the State Senate of Alabama from Macon and served 2 years. He was licensed as a lawyer in 1867. In 1875 he was elected to the State Constitutional Convention. He found his home in the Lower House of the Legislature in 1880, 1882, and again in 1884 (He was a member-elect for the next term). At the time of his death, he was a candidate for Speaker of the House. Powell had run for governor of Alabama several times and had already announced his intentions to run agaiin in 1886.

Always a strong temperance advocate, he had served as Grand Worthy Patriarch of the Sons of Temperance in 1852 and Grand Worthy Chief Templar of the Independent Order of Good Templars a few years before his death. At the time of his death he was President of the State Temperance Alliance.

Not satisfied with these public roles, Powell also served as co-editor of the Union Springs Herald and had filled the positions of Orator, Vice-president and President of the Alabama Press Association.

All of Powell's obituaries include thoroughly flowing references to his character, honesty, Christian faith and service to his community, country and state. ,

Even before the Civil War, Richard Holmes Powell served his community as Intendant of Union Springs. He was elected intendant in 1858 and served for three terms. The intendant has managerial and decision-making duties of the city before the city government adopted the mayor and council form of government. [2, 3, 6]    http://tree.barrittfamily.net/

**STATE OF ALABAMA**
**DEPARTMENT OF ARCHIVES AND HISTORY**
EDWIN C. BRIDGES, DIRECTOR
624 WASHINGTON AVENUE
MONTGOMERY, ALABAMA 36130
205-832-6510

October 14, 1983

BOARD OF TRUSTEES

EX-OFFICIO MEMBER
GOVERNOR GEORGE C. WALLACE

FIRST DISTRICT
THE MOST REV. OSCAR H. LIPSCOMB
MOBILE

SECOND DISTRICT
ROBERT E. STEINER, III
MONTGOMERY

THIRD DISTRICT
JUDGE C. J. COLEY
CHAIRMAN OF THE BOARD
ALEXANDER CITY

FOURTH DISTRICT
HARVEY J. WRIGHT
GUNTERSVILLE

FIFTH DISTRICT
WILLIAM H. MITCHELL
FLORENCE

SIXTH DISTRICT
JAMES E. SIMPSON
BIRMINGHAM

SEVENTH DISTRICT
MCDONALD HUGHES
TUSCALOOSA

Re: Powell, James Blockman
    Powell, Richard Holmes
    Civil War records

Mrs. Warren H. Anderson
634 Ingleside
Tallahassee, Florida 32303

Dear Mrs. Anderson:

Reference is made to your letter received October 13, 1983.

A compiled roll, by M. L. Stinson, of Company D, published in the Union Springs Herald, shows Captain Richard H. Powell in Company D, 3rd Alabama Infantry Regiment ("Southern Rifles"), Army of Northern Virginia. He enlisted in the year, 1861, and was later promoted to Major and Lieutenant Colonel. Under "Wounds and Hospital Record" is the following: Malvern Hill, July 1, 1861, Spottsylvania, May 19, 1864.

We were unable to locate a service record for James Blackman Powell. You may be able to obtain this record from the National Archives, Washington, D. C., 20408.

Sincerely,

Donald F. Watson
Archivist II

*"A promise made to my Mother,*
*or pledge.*
*Dear Mama,*
*I pledge you my sacred honor, that*
*I will not drink anything of the*
*sort intoxicating during the*
*remainder of this year, and*
*I trust that I may be so firm*
*and resolute as to resist the*
*insatiate monster in any of its*
*hideous forms —*
*Your devoted Son,*
*H. B. Powell*
*Dell Rosa*
*Jan 28th 1872.*

Homer Blackmon Powell's letter of promise
to his mother, Mary Ann Blackmon Powell,
wife of Richard Holmes Powell.

# James Blackmon
# 1822–1855

brother-in-law of Richard Holmes Powell
and
older brother of Mary Ann Blackmon Powell,
wife of Richard Holmes Powell

Portrait of James Blackmon, older brother of Mary Ann Blackmon Powell, the wife of Richard Holmes Powell and namesake for all the James Blackmon Powells.

The portrait was passed down and hung in the homes of the James Blackmon Powells, both in Union Springs and Asheville. It has been restored and given to the First Methodist Church in Union Springs where it is now "home." Both James Blackmon and his brother-in-law were founders and major contributors to the church. The original building stood on the corner of Blackmon and Powell Streets. On the same site, a new church building was constructed in 1903-1904, with stained-glass windows, one honoring the memory of R.H. Powell.

| | |
|---|---|
| James Blackmon | 11/28/1822 - 2/2/1855 |
| Gravesite | Oak Hill Cemetery, Union Springs, Bullock County, Alabama |
| Parents | John P. Blackmon<br>Mary Ann Mobley |
| Siblings | Homer Blackmon<br>1816 - 1880<br>Mary Ann Blackmon<br>1824 - 1872 |

# NORBORNE BERKELEY POWELL
# "BUD"
# 1849–1909

son of Richard Holmes,
grandson of Dr. N.B. Powell

# Bullock County

VOL. 8.    Union Springs, Ala., Friday Aug. 20, 1909.

HON. NORBORN B. POWELL.

## HON. NORBORN B. POWELL.

"Thus nothing dies, or only dies to live,
  Star, stream, sun, flower, the dew drop and the gold,
Each goodly thing instinct with buoyant hope,
  Hastes to put on the purer finer mold.

Thus in the quiet joy of kindly trust
  We bid each parting saint a brief farewell,
Weeping, yet smiling, we commit thee to the dust,
  To the safe keeping of the Silent One.

Softly within that peaceful resting place,
  We lay their weary limbs, and bid the clay
Press lightly on them 'till the night be past
  And the far east give note of coming day."

# JAMES BLACKMON POWELL
# 1854–1887

| | |
|---|---|
| James Blackmon Powell | 6/27/1854 - 10/4/1887 |
| Gravesite | Oak Hill Cemetery, Union Springs, Bullock County, Alabama |
| Parents | Richard Holmes Powell<br>Mary Ann Blackmon |
| Wife | Almyra Hinson Brown<br>2/2/1856 - 5/1/1888 |
| Children | Richard Holmes Powell<br>Benjamin Philip Powell<br>Floyd Berkeley Powell<br>James Blackmon Powell<br>Alto Lee, 1882, died in infancy at 22 months |
| Community Service | Farmer, Lawyer, Mayor of Union Springs, Alabama<br>1883 - 1885 |

Our Union Spring special this morning announces the death of James B. Powell, Esq., at his home in that city yesterday after a brief illeess. Mr. Powell was a young lawyer of marked ability and stood in the front rank of the southeast Alabama bar. Though a young man he had already acquired considerable reputation, and was looked upon as one of the rising men of his section. He was ex-mayor of Union Springs and was an influential factor in the politics of his county and congressional district. Mr. Powell was the youngest son of the late Hon. R. H. Powell who was a prominent figure in Alabama affairs and at the time of his death was considered among the gubernatorial possibilities. Thus passes away another of Alabama's young sons—taken while yet the future full of honors lay out smiling before him. To his beloved wife and little orphans the DISPATCH extends its deepest sympathy.

The following is a letter written by James Blackmon Powell, while a student at Randolph Macon College, to his father, R.H. Powell.

R. M. College,
Ashland, Va.
April 14th 1874.

Dearest Father,

Enclosed you will find my report for last month. It is not as good as I would like for it to be; but, when I inform you that I had to write a speech weekly for my Society during that time, I know you will say I did very well under the circumstances. You have heard through my letters home of the great success I have met with in my Society. Yes father I am proud to inform you that I have received every honor my Society could give. I have, in that respect, followed in the steps of my honored progenitor. I was elected Medalist by the greatest vote ever cast for it. For I received by far the greatest majority on the first ballot. Heretofore several ballotings were necessary before one man could get 2/3 of the votes cast. I certainly felt happy when I was announced as the fortunate one. My friends gathered around to offer their congratulations. I was completely embraced on all sides. Great joy was manifested by every one. I shall ever strive to be worthy of their high appreciation of my merits as a speaker. I have at last realized long expected hopes.

The Session is rapidly drawing to a close, so I must give you an idea how I stand financially. I have received from home this Session I think, $140. including Homer's & sister's gift of $5. each & I _____ receive the above am'ts; my board & other expenses had been accumulating ever since last Summer. So you see father that amount hardly defrayed my board & washing bills. I owe, therefore, for my tuition & College fees, books, paper &c yet. Mr Brown, the Financial Secretary, has been, indeed, kind to me. He has proved my true friend ever since I landed in a land of strangers. I owe him for the above, amounting to about $135.00 I will owe on the 25 inst for two months board, & three months washing. Board $16 pr month washing 7.50 Amounting $34.50. I owe for clothing I got in Richmond last January $22.00 I owe for incidentals in town $17.00 So I owe at present $208.00. I will need $45. more to pay for my board & washing till commencement, counting from the middle of this month. Add the $45. to the $208. & you will perceive the amount necessary to defray my really college indebtedness. Making $253. say $260. Now father besides that amount I will need $50. to buy me some decent clothing to speak in, to return home with. I have but one suit of clothes to my name. So I will have to buy a complete Summer outfit. I prefer buying them myself, because I can get them much cheaper, & make them suit me better. Now comes the last item of expense. Money is yet name on. It will take $45. to carry me to "Dell Rosa". So it makes in all $355. That amount I must have. It will make my expenses for the last this session, including last Summer's expenses, & money to return home with, amount to $500.00 I can assure you, father, I have been, indeed, economical. Now father I have given an account of my indebtedness, also the money that will be required to finish the term & take me home. I trust you & Horner will obtain the $355.00 as soon as possible for me. I am in great need of money. Must have some immediately. If the Commission Merchants are advancing, please draw that for me, & let me be placed in a position where I may enjoy the remaining days of my college life. If they are not advancing, get it, father, the best way you can for me.

I have read with much pleasure the various compliments paid you by the press. I do hope you will be nominated to Lieut. Gov. I wish you could come on with Mr Clopton. Are you going to the General Conference in May? If you do, you will meet Dr Duncan, who will, I trust, speak highly of your son. Well father I have written all the news of interest. Please tell Nat. that Bennie Baldwin is not studying for the ministry. Give my love, & write me soon.

Your Affect. Son,
Jas. B. Powell

(Written hastily)

## Mayors of Union Springs
### 1872-1887

**SESQUICENTENNIAL 150TH ANNIVERSARY UNION SPRINGS, AL**

*1844 — 1994*

JAMES BLACKMON POWELL was appointed by the governor as mayor of Union Springs in November 1883 and served until 1885. Mr. Powell was a lawyer practicing in Union Springs at the time of his appointment. Mr. Powell's father, Richard Holmes Powell, had served as intendant in the 1850's. This photo is shown courtesy of James Blackmon Powell who presently resides on Chunnenuggee Avenue in Union Springs and he is the grandson of mayor (1883-1885) James Blackmon Powell.

TWO OF OUR MAYORS of the 1800's listed in today's article are shown in front of the Courthouse around 1874. Note the slight differences in the appearance of the Courthouse then and now. Some of the men are J. B. Hunter, J. B. Powell, N. B. Powell, J. L. Tarver, A. H. Pickett, Maj Culver, and George Williams. Photo courtesy of James Blackmon Powell, grandson of J. B. Powell, mayor 1883-1885.

# The Lineage Generations of James Blackmon Powell

These three brothers were orphaned at preteen ages after both parents, James Blackmon Powell and Almyra Hinson Brown Powell, died at ages 32 and 33, respectively. The brothers were adopted into the Pickett family and their home, Del Rosa, which had been built in Union Springs by Richard Holmes Powell for his firstborn child, Virginia Eliza Powell. Virginia had married Alexander Hamilton Pickett; they had eight daughters! So eleven children grew up together. Stories were told and retold about mealtimes, school and gatherings—mostly happy, but clouded by the hardships of post-war reconstruction times.

[Editor's note: Del Rosa was occupied during my life in Union Springs by two of the eight sisters—Callie(1887-1992) and Virginia ("Gee Gee" 1877-1964), who never married. Bitsy and I, as newlyweds in the 1960s, were given a sideboard from Del Rosa, which I refinished. Del Rosa was razed and replaced by "affordable housing" in the 1980s.]

Circa 1923

| Richard Holmes Powell | Floyd Berkeley Powell | Benjamin Philip Powell |
| 1875-1947 | 1883-1952 | 1878-1950 |

# The Lineage of Richard Holmes Powell

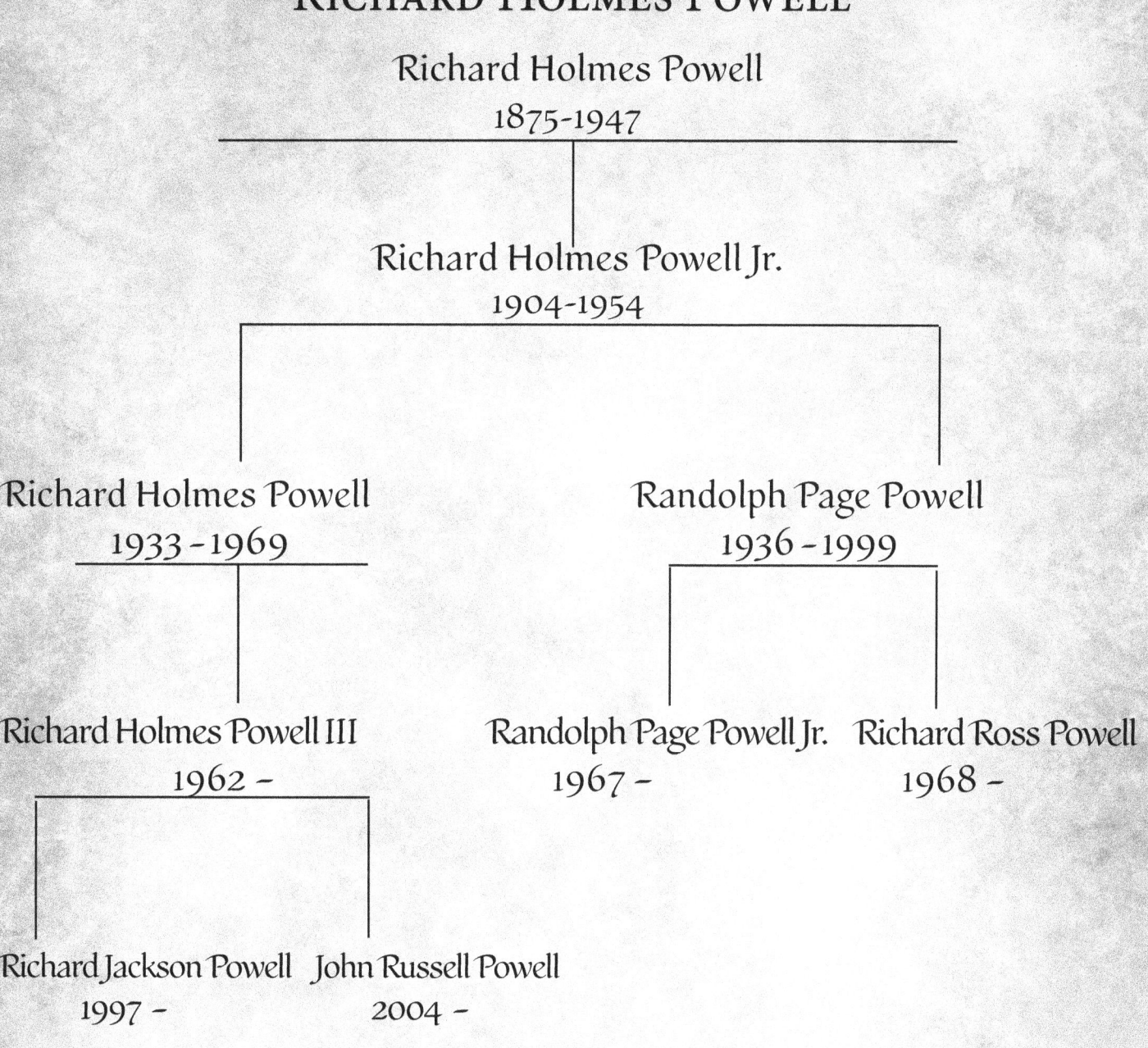

# RICHARD HOLMES POWELL
# 1876–1947

Unfortunately, I had little information about Richard Holmes Powell, my grandfather's older brother. He was a lawyer in Tuskegee. My research provided minimal information and contradictory dates of birth and death. His living progeny may wish to research and add more for the next edition of this book.

# RICHARD HOLMES POWELL JR.
## 1904–1954

Richard Holmes Powell Jr. was the oldest of the four first cousins of the generation of my father, James B. Powell.

R.H.P. Jr. was the possessor of "The Pitcher" at the time of his early, unanticipated death at age 51, while attending an Auburn football game in Auburn. Subsequently The Pitcher was passed to my father, James B. Powell, then to Dr. N.B. Powell, Berkeley's father, then to the younger brother, Key, then to me.

I recall visits to Tuskegee as a preteen with the Powells and their sons, Dick and Page. I also recall their visiting Union Springs, the communities only twenty miles apart. They visited most often for a Sunday dinner at the home of "Mom" and "Pop," where the adults traditionally dined in the dining room and the "children" ate in the breakfast room.

Page      Mother      Dick

Floyd Berkeley Powell     Wife of RHP Jr.     Richard Holmes Powell Jr.

# RICHARD HOLMES POWELL
## "Dick"
## 1933–1969

Thoughts on Dick Powell by the editor

When I was a Congressional Page in the House of Representatives in Washington, D.C., (January–August 1957), Dick was active duty U.S. Army Intelligence, stationed in Maryland. He occasionally called, and we would have dinner together on "The Hill."

Early in July, we were invited by "Old Maid" Pickett family cousins to visit for a weekend at their summer home in Charmian, Pennsylvania, just outside Gettysburg. Dick picked me up, neither of us knowing what to expect. The Pickett cousins were perfect hosts in a setting of beauty—flowers, rolling hills, green pastures and the Battlefield. Their neighbor, a retired Army general, who had taught the Battle of Gettysburg at West Point for twenty-five years, spent two days taking us over all the sites, reenacting the battles, tactics and tragedies of this turning point in our country's history—a weekend still vivid in my memory.

Dick's duty ended, and he returned to Tuskegee to practice law. Returning to Union Springs for my senior year, occasionally I visited with him in his family home where we talked and listened to his extensive Sinatra records. He had a remarkable voice and could sing Sinatra quite well; he was a good mentor.

Dick married Ann Cochran, my father's business partner's middle child. They had a son, Richard Holmes Powell III, but the parents divorced soon after his birth.

Dick later remarried. His death came in a single-car accident.

## MASTERPIECE | 'ONE FOR MY BABY (AND ONE MORE FOR THE ROAD),' WRITTEN BY JOHNNY MERCER AND HAROLD ARLEN, AS RECORDED BY FRANK SINATRA IN 1958

# He Sang One for The Ages

BY JOHN EDWARD HASSE

ONE OF THE PREMIER popular music recordings resulted in no small part from the failed romances of two musical figures: lyricist Johnny Mercer and singer Frank Sinatra. Both also loved their liquor, this song's sub-theme.

*It's quarter to three,*
*There's no one in the place except you and me,*
*So, set 'em up, Joe...*

"One for My Baby (and One More for the Road)" was written by Mercer and composer Harold Arlen. From dissimilar backgrounds, they shared a deep devotion to jazz and blues, and became each other's best-matched collaborator.

Mercer boasted a remarkable grasp of American vernacular language. He was something of a musical polymath—lyricist, singer, record company executive (co-founder of Capitol Records) and talent scout. He was also unhappily married while in love with young Judy Garland, who became a muse for some of his most resplendent lyrics—"I Remember You" and "Skylark." When she broke off the relationship, he was devastated and evidently channeled his grief into "One for My Baby," written for a largely forgotten 1943 film, "The Sky's the Limit."

Arlen wrote the music first—with a winding chromatic melody, a change of key, and an uncommon length of 58 bars instead of the usual 32. Mercer fit his lyrics to the tune impeccably, creating a dramatic monologue that's a masterpiece of urban loneliness and loss. The singer tells the bartender about "a little story / I think you should know," but—in Mercer's clever lyric—holds back and never reveals his tale. Yet his emptiness and despair rouse our compassion. Who can't identify with an unhappy end to a relationship?

Jazz singers and instrumentalists have recorded the song more than 250 times, making it a standard of the repertory. Pop singers as diverse as Marlene Dietrich, Chuck Berry, Marvin Gaye, Iggy Pop and Bono have performed it, too.

Emotional credibility and tempo are key to interpreting this song. Singers have recorded it at many different tempos, ranging from a languid 63 beats per minute to a frisky 141 bpm. Sinatra first recorded it in 1947, at a moderate 84 bpm. In the 1954 film "Young at Heart," he slowed it to 76 bpm. On his third try, in 1958, he decelerated further to 63 bpm and gave the song its definitive rendition—the final track on his capstone album "Frank Sinatra Sings for Only the Lonely," released in September 1958. It's the darkest record he ever made, with such torch songs as "Blues in the Night" and "Good-Bye," and two songs set in bars—Sinatra called them "saloon songs"—"Angel Eyes" and "One for My Baby." Last

Frank Sinatra in 1956; the definitive version of the sorrowful saloon song is from 'Frank Sinatra Sings for Only the Lonely'

month, Capitol Records issued a remastered "Only the Lonely" in multiple formats.

At the time he recorded the album, Sinatra was still reeling from his on-and-off, then failed, relationship with the glamorous Ava Gardner, the greatest love of his life. Throughout this album, he conveys a sense of loss and aloneness from intense personal experience.

In Sinatra's 1958 "One for My Baby," five elements come together—lyrics, music, singer, accompanist and orchestra—to produce a classic of American music. His slower tempo makes a huge difference, allowing the singer to milk the story for all its melancholy emotion. He brilliantly uses the element of time in another way, personalizing the written rhythms to insert pauses and hesitations, all in the service of drama and emotion.

Bill Miller's bluesy, transparent piano lines frame the vocal empathetically, allowing Sinatra's voice to shine through. Nelson Riddle's elegant orchestra comes in and out to underscore the lyrics and add color.

Sinatra's rendition presents not just a song and story, but also a vivid scene. Indeed, in TV and stage performances, which can be found online and in DVDs, he smokes a cigarette while looking forlornly at Joe the bartender, or stabs his fingers in the air to drunkenly punctuate his sorrowful lines.

Whether in audio, on screen, or in person, Sinatra was the supreme musical actor of his time. Sinatra vivifies, inhabits, and lives the lyrics. Duke Ellington called his singing "the ultimate in theater." Sinatra's convincing, conversational delivery; his personal, instantly identifiable sound; and the impression that he was singing directly to you—all these enabled him to connect strongly with his listeners.

When he recorded "One for My Baby" for the last time—in his "Duets" album of 1993, his penultimate year of studio recording—the singer sounds years beyond his best voice, but his life experience has deepened his feeling for this song. As he stretches out the final line—"that long, that long, man it's long, it's a long long long road"—you hear a catch and a near-break in his voice. You can't help but share his pain.

*Mr. Hasse is curator emeritus of American music at the Smithsonian Institution. His books include "Beyond Category: The Life and Genius of Duke Ellington" (Da Capo) and "Discover Jazz" (Pearson).*

# RANDOLPH PAGE POWELL
## "Page"
## 1936–1999

# Dr. Randolph Powell, Sr.        "Page"

Born March 23, 1936 in Tuskegee, Alabama

Passed away after a relatively brief illness December 23, 1999, in Johnson City, TN. He was just 63 years old.

Nearly 2000 friends, family, colleagues, patients, and others whose life he touched attended his pre-funeral receiving of friends.

Undergraduate: University of Alabama
Med School: University of Alabama – Birmingham Residency: Mayo Clinic and University of Alabama

My father, Page, Sr., lived in Johnson City, Tennessee, for most of his professional life. He was an elite, highly regarded general and vascular surgeon. While maintaining a thriving private practice, he was appointed Chief of Surgery at Northside Hospital in Johnson City. He and my mother, Jayne G. Powell, divorced in 1986. They have four children: Laurie P. Webb (currently age 55), Page Jr (51), myself (50), and his youngest, Lindsay P. Fooshee (46). My father was a dyed-in-the-wool Alabama football fan, something he and my brother, Page Jr., had in common from my earliest childhood memories.

  My father and I grew much closer during my college years, and even more so in my Dental School years as medicine became not only a common passion but a source of great pride and respect for each other. I deeply regret that he passed away before seeing me graduate from MUSC.

                    – by Ross, his son

Thoughts on Page Powell by the editor

Even though Tuskegee and Union Springs were only separated by twenty-one miles, visits to Tuskegee were usually to see cousins in my mother's family. However, I recall visiting in Page's home in the early 1950s. I knew of his father's untimely death at an Auburn football game and that "it was decided" that his mother needed someone, so he left the University of Alabama in his undergraduate years. He came home and lived with his mother in their home in Tuskegee. He continued his undergraduate education at Auburn, often commuting.

Tuskegee vs. Union Springs was a significant high school rivalry, but our ages were four years different, so we never competed against one another. However, I knew of his reputation as a "quick-draw" fanatic, having several "cowboy" 22 caliber pistols and holsters. Tales were many, but later he confirmed that he had shot himself at least twice in learning this art—once in the right foot and once in his right buttock.

In August of 1964, as a senior medical student, at the University of Alabama Medical School in Birmingham, I was honored to rotate that month on the service of Dr.

Champ Lyons, Chief of Surgery. Dr. Lyons was feared and respected by all with many, many stories about him that grew with each retelling. Saturday Morning Grand Rounds often pitted him against Dr. Tinsley Harrison, Chief of Medicine, in the same arena, both giants of medical education—playing to a packed house. Two exact opposites—Dr. Harrison, the diminutive, "ape-faced" intellect and Dr. Lyons, the "damn the torpedoes, get it done and get it done right!" surgical personality.

Page was Dr. Lyons' third-year surgery resident that July-August-September, so I spent the entire month of August in University Hospital with Page, me, and a junior staff surgeon in Dr. Lyons' entourage, caring for more than thirty hospitalized patients referred for diagnosis and possible surgery—from all over the state of Alabama, including the wealthy, the socially prominent, the poor and the emergency room patient—all usually quite ill.

I left the hospital only twice during the entire month—to go home and wash underwear and "whites." We wore scrubs 24/7. Page was to be emulated: quiet (even with Dr. Lyons' tantrums), open, listening to patients and their families, empathetic and respectful.

The month with Page helped to make me the doctor I became.

Twenty years later, in 1984, Page was practicing in Johnson City, Tennessee, and I was in Asheville. He arrived at my home in a purple Jaguar sedan, picked me up, and we drove to the "Keyhole Reunion," recalling our times together and our families. We vowed to keep up. Alas, he separated and divorced not long after, so we lost contact. We have since "rediscovered" his sons, who are participating in this book effort.

# RICHARD HOLMES POWELL III
## "RICHARD"
## 1962–

From: **Richard Powell** richard.powell@jacksonthornton.com
Subject: family
Date: April 26, 2011 at 9:48 AM
To: powell710@bellsouth.net

Jim:

Thank you for your recent letter. I am Richard Powell the son of Dick Powell. My mother is still alive and doing well and living in Union Springs. My contact with my father's brother Page has been minimal over the years. I believe he died a couple years ago. I do not have much information on his children.

I have three children: Margaret Ann Powell ( Maggie) 9/4/95, Richard Jackson Powell (Jackson) 12/18/97 and John Russell Powell (Russell) 12/30/04
I am married to Celia Slate Powell

I look forward to hearing back from you.


**Richard Powell, CPA**
Principal
JACKSON THORNTON
T (334) 240-3672  F (334) 956-5072

From: **Richard Powell** Richard.Powell@jacksonthornton.com
Subject: RE: The Powell Tradition book
Date: October 18, 2018 at 11:19 AM
To: Mary Powell powell710@bellsouth.net

Here we go:

I (Richard Holmes Powell IV) was born on July 29, 1962. I grew up in Union Springs, Alabama and graduated from Auburn University in 1985 with a degree in Accounting. I am a Principal at Jackson Thornton & Co. PC and have worked there my entire career. I am married to Celia Slate Powell and we have three children: Margaret Ann Powell (Maggie), Richard Jackson Powell (Jackson), and John Russell Powell (Russell). Maggie was born on September 4, 1995. She is studying to obtain her Doctor of Veterinary Medicine degree at Auburn University (in her first year). Jackson was born on December 18, 1997. He is a junior at Auburn University majoring in Agriculture Economics. Russell Powell was born on December 30, 2004. He is in the 8th grade at Trinity Presbyterian School in Montgomery, Alabama.

I do not have much information on my father (Richard Holmes Powell III). He was born on September 16, 1933 and died in an automobile accident in Macon County, Alabama on March 18, 1969. (I was only six at the time of his death). He married my mother (Ann Cochran) in 1959 and they were divorced in 1963. He had remarried at the time of his death. (Most of his personal effects went to his second wife). My father grew up in Tuskegee, Alabama and graduated from the University of Alabama. He was practicing law in Tuskegee at the time of his death. Maybe there is a cousin of his generation that can add more information.

My grandfather, Richard Holmes Powell Jr. was born on May 5, 1904 and he died of a heart attack at an Auburn University football game (per my mother) on September 25, 1954. He graduated from the University of Alabama and also practiced law in Tuskegee, Alabama. He was married to Ann Page Powell and they had two children (my father and Page).

I have attached a copy of a genealogy report that my daughter prepared for Alabama history a few years ago.

Growing up in Union Springs I do remember that there is a stained glass window in the First United Methodist Church in honor of "R. H. Powell". I believe that this "R.H. Powell" fought in the Civil War with the Army of Northern Virginia. You probably already have this information.

My contact information is 9272 Pennington Pl, Montgomery, AL 36117; (334) 649-1629; rpowell6131@charter.net & richard.powell@jacksonthornton.com

Thanks and good luck with the book.


Richard Powell, CPA    Principal
JACKSON THORNTON
t (334) 240-3672  f (334) 956-5072
w jacksonthornton.com

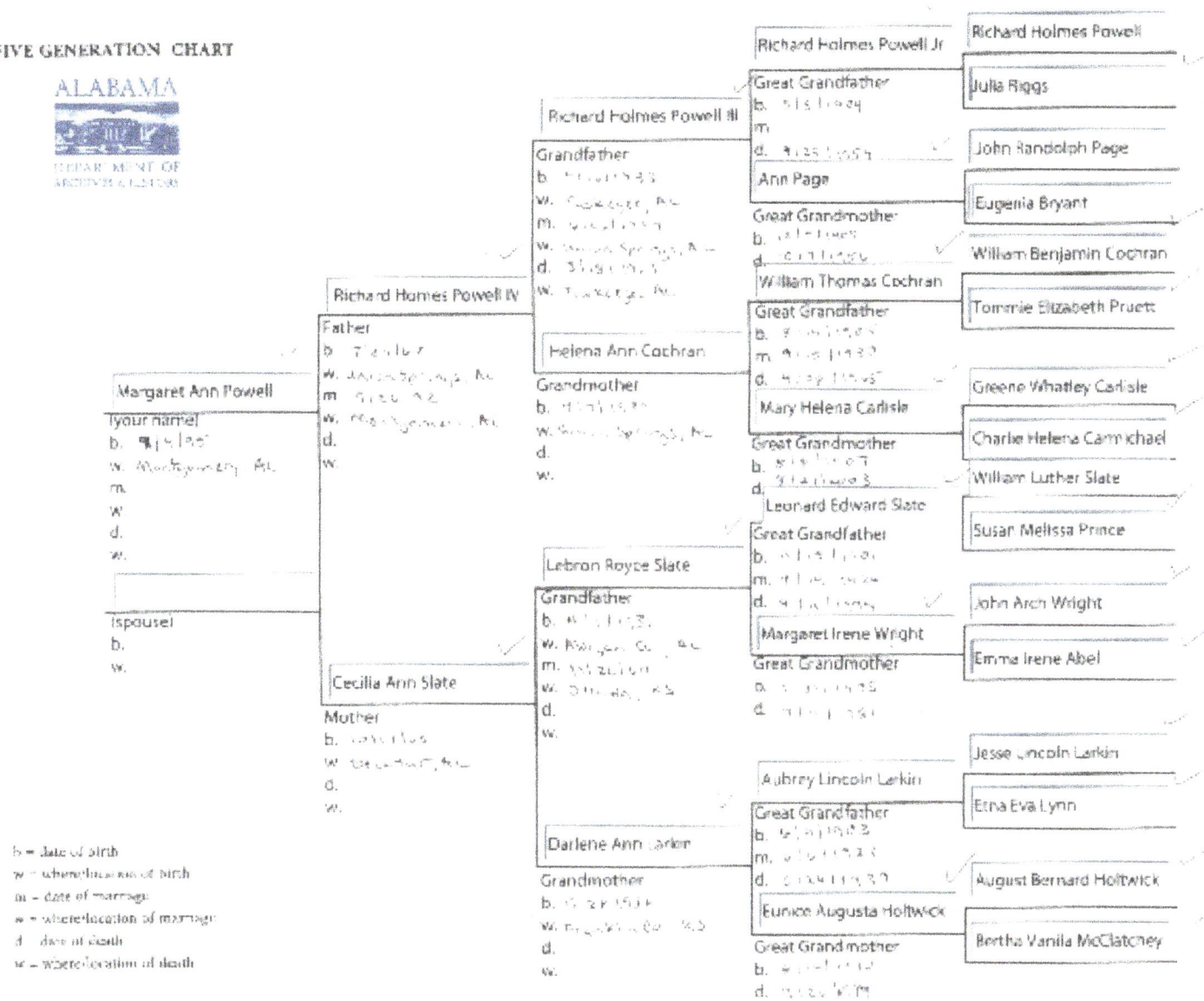

# RANDOLPH PAGE POWELL JR.
## "Page Jr."
## 1967–

# Randolph Page Powell, Jr.     (Page)

Born April 7, 1967 in Birmingham, AL

Undergraduate:  University of Alabama ('89)
Graduate:  University of Georgia School of Law ('93)

lawfirm:
Huff, Powell & Brady
999 Peachtree St, NE #950
Atlanta, GA 30309

My brother, Page, has become an exceptional man in many ways. Back in the 1980's, as his high school years were ending, he had elected to pursue a career in journalism.  Which in my opinion would have been a mistake, given his natural strengths of strong leadership ability, high level of self-confidence, as well as his persuasive and often eloquent speaking skills.  The man was born to be a trial lawyer.

Page reconsidered his decision, and attended the University of Alabama, like his father. Page then moved on to the University of Georgia School of Law, where he graduated with honors.

He has been living in Atlanta ever since (25 years +/-).  After spending five years as an associate in a large firm in Atlanta, he and two colleagues branched off to form a new firm, Huff, Powell, and Bailey LLC, where he is a Managing Partner.  Page specializes in medical malpractice <u>DEFENSE</u> cases, which of course pleased our father.  (Med-Mal prosecution would have been a far different story, as you can surely appreciate.)  As I expected, Page has thrived in the courtroom, and his rapid success in this role is remarkable. He was named 'Georgia Litigator of the Year' in 2015.

Page has never been married, and still resides in Atlanta.  He is the most fanatical Bama fan I have ever known, which some, including myself, find completely obnoxious.  He is an outstanding golfer, still shooting in the 70's at many of the best courses in the world.

By Ross Powell, his brother

# RICHARD ROSS POWELL
## "Ross"
## 1968–

From: **Ross Powell** rrpdmd@outlook.com
Subject: Dr. Ross Powell
Date: March 4, 2018 at 3:38 PM
To: powell710@bellsouth.net

**Dear Dr. Powell,**
**(James)**

Hello, this is Ross Powell. I received a call recently from a physician in Johnson City, TN, that you have been trying to locate me for some time now. He told me that you are my father's cousin, and that you are an ENT Physician in Asheville.

You can understand my skepticism, having never met you. But he also mentioned that you attempted to reach me at my childhood address (Crestwood Dr.), obviously you knew that our family is from Johnson City, and that you were aware of my father's untimely passing in 1999, so I decided to take a closer look. With a simple internet search I easily located a Dr. James Powell, MD in Asheville. An ENT, no less.

I must admit, I am intrigued by the idea of having a first cousin, once removed. (I had to look that up.) found it interesting as well that your career is in medicine. I am a General & Cosmetic Dentist. It only took 4 months of gross anatomy to not only elevate my respect for physicians, but to also maktoiAnd I appreciate your efforts and persistence, despite what I assume were many dead ends.

Perhaps you could reply to this email (rrpdmd@outlook.com) and explain this whole situation in some detail,

Richard Ross Powell, DMD
322 Chick Springs Road
Greenville, SC  29609

rrpdmd@outlook.com
(864) 907-7722

## Dr. Richard Ross Powell     (Ross)

Born July 9, 1968 in Johnson City, TN

Undergraduate:  University of Tennessee  ('90)
Graduate:  Medical University of South Carolina  ('01)
Residency:  University of Connecticut Health Sciences Center

My personal story is not as linear as that of my father and brother.
After hearing "Roll Tide" for two decades, I had had enough.  So naturally I chose the University of Tennessee.  I graduated with a BS in Marketing, which unexpectedly funneled my career into a sales role.  After 5 years and two corporations, I knew I could accomplish more.  Excuse the pun, but I was absolutely certain that I was selling myself short.  I wanted a challenge. So after researching various medical career paths and their respective future outlooks, I chose to pursue a career in dentistry.  Such a seismic career shift caused some concern for some, as I did not have a science background, and would be in my mid-30's if and when I would graduate. Granted, I was rolling the dice a bit.
But my decision paid off. After two years of prerequisite coursework in order to merely apply, and a single attempt at the entrance exam (DAT), I was immediately accepted into the Medical University of South Carolina (MUSC) College of Dental Medicine, in Charleston SC, in 1996.  Apparently very few first-time applicants are accepted, so my new career was off to a positive start.  I was the sole recipient of the Hirsch Scholarship for "achievement and Advancement in Dentistry."  In 2001 I graduated with a DMD.  I took a post-doc residency in Advanced General Dentistry at the University of Connecticut Health Sciences Center in Farmington, CT.
After only four years in practice, I suffered a severe injury to my right hand.  Soon thereafter, I underwent two surgeries on my lower back.  This is perhaps the worst combination of injuries a clinical dentist could suffer, and quite unfortunate brought my career as a practicing Dentist to a screeching halt.  Once again I had to re-evaluate my future.
Since that time I have served as a dental practice management and marketing consultant, a treatment plan coordinator, a teacher and private instructor, and a free-lance writer for several websites and blogs.
My wife, Aimee, and I recently celebrated our 15th anniversary.  We chose not to have children.  We currently live in beautiful Greenville, SC, and are in the process of building a new home.
Not once have the words "Roll Tide" been heard in my home.  Rather, Rocky Top echoes through the halls!

# The Lineage of Benjamin Philip Powell

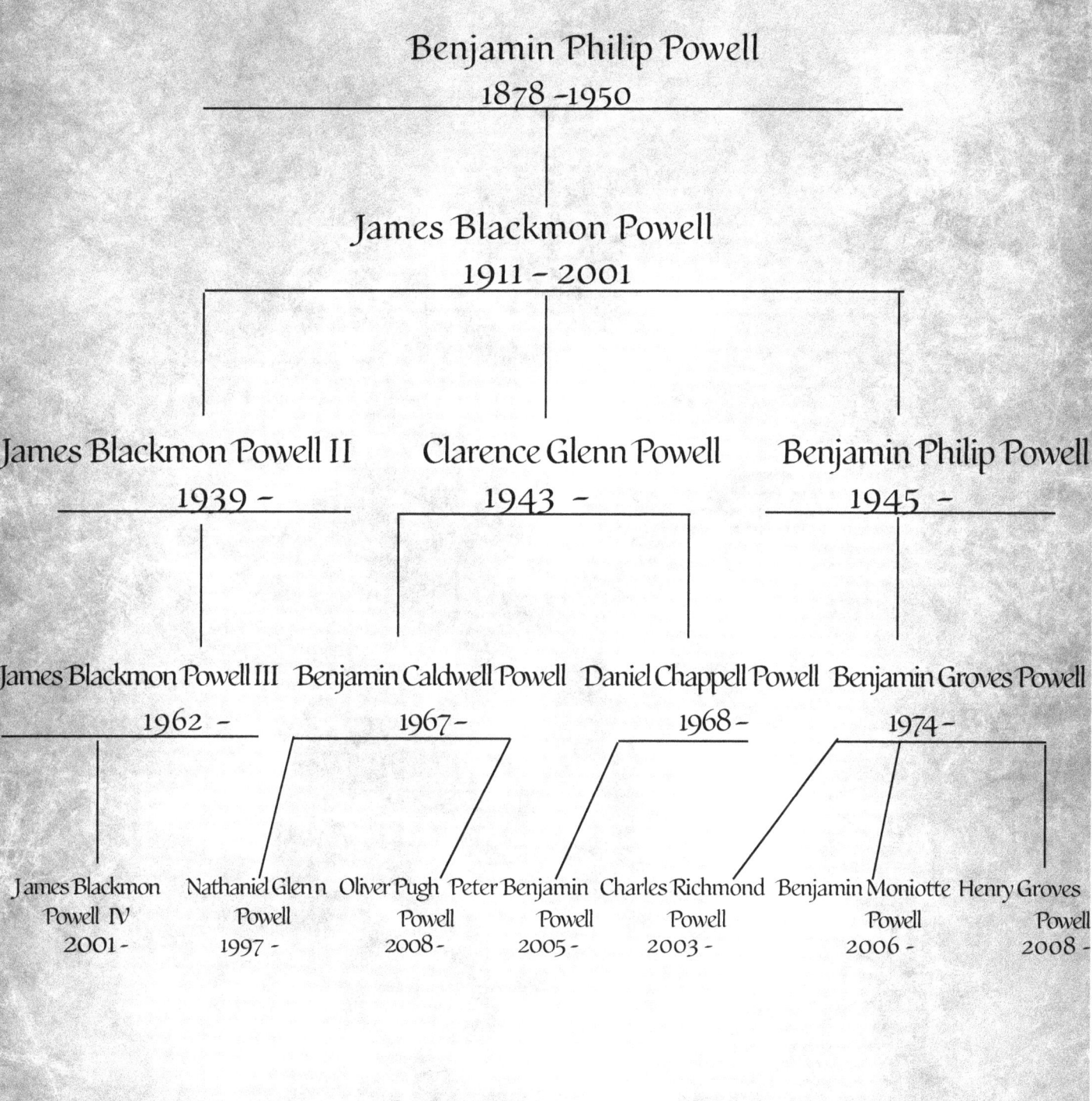

# BENJAMIN PHILIP POWELL
## "Pop"
## 1878–1950

Benjamin Philip Powell Sr. b Oct 8 1878 Fitzpatrick, Ala. d Sept 13 1950 Union Springs, Ala. son of James Blackmon and Almyra Hinson Powell.

Benjamin Philip Powell on his mother's side was a descendant of Benjamin Fitzpatrick, early Governor of Alabama. On his father's side he was a descendant from Dr. Norborne Berkley Powell, member in 1836 of the Ga. Legislature where he was instrumental in the passage of the act which located Wesleyan Female College in Macon, Ga. He later moved with his family and other families to southeastern Ala. This group finally moved to the present site of the Town of Union Springs, Ala. Both parents died when he was about 8 years old and he and 3 brothers were raised by his aunt, Virginia Powell Pickett, and her husband, Alexander. Benjamin Powell was a graduate of the University of Alabama in 1899 and for the year 1898-1899 served as Business Manager of the Year Book "Corolla". Member of Sigma Nu fraternity and several clubs. Founded a business and partnership with a childhood friend, E. G. Branch in Montgomery known as Branch and Powell General Agency, representing Penn Mutual Life Insurance Company. During World War I he was active in Red Cross work, being President of the Area Chapter. Member of Masons and Shriners, and of the First Methodist Church which stood on the land donated by his grandfather, Richard Holmes Powell. Served for several years as a member of the school board. Engaged in farming interest on the family plantation. He was a charter member of the Exchange Club.

B.P.P.

I cannot remember the time when I did not know and love my dearest friend, Ben Powell. Our friendship seemed to be from the beginning, and perhaps partly an inheritance, because my grand parents and his were neighbors and devoted friends and my parents and his Uncle Pickett and Aunt Jennie were devoted friends. As little boys and adolescents we were inseparable up to the time we finished school in Union Springs and he left for the University and I went to work. During those four years we never failed to either write or receive a letter every week; one Sunday he wrote to me and the next Sunday I wrote to him. These letters were full of our most intimate thoughts and aspirations. As small boys we made great plans for the future, always to be together. Court would convene and we would sit entranced as the lawyer of the plaintif would plead eloquently for his client on trial for stealing a pig, we would thrill to his eloquence and decide to be partners at law. Then some gifted preacher would conduct a revival, and for a very brief period we would consider the ministry, then it would be medicine— but always we hoped and planned it would be a partnership. That plan was fullfilled; soon after his graduation he and his splendid brother Holmes and I became partners as General Agents for the Penn Mutual. This partnership between Ben abd Me continued to September 15th, 1950 when God called him to his reward which he so richly deserved. During those forty eight years our friendship was never impaired with any serious differences and the memory of that love and friendship will be with me as long as I live. There has not been a day since he left us that I have not thought of him and missed him.

As far as I realize and remember I have never been guilty of practising fraud at any time or on any individuals except once. That was when I organized a class of three and agreed to teach them violin lessons for one dollar per month each. These "pupils" were Ben, Flora Menafee abd Mr. Rothburgh. There was never a more fraudulent deal in the entire history of get-quick rich-quick schemes, because I knew practically nothing about playing the violin and Ben and Flora had no earthly reason to waht to learn. It will always be one of life's unsolved riddles how I ever put it over on them for they were unusually intelligent young people However I needed the money so that was that, and as far as they were concerned my conscience has never hurt me. But in the case of Mr. Rothburgh my conscience does hurt me because he really played very well, knew a good deal about the violin and read his notes much better than I— in fact I could hardly read music at all, played almost entirely by ear.

About 1906 Stella Clay married here in Montgomery, I was one of the attendants and Sarath was a bridesmaid. She was a most lovely and charming young girl and told me she was going to visit Mary Eley in Union Springs. I wrote Ben of meeting her and told him she was just the girl he had been waiting for all these years and to be sure and call on her. A while later I had occasion to call him over long distance and asked if he had called ob Miss Smith. He said "Hell no- I dont have time to meet all the giddy little girls that visit Union Springs." I told him she was not a giddy little girl and he would be missing a bet if he failed to meet her. "Allright," he said"I'll try and get by".  On the night of the wedding just as we started down the aisle he leaned over and whispered to me "You got me into this. If it don't turn out well I'm going to beat you up". He never did beat me up, and if he had looked the whole world over he could not have made a happier choice.

As I look back over a long and happy life I find many things for which to be thankful and I shall always count knowing and loving Ben as one of my richest blessings. He was one of God's Noblemen; the soul of honor and honesty; one of the finest characters and most delightful personalities it has ever been my privilege to know.

EGB

*Edward G. Branch*

# The PENN MUTUAL Life Insurance Company

**BRANCH & POWELL, GENERAL AGENTS**
703-07 SHEPHERD BUILDING, MONTGOMERY 1, ALABAMA

Union Springs, Ala., 8-7-45

Dear Glennie;-

Congratulations and all good wishes to you and the little shaver and I want to tell you how smart we think you were to - pull off your frolic with so little trouble to all. Jno. was back here on time, we all had a good nights sleep and you were through with your job by one o'clock. I dont think you could have planned it any better.

Know you and Jim preferred a little girl, but that's where I got a break; three boys, three of a kind, is a good hand to have and wins often; then, it is also a good hand to draw to, for it could be filled, 3 kings and two queens, or four kings, and those hands will win nearly all the time, in anybodys game.

Then too, think of three boys in a room and the good times they will have; and the hand me downs, you remember the song I told you of when Glenn was born - "Papa's pants will do for Willie"; quite important items in this day and time.

I think it will be great fun; three healthy, husky, fine boys, playing, fussing, bawling, boisterous, running all around the place like wild indians and driving you nearly to distraction but you will be craz about all of them and would'nt swap the worst one for all the girls in the world. And then after a little while, you will have four males- counting Jim, if he still counts, to lean and four stalwarts to make a fuss over you, and that's a good bunch for a young, attractive matron, like yourself.

You know my father had five boys; one died early but the other four grew to manhood and the good times we had as boys were hard to beat and while that was many years ago, the memories are happy ones. Now, in a more serious vein, I want you and Jim to know that I am ver proud of my little name sake, the first one to bear my full name, and greatly appreciate your nampmg him for me. It is good to know that some will be when you are not, to tell that you have been, and so I am proud of little Ben and of the other two little Powell boys and counting on their growing into good, clean, useful, serviceable citizens; clean-cut, hightoned, honorable, sincere, fearless and true, with the courage of their convictions and standing for the right. And I feel sure they will measure up to the standard, for they have the proper background and will have the proper care and traing, becoming a valued addition to the citzenry of any place; and that is as it should be.

You know there have been Powell's in this county for the past I00 years and I am happy that there may be Powell's around here for the next I00 years, unless this new atom bomb which has just come, and which I hope means the early end of the war, detroys everything, and if that should come to pass, why we wont know any thing any way. May be Ben and the bomb coming along together, means a combinations of much better things to come. Who knows ?

We miss you and will be glad to have you and Ben home as soonas you are able to come, for we love you and want you back. The boys and are thinking of a good indian name for him, and maybe, God willing, as Mr

# The PENN MUTUAL Life Insurance Company

**BRANCH & POWELL, GENERAL AGENTS**
703-07 SHEPHERD BUILDING, MONTGOMERY 1, ALABAMA

Churchill would say, I will be taking Ben with me to the plantation, playing birds, cows, cars, or something else, with him and showing him the cotton and potatoes and corn.

By the way, what shall we call the little fellow? Callie and Virginia suggested "Ben Phil"; that was what they called my uncle for whom I was named and that was what they called me about 45 years ago when I was at the University of Ala. We will have to decide on what to call him when you and Jim make up your minds.

I am hoping that Jim will be able to get a good stay here and be with you and the boys before being moved, if he is moved, and I suppose he will be; but I am still hoping he wont have to go out of the country for awhile, any way.

We are getting along all right and the boys and I have had some good times together; they sleep next to us down stairs and are not hard to manage even about turning in; so dont worry and hurry up and get strong and bring old Ben home.

All join in much love and remember us to S. L.

Affectionately,

"Pop"

# Memories of Pop
## (and Mom)
## Benjamin Philip Powell
## and Sarah Asenath Smith Powell

### (Written in October and November 2018)

He wasn't a cowboy but he loved reading about them. He had a bunch of fictional paperbacks about cowboys and gunslingers that he read in his bedroom and other places in their spacious home. He wasn't Randolph Scott but Scott was his favorite cowboy, and he looked a lot like him. (See Pop's and Randolph Scott's pictures below). But Pop looked more like a banker than a cowboy—often wearing a bow tie but never a bolo tie.

I remember once when Glennie and Jim (my parents) were away, probably at an Alabama football game, and Mozelle (my good buddy and second mother and Glennie's maid) was keeping us, but Pop was coming by to pick us up and take us to the Saturday movie at the Lilfred to see a Randolph Scott western. They were paving (or repaving) the road around our house, and little brother Ben decided it would be fun to take off when no one was looking and go scooting out into the recently poured tar on his little bike. You guessed it. He hadn't gone far before he slid in the tar and crashed and rolled over in it. When Pop and Mozelle extracted Ben from the tar, if we had a briar patch, we would have sworn he was the tar baby. And Pop was in an unusual irritated and impatient mood----he would not miss Randolph Scott. So he and Mozelle got a big pot and a bunch of turpentine and stuff, a little soap and a couple of horsehair brushes and scrubbed off most of the tar and Ben's skin. We took a red, whimpering, in pain, little boy to the Lilfred and saw Randolph.

Pop

Randolph Scott

Pop didn't wear cowboy or Texas style clothes or boots but I remember him as a dapper dresser—almost always in a stiff shirt, bow tie, and coat. He was a businessman, partners until death with Ed Branch as General Agents for Penn Mutual Insurance Company. He also was a part time farmer and rancher and owned a bunch of land out of Union Springs--- I think a couple thousand acres.

But before I go further, it's time and appropriate that I give a warning. Pop died when I was in the third grade, literally in Mrs. Moore's third grade classroom where they came to get me and tell me that Pop had died. It didn't register for a while, probably because my heart and mind wouldn't accept it. Both of Glennie's parents died long before I was born so Pop and Mom were my only grandparents. And living with four females (Mom and their three daughters), Pop probably had a hard time keeping my two brothers and me straight and peaceful, although he grew up living with his two (for a while three) brothers as orphans with the Pickett sisters, Callie and Gee Gee (Virginia), who were their sweet, straight-laced aunts. They lived in Della Rosa, a fine old antebellum home not far from the railroad station, originally built and owned by Col. R. H. Powell, later occupied by his granddaughters, Callie and Gee Gee. Della Rosa was named for the 100 varieties of roses that grew on its seven acres. Built in 1857 by architect Quinling, the construction took a year. It was two stories with a large central hall, 12 rooms, verandah supported by columns. In 1957 on the occasion of its 100ths anniversary, it was recognized as the only house in Union Springs that has not changed hands during those 100 years.

I had little time with Pop for memory building experiences, and what I do remember is foggy and maybe sometimes questionable. My memory comes more from emotions and feelings than from facts---and I have some fond memories and mental snapshots of good times with Pop and in their large and magical house above the bluff on North Prairie Street.

Pop was stately and somewhat solemn but not hard or distant. His brother, Uncle Toy, was the frisky, funny, if not sometimes frightening personality, especially when he pulled apart one of his fingers at the knuckle---quite a trick and one we learned to repeat many, many times. He smelled of cigar smoke and usually had one or a piece of one in his mouth. I'm sure Pop played with us, especially when we lived with Mom and him while Jim was saving America at the end of WWII. I have a vague recollection of "riding horsey" on Pop's ankle as he rocked his crossed leg back and forth. I also have a very clear memory of him lying flat on his back on the stiff divan in the parlor on the main floor in the front of the house. It was a cool, dark, a little spooky room with large windows around the front and side wall that provided soft light and views to the wrap around front porch, Prairie Street, and the houses beyond. Sometimes he would be asleep, fully dressed, bow tie and all (he was a stiff collared, dapper dresser), sometimes with his mouth open, looking very much like a cadaver or a royal person lying in state. We were forbidden to bother him during this time or Mom during her daily afternoon nap in their bedroom.

I remember Pop driving us in an older standard shift car. No cars, commercial trucks, or auto parts were made or sold during WWII from February 1942 to October 1945. So we probably were riding in a pre-1940 straight stick. I remember he proudly boasted that he had one of the few cars that could pull up the Chunnenugee Street hill in third gear.

As I said, he was a general agent for Penn Mutual and that produced a couple of insurance policies on my life, taken out when I was just a child and which I still have, providing a whooping $5000 death benefit, although that was quite a bit back in the mid-1940's. He had a narrow but deep office on main street (Prairie) in the town center right at the Confederate soldier monument that stood in the middle of the street. His partner for life, Ed Branch usually was located in Montgomery. One of the best things Pop ever did was marry Mon, Sarah Asenath Smith (Powell). She was a sweetly, refined, privileged somewhat pampered lady but with a toughness and strong will when she felt the need, which was not very often (like when my brothers and I got into sibling war or sneaked away to the bluff behind their house or the Blount grounds next door).

Mom was the daughter of Lila Hannah Smith ("Little Mother") and McQueen Smith (married February 20, 1879) who had four daughters, Mary McQueen ("Queenie"---Mrs. Hopson Owen Murfee); Sarah Asenath (Mom—Mrs. Ben P. Powell); Eugenia Graham ("Genie"--Mrs. Edward Northington); and Julia Pratt (Mrs. Searcy B. Slack) and four sons, only two of whom lived beyond childhood: William Howard (who married his Iowa sweetheart, Louise Maytag) and Hazen (who married Ruth Slack of LaGrange). One of the other little boys was Ray, who died when he was five. Although there were rough and hard times, McQueen and "Miss Lila" and Will Howard and Haze added more and more to the McQueen Smith Farms over time. In 1919 McQueen Smith died and two years later, Hazen died.

Of Mom, her mother Lila wrote: *"Our oldest daughter [Queenie] was not afraid of anything and never minded being sent into a dark room, but Asenath was afraid of the dark. One night I wanted her to get something out of a closet and she said: 'Rats in there.' I said if a rat saw you, he would run from you.' She said: 'He afraid of me, Me afraid of he.'*

I found that Pop's partner, Ed Branch, best captured Pop's introduction to Mom in his wonderful tribute to Pop, attached in the appendix to this scrapbook. Here is a special part of it about Pop's initial relation to Mom, revealing his somewhat sassy personality: *"About 1906 Stella Clay married here in Montgomery. I was one of the attendants, and Senath was a bridesmaid. She was a most lovely and charming young girl and told me she was going to visit Mary Eley in Union Springs. I wrote Ben of meeting her and told him she was just the girl he had been waiting for all these years and to be sure to call on her. A little while later I had occasion to call him over long distance and asked if he called Miss Smith. He said 'Hell no-I don't have time to meet all the giddy little girls that visit Union Springs.' I told him she was not a giddy little girl, and he would be missing a bet if he failed to meet her. 'All right,' he said. "I'll try and get by.' On the night of the wedding, just as we started down the aisle, he leaned over and whispered to me 'You got me into this. If it don't turn out well, I'm going to beat you up.' He never did beat me up, and if he had looked the whole world over he would not have made a happier choice,"* [Some light editing has been done.

Pop graduated from the University of Alabama, Class of 1899. The 1899 Corolla has the following information about Ben Phil Powell: *Sophomore Speaker; Sophomore Honor Roll; Vice President Erosophic Literary Society; Assistant Business Manager Crimson=White; Vice-President Junior Class; Junior White [?]; Lieutenant*

*[?] Junior Honor Roll; Business Manager Crimson White; Vice-President Athletic Association---[Sigma Nu].* In one of the entries in that Corolla about the Class of 1899, it reveals that Pop's "alias" was "Benny" and that he said he will be a lawyer but "they" believed he would be a "book agent."

Probably because of the connection with Will Howard and his wife, Louise Maytag, and the Maytag family, mainly Lewis B. (Bud) Maytag, Pop quietly bought up several thousand acres of land for Maytag, near land that Pop owned. That became the Sedgefield Plantation of some 14,000 acres and among other things the home of the national amateur shooting dog championships.

I close these memories with one that is closest to my heart. Pop's land was out from Union Sprigs toward Tuskegee. I remember he would load some or all of my brothers and me in his car and take us to his "farm." Probably to keep us somewhat calm and a little quiet, there were landmarks all the way out. We had to identify and name each one as we rode by. Some required a short story. Sadly I don't remember them all but here's a few: the house that was burned down and built back in the same place; the hawk tree (where often there was a lone hawk perched in the very top); Alamo flat; the bumpety bump red bird road; the site of the circus; the place of the landing of the out of space machine (actually a weather balloon with instruments attached); Henry's house (sometime more appropriately called Margarite's house; Blue's house; the ghostly swamp; the Last Chance; the cane syrup mill; and a lot more. It sometimes meant a stop for a soft drink or hard candy. Those were special times with a special person who was taken too soon out of my life.

I end this by joining with Ed Branch in his closing to the warm tribute to Pop he wrote: *"I shall always count knowing and loving Ben as one of my richest blessings. He was one of God's Noblemen; the soul of honor and honesty; one of God's finest characters and most delightful personalities it has ever been my privilege to know."*

Glenn Powell (son of James Blackmon Powell, who is the son of Pop)

# JAMES BLACKMON POWELL
## "Daddy" "Jim"
## 1911–2001

Jim with the PITCHER, outside his home on Chunnenuggee Street (circa 1986)

## Death claims James Blackmon Powell

Mr. James Blackmon Powell, a resident of Bullock County, died in Tuscaloosa Thursday, June 28, 2001. With his death goes the last of a long line of Powells in this county. His ancestor, Dr. Norborne Berkley Powell, came into Alabama (that part which is now Bullock) in 1838. He and several friends settled on the Chunnenuggee Ridge. A direct descendent of this illustrious family has lived in Bullock County ever since that time.

The family was always active in the life of this county, both the social, political and business life. They have served in all capacities from doctor, to legislator, to businessmen and church leaders.

In 1857 the Methodists of Union Springs were without a place of worship. Col. Richard H. Powell gathered all the children and their parents together and began a Sunday School in his home. Later they held church services at the Presbyterian Church but in 1858 they decided to build a church of their own.

The Land Company comprised of several men including Col. Richard Powell and Col. Homer Blackmon (these two families were later joined by marriage) donated the land where the present day church building sits. In 1861 Dr. George Pierce was here to dedicate the church. He asked, "Brethren is there any indebtedness on this building?" The treasurer answered, Yes Bishop, $1,600 is due. Dr. Norborne Powell, sitting in the amen corner, arose and said, "Bishop, I will assume $500 of the debt and my son, Richard, who is now with General Lee in Virginia, $500. Seconds later the entire balance of the debt had been paid and Bishop Pierce dedicated the First Methodist Church to the glory of God.

Years later when the streets of Union Springs were named the two streets that intersect at the church building were named Blackmon and Powell. That alone tells you how influential these two families were in this church. James Blackmon Powell, or "Jim" as he is known to his friends, was a lifelong member and has held just about every office in the church. He has always given above and beyond the call of duty both of his time and anything needed.

Benjamin Phillip Powell, father of Jim, was a well known cotton broker in Bullock County. When Jim graduated from the University of Alabama he joined his father in the business. His mother was Asenath Smith Powell, both predeceased him as did two sisters, Myra Powell Anderson and Mary Powell Carroll. He is survived by one sister, Asenath Powell Dooley.

Jim Powell was an outstanding citizen of this county, contributing in so many ways. To list a few, he served as Chairman of the Board of Directors of the then First National Bank and as a director for many years. He served on the Board of Education, was a member of the Exchange Club, a Legislator and he served in World War II.

Jim married Anne Glenn Caldwell from Eufaula who also pre-deceased him. They had three sons, James Jr., who now lives in North Carolina, Glenn, who lives in Tuscaloosa and Benjamin who also lives in North Carolina. They have seven grandchildren and six great-grandchildren. Though sadly there is no longer a Powell from this line in Bullock County we can be sure the traits these children inherited and learned from their parents will leave a mark where ever they live.

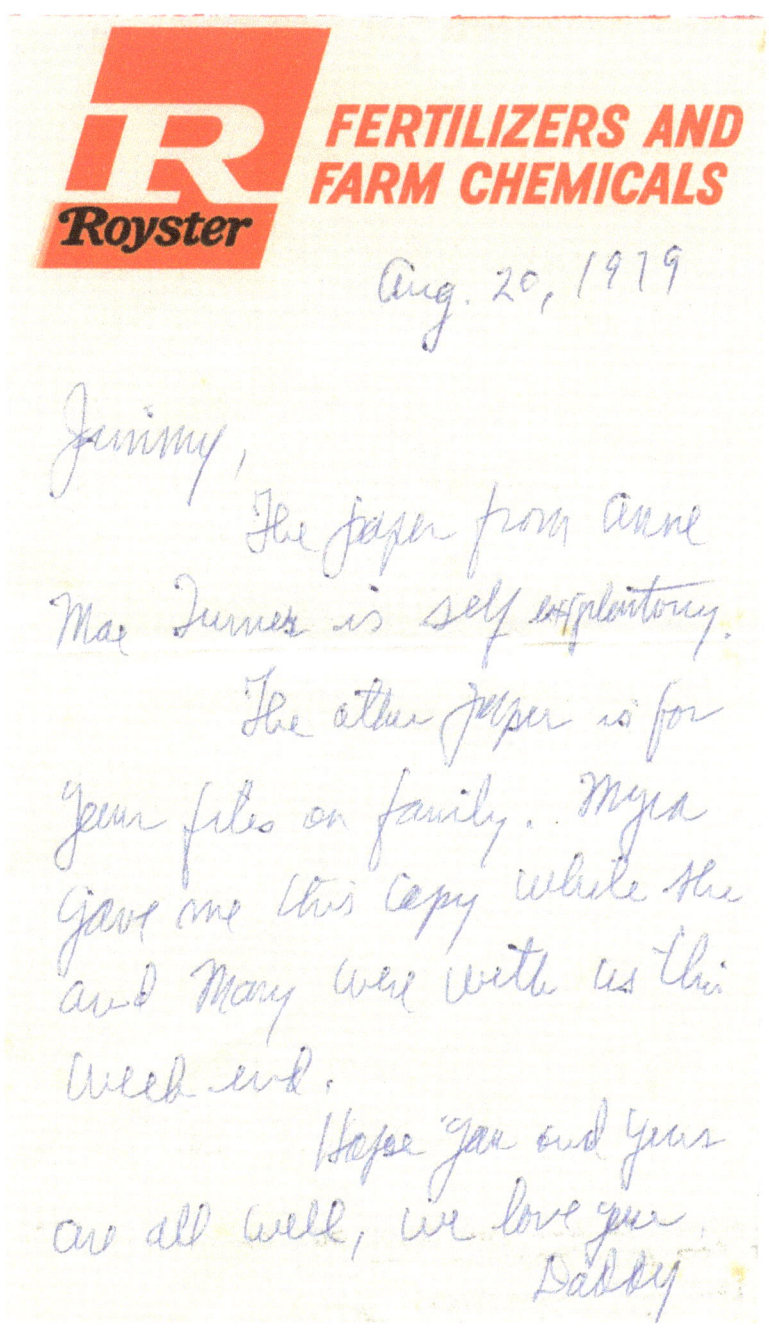

A note explaining the
following church history
JBP II

# First United Methodist Church

101 South Powell Street
Union Springs, AL 36089
Rev. Asbury F. Wolfe, Jr., Minister

Office: 738-3282

Parsonage: 738-3345

April 21, 1979

In the year 1857 the Methodists of Union Springs were without a minister and a church, so Colonel R. H. Powell gathered the few Methodist children and their parents and organized a Sunday School. The meetings were held every Sunday afternoon in his parlor.

In 1858 the first scheduled services were held by the Methodists in the Presbyterian Church. The congregation was without a minister, so the Presiding Elder preached when his schedule would permit him to do so.

In 1859 it was decided the time had come to build a church for the growing congregation. The Land Company, composed of Doctor J. M. and S. J. Foster, Colonel R. H. Powell, Colonel Homer Blackmon and Arnold Seales, gave the lot for the church and parsonage. One year later the church was completed. Its first minister was Rev. John Williams.

The membership grew and the Church prospered, so that a new building was needed. The present building was built in the years of 1903-04. The origional building faced Blackmon Street, but it was decided that the new building should face Powell Street. The building committee who looked after the details of construction were F. M. Moseley, Sr., Chairman; T. S. Durr, J. B. Hunter, G. H. Harris, and W. R. Bickerstaff, Sr.

# A memory of Jim by his grandson, "B.G."

Every May when the temperatures here rise and the humidity gets worse, I think of Jim and the nights I spent in Union Springs towards the end of his days. We would watch Braves games on the highest volume setting and he would fall asleep in his La-Z-Boy after a couple of 'Jimmies' and a few handfuls of Goldfish. I would turn the volume down to maybe a jackhammer setting and sit there in the heat and humidity… Jim would usually get up around the end of the game to find the Braves had pulled out another one…good times.

"Jim"
College years
1929-1933

# Memories of Jim
## (and Glennie)
## James Blackmon Powell
## (and Anne Glenn Caldwell Powell)

### (Written in November/December 2018)

In the last part of Jim's life, he had an expression that he often used: "Thank you. Thank you. Thank you." And so, with a toast to Jim with his famous invention, a "jimmie" consisting of a healthy portion of rum, cranberry juice, and Diet Coke, I begin this short journey with Jim and say "Thank you. Thank you. Thank you Jim" for your gentle, friendly, and warm life.

The son of Benjamin Philip Powell ("Pop") and Sarah Asenath Smith Powell ("Mom"), Jim was born in Union Springs, Alabama on September 11, 1911. He was the third child with three sisters wrapped around him: Myra, Mary, and Asenath (Senie). Jim came after Myra (the mature, serious sister) and Mary (the docile and sweet sister) and before Senie (the baby who could drip honey and a lot of action). The sisters were both a blessing and curse to him; he didn't dare cross one or he would risk gang retaliation. Jim had a black spot on his rump where sister Senie, on their way walking to school, told Jim to move faster and when he didn't move at the speed Senie wanted, she poked her pencil in his rear; he bore that black lead under his skin for the rest of his life.

Jim was probably a bit of a rover, not quite a gadabout, but he loved hunting and moving around with his buddies. He was reasonably good looking but not in the market for a wife. I know very little about it, but there was a tragic accident on the Alabama/Florida coast; the car in which he and some other guys were riding ran off the road into the soft sand and overturned and one of his buddies was killed. I have reason to believe that something like that happened because as I was learning to drive, Jim would go hyper if I drove close to the shoulder of the road or to the edge of any bridge we were crossing.

He attended the public schools of Union Springs and the University of Alabama, where he was a Sigma Nu. He graduated from the University on May 3, 1933, in the middle of the Great Depression of 1929 to 1939 with a Bachelor of Science degree in Commerce and Business Administration signed by Dr. Denny as President and Dr. Bidgood as Dean of the Business School. Times were bad and jobs were scarce. But with no job and a somewhat carefree attitude, Jim bought a car and went off to the Chicago Worlds Fair. Reality must have set in soon because upon his return, with little more than his accounting major, he began work as a roustabout in the Louisiana oil fields, pulling up used and abandoned pipes.

He eventually returned to Union Springs where he resumed his bachelor life of working, hunting, farming, and starting his eventual life occupation of cotton brokerage. He met Glennie, who had moved to Union Springs and was teaching PE in the public school. Glennie was Anne Glenn Caldwell from Eufaula, Alabama, born on June 19, 1912, to Clarence Groves Caldwell and Mattie Crawford Green Caldwell, the last of whom, her mother, died when Glennie was a teenager. She had a sister who died in infancy before Glennie was born and a brother, Rye, who died as a very young man in a car accident in Eufaula. She had another brother, Clarence Caldwell ("Uncle Clarence"), who was the only member of Glennie's immediate family alive when she went off to the Woman's College of Alabama (later Huntingdon College, a Methodist institution) in Montgomery at the age of 16. She graduated from The Woman's College with a BA on May 30, 1932. Her good friend and next-door neighbor, Joy McDowell (Crook), had taken a teaching job in Union Springs and convinced Glennie to join her because the male market was good. Joy married a banker, John Allen Crook ("A. Crook," president of the bank as recognized in Ripley's). Glennie went to Union Springs, took a job teaching PE, and eventually hooked Jim. Following her mother's death, she was cared for by her Aunt Susie, who lived in Opelika, Alabama, and it was in Aunt Susie's house that Glennie and Jim were married in 1938 when she was 26 and Jim was 27. Glennie was vivacious and fun and a great entertainer. Her clothes were an explosion of color and movement, and she was often draped in jewelry, much of which I discovered after her death was costume. She taught us three boys housekeeping and cleaning, some cooking (with a lot of help from Mozelle Young), and how to set tables and entertain. And she gave us a modest but strong spiritual life---bible reading and references and routine prayers. Though Jim was fun loving and social, his more somber and serious side needed a Glennie. I think they had a loving and exciting relationship for much of their lives, although it got bad and sometime ugly in their later years.

When Pop died, Jim acquired the interests of his three sisters in 960 acres of farm and timber land about 7 miles from Union Springs out Highway 29N toward Tuskegee. Over the years I heard a bit of a conflict about this transaction. Some of the sisters felt that Jim underpaid and Glennie felt that he overpaid. Mom still owned a large piece near this property, out the bumpety-bump red bird road that turned off Highway 29 at Noose Ball's black club (later to become the Bullock County/Union Springs Country Club). The "farm" had two adjoining large ponds, a smaller watering hole, a few small creeks, and a swamp. There were several black families and at least one hearty sharecropper living on the land. Two of those, Blue and Henry, "managed" the farm, tended the cattle, planted and harvested the cotton and a little corn (feed for the cattle and a few pigs) and generally kept up the place, including maintaining the sometimes crude fences. Most of the residents picked cotton in season. No one, including Jim, made much money from their often very hard work. Theirs was a meager existence. Their "homes" were crude shacks with newspaper on the walls for insulation.

Jim was a hands-on owner. Although he didn't pick cotton, he was there during picking time and often helped with the collection and weighing. He took part in the cattle round-ups and "cuttings," the bloody conversion of male calves to steers. He roamed the land and often hunted, mainly quail and a few doves around the water holes and corn fields (and on some baited fields). Some of the land was in large open fields that provided hay and grazing and required bush hogging (the bush hog was invented in Selma, Alabama).

Jim taught us to shoot. I'll never forget the first time I fired the 20 gauge shot gun at the place where a snipe had been. I think I put the shotgun down and ran for the car, thinking I would never hear again. But over the years, I got a lot of good shooting practice by trying to hit those snipe around those ponds. And there were also the majestic and elusive geese that sometimes dropped by our pond. I spent many an hour crawling on my belly trying to get close to them but they were too good for me.

Jim took a real chance in taking us hunting. Many a Thanksgiving morning, Jim would load the three of us up along with an assortment of guns (22 rifle, pistol, shotguns) and stop by and hook up with Shorty Benton and his wild son Aubrey (he often had a flying squirrel climbing all over him and in his shirt pocket) and their pack of beagle squirrel hounds. The problem came when Shorty and his dogs sniffed out a squirrel high in a tree, usually in a nest, and we would open fire and continue to fire at the squirrels as they scattered, often up and down. I can still see Jim and Shorty eating leaves and dirt as we fired indiscriminately as they screamed for us to stop shooting.

And there were the exciting late afternoon dove shoots over a water hole deep in the farm. It was a thrill just to wind your way around to the place with no trail or markings and then suddenly, there it would be. Tall trees largely surrounded it so that as the doves flew in fast and hot, diving and turning wildly, dropping low to the water, we would fire away, sometimes toward Jim or a brother on the other side of the hole. And I will only mention shooting at doves in early morning in a corn field before the corn had been harvested as they swooped and dove in and out of the corn, praying no one was within the range of my shotgun blast. But we never shot anyone and actually learned safe hunting and shooting from Jim ----- and had some very special times with him. He was patient and tolerant, especially on those many occasions when he and Glennie loaded us up with poles, worms. crickets, and corks, and, after stopping for a couple of Miller beers and malt crackers, drove out to some club ponds out from town. Imagine if you can, Glennie, who required at least two full time assistants, rocking the boat as she moved with no thought of its precarious condition, quick to scream or yelp when she saw a snake, caught a fish, hooked her line on a limb or stump or in Jim's head, back, or hand. And she was better than we drowned worms and crickets. Picture two adults and two or three high strung boys in a boat with nothing to do but cause trouble. At least Jim couldn't use his belt. But those we very good and fun times---we were a family. Jim made us clean the fish when we got home, but I never ate any we cleaned because of the remaining scales and bits of entrails.

The farm provided a wealth of adventure and education but its distance from where we lived was a barrier. Until I got a driving license at 16, I had to depend on Jim or someone to get me there. And even after I got a license, I had no car until my second year in college. So I was limited to a very occasional walk (about 45 minutes to an hour each way), an even more rare hitchhike, or a friend with a license and car. And then by the time I had a car. I was off at college and distant summer jobs. But somehow I did get there----hunting duck in the swamp at dusk with brother Jimmy and his friend Crook, "borrowing" Jim's rattle trap truck, using Glennie's car when she wasn't, and eventually having my own car.

I worked on the farm on occasions, clearing out Cherokee Rose, planting pines, bailing hay, spraying weed killer on the cotton fields using Jim's antique tractor, rounding up cows, bush hogging the pastures, and paying the cotton pickers, which took some doing. With Jim's oversight, I had to determine the amount due each picker from the amount of cotton picked and apply the per pound rate. Then using those amounts, I had to determine the number of bills and coins necessary to pay each picker the exact amount due them, total it all and get Jim to write a check. I would sweat it out as I got to the last payment, praying the coins and bills would come out right. If they didn't, I would have to empty the envelopes and start all over.

I think Jim would have liked to be a full time farmer/cattleman/hunter, but he didn't have the time or resources to do that. He had to squeeze out of the farm every nickel he could to maintain the farm and to support us and our lifestyle and three college and professional education expenses. I remember the night when we were children and Daddy loaded us in a car and drove to the farm to see a raging forest fire, spread from a Maytag burn off that had jumped its fire lane and onto the farm. Jim told us that we were watching our college funds go up in smoke. Although he and Glennie (and we boys) found ways to cover those costs, it did show the pressure on him and the tight financial margin he had between making it and not making it.

And that takes me to his main livelihood---the cotton brokerage business and the Loving, Cochran, and Powell partnership. These are childhood memories and may not be completely accurate but it is what I remember. Mr. Loving was a kind of absentee partner, probably mostly involved in financing, connections with the cotton mills, and the fertilizer, boll weevil and weed control business. Bill Cochrane was an active partner until his death; he had a very athletic son, Bill, who drowned while swimming with brother Ben and a group of friends at Chewacla State Park out f[rom] Auburn. He had a daughter, Ann, who married cousin Dick Powell. I believe th[ere] was an older daughter too, Mary Jo??

By the time I reached the age of awareness about Jim's business world, he was th[e] sole owner of the brokerage, warehouse, and fertilizer and weed and boll weevil control business. He was assisted by Ben Cochrane, who was not a partner but a kind of office manager. So. Jim was both a buyer and seller of cotton---a jobber. Using a letter of credit and loans, each year Jim would go deep in debt to get the funds to buy cotton that usually was taken to and stored in his large warehouse u[ntil] he could sell it to a mill, hopefully for more than he paid for it----but there were [no] guarantees. He had a group of powerful and fun loving black males who could l[ift] and toss the bales around like bags of fertilizer. He had a couple of open long-be[d] trucks that looked like they were more appropriate for the dump than the highw[ay]. Those black men drove those trucks and did a good job, considering the equipm[ent]. But don't take this to mean that Jim was reckless with his men or careless with t[he] condition and safety of his trucks and equipment. Hear it as the strife and pressu[re] under which Jim had to operate to be profitable and safe.

Often we had the run of the warehouse (and later, when we drove our own junk cars, access to his gas pumps), and what a wonderland it was. If we could get aw[ay] with it, we would romp all over the tops of the bales of cotton, sometimes two bal[es] high and in the huge, very dark, wren and pigeon infested back area, bales sometimes stacked three high, often rocking precariously from our explorations a[nd] climbing. As you ran over the bales (Jim threatened us about knocking off the ta[gs]) you tried not to fall into the sometimes small spaces between the bales, and you could hide in the those spaces. Better than all of that was the loose cotton bin, ab[out] 10 to 12 feet high, usually filled with discarded samples and cotton swept up from the floor. We would climb to the top of the bin and dive, flip, jack knife, belly bu[st] and cannon ball into that fluffy, soft, dirty, DDT infested cloud. You could do no[thing] wrong in your dive. The only problem was that as you sank deep into the cotton [and] pushed it away from your face (assuming it was not packed around your head), y[ou] had no idea about which way was up and which way was down. If you didn't br[eak] surface fairly soon, panic would set in and you would start with a gentle yell and then progress to a scream. Hopefully Clive or one of the other men would rescue you but only after saying loudly to others that they were loading up the loose cot[ton] in the bin to be baled. And there was in the dust as we ran over and among the b[ales] and dove in the loose cotton in the bin, the sweet smell of DDT and other pesticid[es] and herbicides.

There were other big city jobbers and brokers (e.g., Weil Brothers Cotton, headquartered in Montgomery) with deep pockets and numerous employees and heeled competition, Jim usually was successful in maintaining his customers because he was honest, hard working, personable, and fair.

To know Jim, you need to know a little about the cotton business (before the day of automated picking and round bales). Pickers pulled the raw cotton from the sharp, prickly bolls and put it into cloth or burlap bags that the picker had on their shoulders or pulled along. At the end of the day, those bags were weighed to determine what was due the picker. Then the cotton was combined and hauled to the gin where the seeds were removed along with some of the trash and packed into burlap with steel bands holding it in, looking like a very fat and stuffed Santa Clause. Each ginned bale was weighed (around 500 pounds) and tagged with a flat paper card with severable portions with an identifying number on each portion. Using a very sharp knife, two crescent shaped cuts were made on each side of the bale, a sample was pulled out from each side, and one of the severable tags was separated and placed between the two samples and then rolled, sometimes in paper, and packed with other samples. It was those samples that Jim used to grade the bales and determine a price.

So that sets up my best and most extensive time with and knowledge about Jim (hunting and fishing being a close second). During summer and sometimes during school breaks, I would go with Jim on his buying trips, usually in southeast Alabama---Clayton, Louisville. Clio, Bertha, Abbeville, Midland City, Newton, Headland, Pinckard, sometimes Dothan, Ozark, Eufaula, and Troy and a number of gins not in a town. Sometimes I would make a trip with him during the fall during school breaks. Jim was a very good driver and did a lot of driving (and smoking, Camels and then filtered Salems, and later eating hard candy when he tried to stop smoking). My job during the drives was to keep him awake. With the thousands of miles he drove, I don't know of a single accident during one of these trips.

We would go to his contact, at a gin office or in a store or a bank. His customers knew him well and clearly liked him and respected his honesty and integrity, but some were greedy and hard, quick to sell to another if Jim's price wasn't enough for them. Around Christmas, we could take giant peppermint sticks and other small gifts for them. Jim and his customers would talk at length about cotton and the market and hunting and fishing and of course, football. Eventually we would go to the place where the samples were rolled and usually packed in a large, round wicker basket. My job was to carefully lift out a sample and hand it to Jim and then, when he finished grading, make sure the tag was back in the middle, roll it up, and put it in a second wicker basket. Jim would unroll each sample, record the number, smell it, look though it, and use a small amount to estimate the fiber length and quality (he later had some equipment in his office that would do this and some special lighting). Bad or poor lighting could affect the test of the quality of the cotton, so he sometimes would move around for better lighting.

One of the best parts of these trips was the freedom to explore gins, warehouses, and other special places and the lunches at the rustic but very good cafes and the occasional "Green Spot" and "Orange Crush" and Ike and Mikes or his favorite, malt crackers.

Jim had perfect printing skills. He wrote down the bale numbers, the weight given by the seller, his grades (strict low bright, fair to middling, etc.), fiber length, etc. in perfect print form. Then he would add the weights and offer a price. He was an artist on the adding machine---fast and always accurate. I was the opposite, coming slowly up with a different total each time. But Jim was infinitely patient, and I provided good fodder for his fun loving customers and bystanders.

What follows next are a few of the snapshot memories I have of Jim and my life with him.

As a young child struggling for one of two window seats in the car (Glennie always had shotgun) and after being shoved, pinched, and harassed by the brothers even when it was my turn, I sometimes opted for the space behind the rear seat under the rear window. Anything was better than trying to outrun Jim's belt that came out when he could no longer abide the struggles and noise. But that rear window was a serene and peaceful spot where at night I could look up at the stars, the moon, the Milky Way and other celestial wonders. Often I would drift off to sleep and be only a little aware of Jim lifting me up and out and onto my bed. It was a dreamy and wonderful---and upon reflection, spiritual event.

Once after yet another loss by our high school football team (we won only one game in each of my junior and senior years), Jim and Glennie came home after a night out, and Jim roused me from a deep sleep and said we were going out to the back yard where he would teach me a thing or two about blocking and tackling. I loved football and was pretty good at blocking and tackling (named best blocker), but I would not cross Dad, even though I was worried that one of us was about to get hurt. Glennie intervened and that was the end of that coaching, although he did continue to come to some practices. I was glad he cared and noticed.

Jim was elected to the state legislature when I was attending the University of Alabama. He also was on the local board of education, maybe chair. He was not comfortable in relating and speaking to large groups but was wonderful one-on-one and with small groups. I remember when our Methodist Church had an anniversary celebration during which Jim presented a paper about the church history and his family's role (the church is located at the intersection of Powell and Blackmon streets). He was so nervous as he presented that he basically read his paper and shook enough that you could hear the paper rattling. But he recognized the challenge and enrolled in and took a Dale Carnegie public speaking program.

When his term in the legislature was up, he ran for reelection but was defeated by a railroad employee. His defeat came largely because of his support as a member of the board of education tor the closing of the Inverness High School, the only high school in Bullock County other than the one in Union Springs. Because of its small size and poor financial condition, closing was the only solution to a dying school, but the Inverness community passionately objected. When I was home one weekend during the election, after a late night with Caroline, I answered a very late call from a furious, vulgar, threatening, anonymous female caller. I'm sure Jim did not like the defeat, but it was not hard for him to get over it.

I remember Daddy as a gentle, soft speaking, but firm father and person---in love with and loyal to his wife Glennie to the end, even in the face or her sometimes blistering assaults. I remember a lot of love and affection between them in my early years but by the time Glennie died, their relationship was often not good, in fact terrible. Jim must have had some role in Glennie's increasing anger but Jim never demonstrated it that I saw. Mom (Jim's mother) was a pain in Glennie's side, and Glennie had only distant kin. And she lived with four males and no girls---and for much of her life, no mother or father. Whatever may have been the root cause of this often tumultuous relationship, as she was dying, Jim was her dedicated and constant caregiver in all her needs. He never forgave himself because Glennie died when he left her at the hospital for a few minutes to go to Hardees to get a sausage and biscuit.

I knew it was going to be a trying time for Jim without Glennie around, a truth quickly revealed during the wake at Jim's following her funeral. When I went in the small pink half bath beneath the circular staircase in their home, hundreds of termites came swarming out, all over the place. I ran and told Jim and he said not to worry---he was having a problem with ants that he could control. He went to the small closet opposite the bathroom door and took out an ant killer spray. There were at least 15 other cans stored in that closet. I did call the termite people who brought a platoon of people to wage termite war, oops, I mean ant war.

Jim's life in their large home after Glennie's death was colorful to say the least. As the closest son and with a serving wife in Caroline, we tried to keep local help feeding him and cleaning. He insisted on walking to the state whiskey store in town, at least a couple of miles and across several dangerous roads and with poor eyesight---he had macular degeneration. Sometimes kind friends would see him and make him let them drive him home.

Glennie and Jim had a large upright freezer in the kitchen that went out after her death. He really didn't need it though because he had ample freezer space in the top of the refrigerator. But when I came home one weekend, he told me that he had bought a new upright freezer. It was so large that they had to take off two doors to get it into the kitchen. When I checked to see what he had in it, I found four or five zip lock bags of locally made cheese straws, a favorite of his with his Jimmies, and nothing else.

Caroline and I had dated off and on (mainly on) for over 20 years, and finally in 1964, we were getting married. On the wedding day, Jim came upstairs where I was dressing and offered me pre-marital advice. Never before had he talked to me about birds and bees or anything having to do with relations with Caroline. He just had one firm piece of advice: "Don't be a brute." I don't know why or from where that came. Maybe he saw the fire in my eyes and worried for Caroline. In truth, although it surprised and amused me, I tried to treat Caroline according to that standard, especially after I broadened the definition to include "Don't dominate, don't close your eyes, ears or mind, don't think 'me first,' look at and listen to her, talk to her, make yourself vulnerable to her----don't be a brute." Good advice Dad.

This writing has taken me back to some memories and emotions that time has sullied and somewhat obscured. As I reread it, I have a strong sense that something important is missing---and I think I know what it is. Jim and Glennie loved the three of us and taught, trained, and watched over us, often at their sacrifice. Much of their resources went to our expensive and never ending education, summer camps, doctor's and dentist's bills for countless cuts, broken limbs, head and foot injuries, boils, braces---you name it, we had it. And there were the wonderful, long trips to Gatlinburg, the Smokies and Blue Ridge, the beach (Alabama and Florida), Mexico, Canada, nearly every state capital and national park and forest, Washington DC, New York, Miami, Atlanta, and just about everywhere else, including a distant relative's grapefruit and orange grove near what was to become Cape Canaveral. We had prayers before meals and devotions every day. We were taken to every church service and revival, Sunday school, and MYF. We consumed most of their resources and time. They took us to and attended endless piano recitals, school programs and plays, PTA and similar meetings, football games and practices, baseball games all summer long (including running the food stand), road trips, trips to out of town doctors and dentists, and much more. They "led" us to piano and some musical instrument lessons (a trombone for me) and even voice lessons (I was fired by the teacher). Before the time of central heat, I remember them bringing a towel heated on the top of the oil firebox and wrapping our feet under the cold sheets. They raised us to excel, two doctors and one lawyer, all with top honors in high school and college. All three of us served in the military, and no one had a criminal arrest, drug, or drinking problem. I say these things, not to boast, but to honor and praise them---that they had the love, patience, and skill to mold three very rough, independently-minded boys into men who are able to and do serve their families, friends, community, and church, instilling in their progeny the good that they learned from Jim and Glennie.

Daddy and Momma: Thank you. Thank you. Thank you. See you soon.
Clarence Glenn (#2 son)

# JAMES BLACKMON POWELL II
## "Jimmy" "Jim"
## 1939–

# James Blackmon Powell II

Info:

jamesandmarypowell@gmail.com

828-274-1696 (Home) 828-275-7865 (cell)

4 Greenwood Road, Biltmore Forest Asheville NC 28803-3111

Bio:

First born of three boys December 12, 1939, in Norman Apartments, Union Springs, Alabama. Birth was at home, attended by "Dr. Charlie" Franklin, the doctor for all in Union Springs.

Earliest memories:

Cocker spaniel puppies bred and raised by uncle Clarence, Mama's much older brother; subsequent puppies Rags and Tags; having Mom and Pop, Daddy's parents, always as support; brother Glenn born 1942; moving into a make-shift apartment with a small kitchen upstairs in Mom and Pop's house when Daddy was drafted and sent to invade Japan 1944-1945; President Truman and his decision to use the atomic bomb, likely saving our father's life; brother Ben born while Daddy was shipboard in Okinawa; duties of bringing coal in for the fireplaces, the only source of warmth, and only able to carry a half scuttle per trip.

Starting to school and having new friends; in the second grade, teaching Mary McElwayne how to tie her shoes; church, Sunday school and summertime revivals.

Visits of our cousins every summer with children segregated to areas away from adults; ghost stories that are still remembered; Sunnyside Beach, the last beach west of Panama City, Florida, with cousins Carrolls and Andersons; being dressed by older cousins, Virginia and Mary, in palmetto frond skirts they made; sand in sunburned skin, sand in sheets, AC did not exist.

School with teachers who loved their jobs and who exposed us to new worlds that seemed almost real; being taught that thinking was good.

Friendships that remain close even today; fishing and hunting as a family and with Crook, a constant companion; occasional trips to Montgomery to shop and dine in a "fancy" restaurant and see a first-run movie; an accident on my Cushman motor scooter on Mother's Day 1952, with some delayed health concussion problems, none long lasting—Glenn and Ben never got a motor scooter; a graduation party hayride to celebrate graduation from 6th to 7th grade, which meant we would be in the high school building across town for 7th-12th grades; scouting, highlighted by two summer weeks at Camp Tuckabatchee, $11.00 per week; tapped and initiated into the Order of the Arrow; by train and bus to the 1953 Scouting Jamboree at Irvine Ranch, Los Angeles, California, Zion National Park; troop disbanded, two merit badges (required) short of Eagle (would have necessitated joining a troop in Montgomery); first real job as a soda jerk at Main's Drug store, age 11.

High school with great, demanding teachers, a very special time with friends in grades ahead and behind. Thirty-three people in my 1958 high school graduation class. All but three went to college, four had football scholarships—Auburn, Miss Southern, UGA.; three MDs, four PhDs, two pharmacists and several local businessmen, entrepreneurs, and land/timber holders. A very special time, 1955–1960. All who experienced it have always looked back and recalled how lucky we were and became. Twentieth high school reunion, a blast.

Junior year, Jan. 1957–Aug. 1957, a page, Washington, DC, in House of Representatives appointed by Congressman George Andrews; Page school in Library of Congress, 6:30-10:30 a.m., depending on House sessions' times; "Coming of age" experience: as great friends, a group of eleven of us, formed a "little" fraternity; reporting to the Congressman's office most days, otherwise duties in the House; Sam Rayburn, Texas, Speaker of the House, respected, revered, admired, POWERFUL; Senator John Kennedy, single, handsome and envied; President Eisenhower's second inauguration in four inches of snow!

Graduation from high school 1958; summer school at University of Alabama, hot humid Tuscaloosa; jump started premed courses; "fast tracked" to medical school after three years before "fast tracking" had evolved. Still had time to take non-medical courses, which were wonderful but not enough. Thinking back, could have had a fourth year of all elective courses non-medical, which would have been a luxury; two younger brothers to be educated, $.

Married summer of 1961, Mary Elizabeth Murphree "Bitsy," after courting for a year; medical school in Birmingham long before UAB; first two years of medical school an immense disappointment with turmoil in the faculty and administration—ensconced poor teachers who fostered promulgation of competition among the doctors-to-be, premed all over again—of the original 76 in the class of 1965, six quit the first six weeks of September 1961, and thirteen were flunked out in May 1962. Seven students in the class ahead were put back in our class. A bad time for all with repercussions for several years, but got to the clinical years intact. A new world there. I thrived; Son Jimbo came along at end of first year.

Surprisingly got a competitively sought-after medical-surgery internship at UVA. There met Dr. Fitz-Hugh and residents in otolaryngology, in which I became more and more interested; previous commitment to return to UA to Dr. Lyon's surgery residency, but he died of a brain tumor as I was contemplating my future in Virginia; settled when Dr. Fitz-Hugh offered me a residency in his program; returned to Birmingham for a year of general surgery, to which Dr. John Kirkland, Mayo Clinic world-famous cardiac surgeon, had accepted the Chief of Surgery position; really great year there but returned to Charlottesville for otolaryngology, finishing in 1970. Daughter Ashley born in Birmingham during spring of the residency year there (1966–67).

Three years active duty (1970–1973) US army, 2nd General Hospital, Landstul, Germany. Three wonderful years both for family, for travel, for my medical practice —a different patient mix, which complimented the residency-training mix; very close friends from those three years; 2nd General Hospital remains the most important US military hospital for all of Europe and Middle East.

Returned to USA and to Asheville in Sept 1973 to begin practice with three doctors from the UVA residency; established a reputation of surgical and diagnostic excellence that continues with the second generation of doctors. The original four have retired, I being the last. I continued a limited practice part-time with our VA Hospital until Dec 2018. So at age 79, now fully retired.

Asheville was a great place to call home in 1973. The medical community grew rapidly from 1967-1985 with specialties and subspecialties being established. This community of physicians offers excellent health care for Western North Carolina and has made Asheville attractive to not only retirees but others. Asheville today is far different than the Asheville to which we came in 1973.

We have had a wonderful life here and continue to be active in what we love: activities and participation outside the medical community—travel, bridge, golf, skiing, fly fishing, family; daughter and son-in-law moved here from London after a ten-year stint in London (investment banking) and have raised three children—Sydney, graduating from Vanderbilt, May 2019 (engineering science); Charlie, rising junior Northwestern (computer science); Nicholas, rising junior in high school; son Jimbo, Decatur, Georgia, (medical information technology) and daughter-in-law Ellen Georgia State University (marketing); Emma, rising senior UGA (physiology); Jake, freshman UGA (engineering). All blessed with keen minds and good health.

Life is GOOD!

# JAMES BLACKMON POWELL III
## "Jimbo"
## 1962–

James B Powell III

Born: Birmingham, AL, April 15, 1962

High School: Asheville School, 1980

College: University of Virginia, 1985 BA History & Economics

I have early memories of staying with my grandparents Glennie & Jim in Union Springs and Mimi and Grandaddy in Troy.  Jim had a cotton business and I would climb up into the cotton bales in the warehouse until I figured out that it was way too hot for that.  One time Glennie once got mad at me for some reason and I told her I want to go to Troy so she obliged me, packed my bags, took me to the front door and said "Troy is that way".  I was back in the house in no time.

We lived in Birmingham and Charlottesville during my early years.  My first dog Fluffy was a black cocker spaniel.  When Dad went into the service we were stationed in Landstuhl, Germany for 3 years.  We had to leave Fluffy behind and I was told she went to live on a farm where she could run free - not sure if it was that or the SPCA.

In Germany I was in 3rd through 5th grades.  I learned to ski and play baseball.  We got a guinea pig as a replacement for Fluffy - who soon gave birth to 2 more guinea pigs.  We also adopted a cat but learned we were not a cat family.

After Germany we moved to Asheville, N.C. in 1972.  My high school had a great mountaineering program and I enjoyed hiking and backpacking.  Family Thanksgivings were spent a in a lot of places but it wasa highlight when the Glenn Powell's would come and we would take their Volkswagen "Thing" up in the mountains.

I went to the University of Virginia and was a member of Sigma Chi.  Basketball was riding high then with Ralph Sampson on campus.  The summer after my Junior year I worked in the Jackson, WY at the Jackson Lake Lodge.  More hiking and camping in the Tetons and Yellowstone.

After college I lived in New York from 1985-1988, working for a real estate developer and entrepreneur.  I knew I didn't want to stay in New York so I decided to take a year off and travel.  I backpacked through Africa, India, Nepal, Burma and Thailand.  One of many highlights was a 6 week trek in Nepal that lead us to Annapurna base camp at an elevation of 20,000 feet.

When I returned I moved to Atlanta, GA in late 1988.  I met my wife Ellen Turney through mutual friends from the University of Virginia.  We have 2 children: Emma Porter Powell a Junior at the University of Georgia and James Blackmon Powell IV (Jake) a Senior at Decatur High School.  We live in Decatur, GA.  I work in healthcare technology and Ellen works at Georgia State University in marketing and communications.

Info:  464 Parkwood South
Decatur, Georgia 30030
404 377 1417
jbp3@bellsouth.net

Jake   Ellen  Jimbo Emma
2018

# CLARENCE GLENN POWELL
## "Glenn"
## 1942–

# Info for Dr. Jim Powell

# (Written July-September 2018)

Your full name and nick name: Clarence Glenn Powell   Nick names:  Sputter, from High School mates; Little Fatty---the name of one of several Tuscaloosa gamblers and worse (Nubs, Peter Hunter, Little Fatty, etc.) given me by their associates, the Animal House gang in Sigma Nu.

Your date and place of birth: March 17, 1942, at Hubbard Hospital in Montgomery, Alabama.

Your addresses, both email and USPS (to send cc's of the book): cgpowell2@gmail.com 13297 North River Farm Drive, Northport, Alabama 35473-7125.  (My home is located in the city of Tuscaloosa but the US Postal Service chooses to give me a Northport mailing address.)

Your phone numbers, good but not required: (205) 345-3070

Wife: Caroline Chappell Powell, born May 13, 1942, in Union Springs, Alabama and died on October 20, 2011, in Tuscaloosa, Alabama.  Married August 28, 1965, in the First United Methodist Church of Union Springs, Alabama.  My everything for all time.

The same for your male children and their male children (spouses and female children info):  From my marriage to Caroline Chappell, I have two sons, namely Benjamin Caldwell Powell, born August 29, 1966, at Madigan General Hospital when I was in military service stationed at Ft. Lewis, Washington; and Daniel Chappell Powell, born January 10, 1969, at Druid City Hospital after we moved to Tuscaloosa, Alabama in June of 1968.  My sons have been my joy and companions, my sometimes advisors and critics, and, in a way that reveals just how blessed I am by God, two of my spiritual cornerstones and inspirations.  It was Ben's good fortune to marry the vivacious, talented, and exuberant Virginia Cherry from North Carolina.  Four children have been born out of their marriage, a son, Nathaniel Glenn Powell, born August 12, 1997; a daughter, Kathryn Drake Powell, born October 7, 1999; a daughter, Genevieve Moore Powell, born May 12, 2006; and a son, Oliver Pugh Powell, born October 10, 2008.   Dan has been blessed by his marriage to the petite, winsome, and bright Nicole Palardy from California.  Two children have been born out of their marriage, a son, Peter Benjamin Powell, born April 22, 2005, and a daughter, Mary Caroline Powell, born October 29, 2008.

Your father and grandfather with their full names, birth and death dates:  My father and mother are James Blackmon Powell (30 years old at the time of my birth) born on

September 15, 1911, and Anne Glenn Caldwell Powell (29 years old at the time of my birth) born on June 19, 1912. They were married in 1938 in Opelika, Alabama. Jim's parents (my grandparents) are Benjamin Philip Powell ("Pop"), born 1875 in Fitzpatrick, Alabama, and Sarah Asenath Smith Powell ("Mom"), born in Autauga County, Alabama in 1883. Mom lived to her 90's but Pop died in 1950 in Union Springs, Alabama, when I was in the third grade. Mom's brother, William Howard Smith, married Louise Maytag, and that got my brothers and me a long supply of wonderful Christmas, graduation, and birthday gifts. Glennie's parents were Clarence Groves Caldwell and Mattie Crawford Green Caldwell, both of whom died when Glennie was a teenager. She had a sister who died in infancy before Glennie was born and a brother, Rye, who died as a very young man in a car accident driving up country club road in Eufaula, Alabama, that runs in front of their house. She had another brother, Clarence Caldwell ("Uncle Clarence") who was the only member of Glennie's immediate family alive when she went off to college at Huntington College in Montgomery as an orphan. She was cared for by her Aunt Susie, who lived in Opelika, Alabama, and it was in Aunt Susie's house that Glennie and Jim were married. So I had only two grandparents at birth and only one from the third grade on. Note: I have not said that I was named Glenn for my mother (although now in my later years, that would not be a problem for me). The name came from a last name in Glennie's family. I remember going several times to my buddy Caroline Crook's grandmother's house (Dan McDowell's house) in Eufaula, Alabama (I actually rode the train from Union Springs to Eufaula a couple of times). Dan was the mother of Glennie's best friend, Joy McDowell Crook. Joy's house was next door to Glennie's house. Behind them both was what I remember as a very young boy was a dark and musty old house of mystery and ghosts occupied by Glennie's very old relative, Miss Glenn (last name)---therein I believe lies the name connection.

A brief (I don't think I know what that word means) bio of you: who, what, where, and why and other interests:

Because my mother, Glennie, had a little trouble with her home town delivery of her first born, Jimmy, by "Dr. Charley" and because Jim was often out working or hunting or whatever, she decided to have a hospital delivery, so on a dark and rainy day, two days after the Ides of March, I was born on St. Patrick's day, 1942, in Hubbard Hospital in Montgomery, Alabama. Jim was a little too old for the Army, and I heard Glennie fussing later in life that Pop, Jim's dad, was on the draft board so he should not have been called up or volunteered to serve. Whether he was drafted or volunteered, off he went to the Army (Infantry) at 31 or 32 years old with the thousands of 17, 18, and 19 year olds almost half his age. Mom and Pop took us in, and Mama, Jimmy and I (and later, Ben) lived on the second floor of their house while Jim was making the world safe. I do know that Jim ended up on Okinawa (after perhaps the bloodiest and fiercest battles of WWII) where he waited with all the other green soldiers to invade a well dug in and prepared Japanese mainland force. They expected 80% or more losses from those soldiers who had seen no combat. The plan was that, as they fell, the seasoned troops would be called up. Glennie was about to become a single mom and Jimmy and I were about to lose a father. But then in 1945, along came brother Ben and the bomb. The war soon ended, and Jim came home to Union Springs. NOTE: This would be a good place to include or reference that great shot of the three us with Glennie sitting in a chair in Mom's yard.

Growing up in Union Springs was being in the center of the universe. School was small and usually fun. Other than school, our time was taken up riding bikes all over, swimming at the Rec pool, almost all day every Saturday going to a cowboy and scary movie at the Lilfred theater, roaming around in and swinging on vines above the trees in the two bluffs, one behind Mom and Pop's and the other near our home on the Hill, summer and weekend jobs at Main's Drug Store, Armstrong's grocery, Bill Cameron's Fair Store, Jim's farm and cotton warehouse, the Maytag Plantation (a hard, educational, and maturing time of blood and sweat) and Blount Brothers Construction on the Atlanta Airport, Montgomery Baptist Hospital, and Math and Science Building at Auburn University, all the while spending every possible minute with my growing love, Caroline. During two Christmas holiday times, John Ogletree and I (at 16 and 17 years old) borrowed a Maytag or Bonnie Plant Farm cattle truck, borrowed money from the First National Bank of Union Springs (Jim was a director), and drove to the Indian River region of Florida and loaded the truck with loose oranges off a processing line. Then we returned to Union Springs, parked on a side street, and started selling them like crazy. Every time we got a little cash, we would take it to the bank and pay down our loan, several times a day. The local grocers tried to shut us down because we had no license, but our lawyer, who was the city attorney, advised us to get a telegram from our seller, who owned an orchard, saying we were selling as his agent---growers were exempt from having to buy licenses to sell their own produce. Thus, we avoided certain bankruptcy and made a lot more than we had been making selling pecans to the ice plant.

It gets too painful to leave out so much and so many adventures but Jimmy said be brief. So dropping back to first gear, here are a couple of random vignettes.

I graduated from Union Springs High School (Salutatorian), president of student body, captain of football team, president of the U Club, and four years of letters (football was my passion), etc. In the summer of 1960, I entered the University of Alabama immediately after graduation from high school, after winning a battle with Glennie (and somewhat with Jim) over having to enroll at the Citadel, where they had paid a deposit. Their idea was that if I went to the Citadel, I would learn some order and discipline and cool my strong relationship with Caroline, who would go to Auburn. At UA, I pledged Sigma Nu (largely because my brother Jimmy was Commander and had a car). I attended under a three-year plan by which I could enter law school after 3 years of undergraduate work. If I succeeded in law school, I would get my BA degree at the end of my first year in law school. Why law school you ask? I really don't know. I think it goes back to something I learned when Glennie was cleaning out a lot of our stuff and sent me a number of report cards from my early school. The teachers were glowing about my academic and social success but all said things like, "We can't shut him up." That line of thinking led those around me to decide that I had to become a lawyer to use all those words to make a living. Actually there was a time when I was fascinated with political science and the study of foreign countries, so I decided I wanted to be in the Foreign Service, as an ambassador to China or France or Switzerland. Anyway, for some dumb reason I accepted an election to be Commander of Sigma Nu during my first and critical year in law school. It was a very precarious time; all the males were flocking to any graduate or professional school they could get in to avoid the draft and Vietnam, plus I had to deal with George Wallace's stand and a campus full of soldiers and secret service with, I felt sure, an off campus group of militant, angry people, ready for battle. I witnessed the infamous George Wallace "stand" from a Law School upper window.

Anyway, I made it through law school in only two and a half years, with an AB and law degree in five and a half years (June 1960 to January 1966). My zeal in wanting to finish in a hurry came from my passion to marry Caroline and relieve Jim and Glennie of the expenses of three sons, two pursuing medical degrees and one in law school. I was commissioned as a second lieutenant in Artillery through the ROTC program, finishing the fourth year requirement during my first year in law school, along with trying to serve the Sigma Nus as their commander.

Those last several years of school were emotionally hard because by then I was madly and deeply in love with Caroline. Other than writing each other, Caroline and I could share little because long distance calls were expensive. We would sometimes call each other person-to-person so that the one called would tell the operator that she/he was not there. Then the one called would call back station to station, but even that was often beyond our budget. When I finally bought Jimmy's green Easter egg, I drove to Union Springs when I could but the exciting trip down at lightening speed was later ruined by the sad and dreary long return trip, especially to a paper mill grunge Sunday night in Tuscaloosa. I drove to Auburn one time and stayed with some of Caroline's kin, but as soon as I put down my bags, I started throwing up and continued until just before I left.

Caroline finally graduated in the summer of 1965 (her Auburn education was a financial challenge for her and her parents, even with her working and commuting much of the time). In 1965, she was offered a teaching position in the Tuscaloosa City system at Northington Elementary, adjacent to the UA Northington Campus married student housing, allowing her to walk to work and me to drive to school. So that cleared the way for our marriage in Union Springs on August 28, 1965. After a very fast three-day honeymoon so Caroline could report to work on time, we returned to Tuscaloosa to her job and my last semester of law school.

A couple of months after our marriage, Caroline's ob./gyn advised her to get off birth control pills. The thought was that with her issues, she would find it difficult to get pregnant but they were wrong and by October, we were drinking champagne toasts to our little baby fetus. That pregnancy was a scary issue for me because I had no idea where I was heading in the military, although Vietnam was a very real possibility. My fear was that I would get orders for Vietnam and leave behind a pregnant wife or a wife and new baby.

I completed law school in January of 1966, took the Bar exam in February and left for Fort Bliss (El Paso, Texas) with Caroline and baby fetus Ben to begin my two years of military service. I graduated in the upper 10% of my law class and was named to the Farrah Order of Jurisprudence (now the Order of the Coif) and served as president and other officers of my law school fraternity, Phi Delta Phi, and in a number of other law school and undergraduate offices and roles.

So off I went, with a sweet, all alone (except for me) pregnant wife. After arriving at Fort Bliss and cancellation of my Germany Nike missile orders (because I had declined to take a minimum four year obligation with the Army JAG, I could hear Jim saying "They're gonna make cannon fodder out of you"' I was sent to Fort Lewis Washington to assist in reopening its North Fort as an Infantry combat training center.

Now I'm really going to take off. After baby Ben was born at and survived several days (jaundiced) in Madigan General Hospital (without Caroline, who just about lost her mind because of that separation) we left the military in 1968 and returned to Alabama and began interviewing for a job, while farming some for Jim. With a good shot at one of the top Birmingham firms and an even more enticing offer from a midsized and highly regarded firm in Montgomery, I accepted an offer from a three person firm in Tuscaloosa that represented most of the good banking and business clients and was looking to build a trial practice that I would lead. So in 1968, we moved to Tuscaloosa, which in a way surprised me. The racial battles and ugly white actions in Birmingham, Montgomery, and Tuscaloosa (dogs, beatings, bombings, and burning buses) made coming home hard and Seattle look better. But home and family won out. Dan, another unplanned but delightful surprise, was born in Tuscaloosa in January of 1969.

I practiced in that firm for 5 years and finally became uneasy with the controlling lawyer and decided to look around. I did not want to go to the big cities in Alabama and wanted room to grow in a firm. Oddly enough I selected Asheville, North Carolina, as a place to consider and secretly arranged an interview with one of its top firms. I say oddly because later, with no communication among us, brothers Jimmy and Ben located there. Anyway, the interview was not good. I was cross-examined by a bunch of very old men who were more interested in knowing why I was leaving a good firm than what I wanted from them. I returned to Tuscaloosa and began exploring starting my own firm with Ralph Quarles, one of the lawyers in my firm. Then I learned the University of Alabama was looking for a business counsel. Although I was totally disinterested in being a house counsel, especially for a university, it did provide a good place to practice and look around, so I took the job. I began to love my work. It was demanding, although not like the legal sweatshops of today. The Office of Counsel provided all the legal services for the University System, including the Huntsville campus (UAH), the Birmingham campus (UAB) and the medical center, and the Tuscaloosa mother campus (UA).

After a couple of years at the University, I got restless and began to look beyond my work. So I took a leave of absence, packed up my family in a U Haul and Volkswagen Thing, and moved to New York City where I enrolled in the NYU tax program. I had very little desire to become a tax lawyer but was looking at what NYC had to offer all of us---and it was exciting and fun, although not everything was easy for the kids. That time had a lasting and positive effect on the boys, although it often was hard for them. For several reasons, we returned before I completed the LLM in tax but making that decision led me to a better understanding of what I wanted, not just for me but also for my family.

I returned with renewed vigor and interest in and commitment to my service to the University. I eventually became its General Counsel, and when I retired, we had 18 lawyers and 14 professional and staff members with offices at UAH, UAB and the medical center and the UAB Health System, and UA. What made it so rewarding was that instead of having many clients with many different problems, we had one client with many issues and the freedom to concentrate our energy and resources as we felt best and proper for the client, without the controlling demand for billable time and fees. But we could and did monitor and measure productivity and efficiency---and we were very busy, working many nights and most weekends.

I retired in 2003, and said a sad goodbye to a disappointed and loving group of lawyers and staff. It was not easy to do but I had ideas of world travel and big time public service that had not been possible from the time Caroline and I married in 1965, and I wanted a lot more time to spend with Caroline and for us to spend with our families, especially the grandkids.

But Caroline used to say, "If you want to make God laugh, tell him your plans." In November of 1994, we found Caroline had what was thought to be breast cancer that had moved into and was dangerously threatening her spine. After instant and prolonged radiation and stuff like Tamoxifin, she was eventually cured of that cancer, so after our retirements, we took off on our travels, Alaska, Ireland, Paris, London and more. In doing extensive gardening and riding in hackney cabs all over London, in May of 2007, Caroline experienced a return of the terrible pain in her back and side. The earlier radiation treatment apparently resulted in sarcoma in her spine (She also was diagnosed with lymphoma that probably could have been managed). After numerous chemo treatments and 9 hours of surgery at UAB in October of 2009 and pins and such, the sarcoma kept roaring back, and she eventually became paralyzed from the chest down, and I became her in-home, full time caregiver. Her disease was a curse, but it gave me the opportunity to love and serve her in a special and demanding way. It was a painful but very loving and spiritual time. She was pain-ridden but always a brave and loving angel, constantly praying for and serving others (especially me). I now look back on those times as gifts to me from an ever present, always loving God and an awesome soul mate. Anyway, she died on October 20, 2011----and I miss her and long for our eventual and eternal reunion (if she can get me in).

I can not cover the many other adventures, events, and experiences of my blessed life---I feel badly that they are omitted, but grab a glass of good wine (preferably from brother Jimmy's cellar) or some very old unblended scotch and sit a while with me, and we will try to cover a few of those memories.

What were some of the other highlights of my life? They're impossible to list but I will mention some. First and foremost by far is my relationship and life with Caroline. Through some bumpy times (what do you expect from a relationship that covers over 60 years), we got better and closer until we were truly united and one, in spirit and soul, with the Holy Spirit gently guiding our relationship. It is a mysterious and deeply spiritual thing that is impossible to describe but unquestionably real and tangible.

Life in Union Springs from birth to graduation from high school was an amazing adventure and blessing---truly a cocoon that allowed largely sheltered but real growth among family, numerous friends, teachers, and a great and colorful community.

Other than Bear Bryant, Joe Willie Namath, George Wallace, the "pool" at the Sigma Nu house, Ship Wreck and other parties at the Sigma Nu Animal House, a couple of temporary alluring beauties along the way (my parents wanted Caroline and me separated, her at Auburn and me at Alabama), some long and lonely times separated from Caroline, and serving as Commander of the Sigma Nus and finishing my fourth year of ROTC, all while taking my critical first year of law school, my five and a half years of undergraduate and law school will not be reported on more here.

My two years in the Army (1966 to 1968) at Fort Bliss, Texas and Fort Lewis, Washington were quite an adventure. Separated from home and family support, my brave wife Caroline went through the birth and care of baby Ben with only Dr. Spock and me to help. With a commission in field artillery, as only the Army can do, I was trained instead with Nike missiles (a couple misfired into Mexico) and quad 50 caliber track mounted machine guns (World War II air defense weapons) to be used in Vietnam as convoy escort and perimeter defense. Armed with that training and with the real possibility of orders for Vietnam, off I went to Fort Lewis, Washington to open its North Fort as a basic combat training center. I have never had more responsibilities or challenges in my life---it was exhilarating and in a perverse way, exciting. On the rare occasions that I could slip away, Caroline, baby Ben and I were off exploring the Oregon and Washington coast, the ski slopes, rafting down the melting snow rivers, the San Juan and Emerald Islands, British Columbia, Mount Rainier, Hood, Baker, Adams and the Cascades. But I'm going back into too much detail.

Other highlights include: Building and operating a "law firm" in the University from 4 lawyers to 18 lawyers and a support staff of 14 when I retired as General Counsel, operating out of 5 different offices in Huntsville, Birmingham, and Tuscaloosa; attending one semester in the Tax program at NYU and personally moving (via U Haul and a Volkswagen "Thing") my family to NYC; starting and managing a volunteer weekend soup bowl program in Tuscaloosa and presiding over the full 7 day program; assisting in and supervising the creation of a prayer garden and columbarium at First United Methodist Church of Tuscaloosa, which is the location of the ashes of my now full time angel wife and eventually of me too (hopefully after my death)..

The editor has suggested that I mention my experiences with Boy Scouts and the Lay Speaker program of the United Methodist Church.

Growing up in a small town in rural south Alabama, one would expect Scouting to be in the radar of any young male. Lieutenant-General Robert Stephenson Smyth Baden-Powell, 1st Baron (22 February 1857 – 8 January 1941) was a British Army officer, writer, founder and first Chief Scout of The Boy Scouts Association, and founder of the Girl Guides. Baden-Powell authored the first editions of the seminal work *Scouting for Boys*, which was an inspiration for the Scout Movement. Though he is no kin to us, that name stirred in me some of his fascination and interest. in Scouting. My relationship with Scouts began as a young person in a small troop led by Bobby Moore and "Preacher" Chappell (Caroline's ex marine dad) that met in a basement area below the state whiskey store which was below the only telephone service in the county and its sole operator, Miss T. Pitts. Mainly we gathered and then ran all over town, going by the body in the window of the morgue next to the Courthouse and on to the large and foreboding Oak Hill Cemetery and the ghosts of Jesse James and many others. We also did a lot of camping and some upchucking from hamburger cooked in a can over potatoes and beans, grease au jus.

Scouting got more serious when my brother, Jimmy, and I, started going to BSA summer camp at Camp Tukabatchee near Prattville in Autauga County, Alabama. It was for real —hot, tough, controlled, military like to some extent. The swimming and life saving training were as tough as Olympic training---diving for and rescuing concrete blocks from the bottom of the lake, trying to rescue powerful older athletes from fake drowning (they usually drowned us), and swimming, swimming, and swimming. There was a compass course through the jungle that took you on and on until hopefully you ended up at your designated marker and not the kitchen, lake, or latrine.

Once a week, we would gather in an amphitheater type place for the show---and what a show it was---better than any I have seen. Sitting in the dark night suddenly you see a shooting star (actually a flaming arrow) slowly arching way up and over toward the dark mound in front of us. As the arrow made its way to the earth, suddenly there was an explosion in the mound, and it burst into flame. As the fire sprang into a blaze of color and heat, you could hear, very faintly at first, the steady and rhythmic beat of bells. And a line of barely dressed Native American braves (we called them Indians) approached the fire from four different directions. As they danced around the fire, suddenly a giant **Pterodactyl** looking form flew out of the woods and danced around the fire, in eagles dress. There was more dancing and magic fire displays. As the dancing died down and the braves made their way back into the woods, with only the slow, steady beat of the drum and toe-step ring of the ankle bells, the black night returned with only a glow from the fire pit. Complete silence. Then all Hell seemed to break loose behind and then all around me. I was stood up by several strong braves, blind folded, and taken off, stumbling and drug along. After a long time, we stopped, and suddenly the blindfold came off and I was told to not say a word. I had been tapped into the Order of the Arrow---probably because my brother Jimmy was also tapped. They put a lariat around my neck with a portion of a small tree branch tied to each end and said that I would now go through an ordeal to test my bravery, strength, and endurance. I was not allowed to speak, but if I did, they would carve a notch in the branch. They said I would be taken to a place of testing and that I could not move. Then they blindfolded me again and led me far into the woods. Finally they stopped, took off the blindfold and slipped away, telling me nothing about where I was or what would happen next and when. So the dark night closed in around me. I was less afraid of bears, wolves, and rabid raccoons than I was of what they would do to me. It was a very long night. It seemed like noon the next day (actually it probably was 6 a.m. or so) that they came to get me. I was lavish in my thanks, but that only got me more notches. By the time the ordeal ended, my branch looked like a family of beavers has been feasting on it for days. Suffice it to say, I passed somehow and became a believing and committed Scout forever.

Before we leave Camp Tukabatchee, I will mention an event. I have said good things about Tukabatchee, but as one of those football coaches said, all that good talk can be rat poison. So, here's a bit of the rest of the story. One day, the adult leaders made all of the campers come to the first aid office where, one by one, we got a shot of some kind. They told us nothing but they did talk to our parents when they came to pick us up and gave them some papers. Later I learned that some of our older boys had sought out some local ladies and secretly taken them to camp for a visit. From that adventure, several of them developed a little health problem from the ladies and required penicillin shots, first for the participants and then for the whole camp. The paper told our parents about the shots and why we had them. You can imagine their pleasure. Never at a loss to try to turn a really bad situation around, the Scout hierarchy said the situation validated the need to remember the Scout Motto: Be Prepared.

Jimmy and I did not have an Order of the Arrow organization in Union Springs, so he drove us to Montgomery where they had one. On one of those trips, we arrived at a horrible wreck that had just happened just out of Montgomery. An elderly couple pulled out onto the busy and fast highway in front of a fellow on a motorcycle. He was knocked him off the motorcycle, and went sailing and sliding down the road. His flesh was torn off on the down side of his face and body and his arms and legs were twisted weirdly like a pretzel. It was frightening and very disturbing---my good first aid training would do him no good. I can't remember whether we went on to the meeting or not.

I was able to pass off at Tukabatchee a lot of the requirements for advancement, but it was not as easy to do that at home as a Lone Scout. I can't remember now but I think I had done all the requirements for everything up to Life Scout but had only made 1st class rank because to get credit and advance for the work I had done, I would have to go before a review board in Montgomery and I didn't want that.

Going forward some 10 or 12 years, in Tuscaloosa, I became active with the Black Warrior Council that serves 12 counties in 3 districts in West Alabama. I was elected to the Executive Board (on which I continue to serve) and became heavily involved in recruiting (chair of School Night for Scouting, etc.), fund raising, long range planning, and policy drafting. I became their legal counsel and served in that role until about 8 years ago. I have been on countless committees and planning groups. A few years ago, I was awarded the coveted Silver Beaver, the council-level distinguished service award of the Boy Scouts of America, given to those who implement the Scouting program and perform community service through hard work, self-sacrifice, dedication, and many years of service. Individuals considered for this award are registered adult leaders who have made an impact on the lives of youth through service given to the council and who are nominated by their local Scout council and approved by the National Court of Honor. It is given to those who do not seek it.

My son Dan is an Eagle Scout and member of the Order of the Arrow. He is a tireless worker for dens, packs, troops, and scouts and eats and breaths the program and activities, now for girls as well as boys His son Pete will soon complete his Eagle requirements in remarkably short order. My son Ben's son, Nathan (Glenn) is an Eagle Scout in Blowing Rock, N.C. where Ben has been heavily involved in the troop and Nathan's advancement. Thank you "cousin" Baden-Powell.

Bubba (Jimmy) suggested I comment on my lay speaker experience with the United Methodist Church. Growing up in Union Springs and with a mother who was a student of the Bible and a praying Christian, I experienced the undemanding but supporting and comforting influence of a great church. There were church services, Sunday school, Vacation Bible School, MYF and its projects and activities, and a revival or two. I had little involvement with church life during college and military service. But when we settled in Tuscaloosa in1968, we immediately joined the downtown Methodist Church. I did that because it was proper and offered a way to meet people and get clients. But the Lord had plans for me. While baptizing our second child, going to Sunday school to replay the Saturday football games, serving on fund raising committees and going fairly regularly to church (I was involuntarily assigned to an Army reserve unit in Greensboro and had to go there for drill on the weekends until I got out), I was a great Laodicean. But the Lord had more plans than those for me. Our senior pastor decided to teach the first of four Disciple series, four outstanding 32 week Bible studies that require 4 to 6 hours of preparation before each session and 2 to 3 hours of class. He recruited me to teach some of the sessions. I also participated in and taught some in another study in the Disciple format entitled Christian Believers, also a 32 week study. I became hooked. Although I had some knowledge about and understanding of the scriptures, my eyes and heart, and eventually my soul, were opened to a deeper, richer and better understanding of not only God's Word but his way, his love, his wisdom and so much more. So I took all four and a fifth in the same format and style called Christian Believers. I even taught a god many of the sessions.. The intensity and depth required to teach only drove me into a deeper into the Bible and my relationship with God, making me hungry to know and do more.

Perhaps because of my participation in those courses and my zeal for them, our pastor asked me to deliver a sermon to our early and late services (he allayed my concerns by explaining that the particular Sunday for my sermon was typically the least attended in the year). He also asked me to offer one of the messages during Holy Week. I also was teaching Sunday school in my and other classes and leading and assisting in small group classes on a variety of subjects. Also my leadership and involvement on the Community Soup Bowl and the columbarium and prayer garden were producing a lot of spiritual soul-searching in me. All of that led me to sign up for Lay Speaker training. I have been taking part in those training sessions for years and have been a Certified Lay Speaker (who didn't speak). I have turned requests to preach at usually small churches in our district that had a temporary vacancy in their pulpit. Recently the Methodist Church changed its terminology to Lay Servants so I am now a Certified Lay Servant. You are certified following a favorable recommendation of the pastor and the Charge Conference and approval by the District. I have attended training in Methodist Churches in Fayette, Reform, and Tuscaloosa. I believe the main reason I am a lay servant is to attend those sessions. They are led by devoted and experienced disciples and ministers, but best of all, they are attended by people from the small, rural churches in our district who have powerful and captivating stories and testimony. I love it.

I cannot write any family history without featuring my remarkable wife, Caroline. It is appropriate because her genetic composition, her DNA, and her blood repose in and flow through a number of these Powell's, currently her two sons and six grandchildren.

Caroline was born in her home town of Union Springs on May 13, 1942, under the care of local Dr. Charlie, who offered her mother Floyd the option of delaying birth an hour or so until the 14th. Floyd's answer was NO, so we have celebrated a number of birthdays on the 13th, including some Fridays. "Sweetie" died on October 20, 2011, at Hospice of West Alabama in Tuscaloosa. She chose to be cremated and inurned in the Columbarium at the First United Methodist Church of Tuscaloosa. I have an urn in her niche for my ashes. A memorial service was held for her on October 24, 2011, at First Methodist.

In all she did, Caroline served and loved the Lord. She was a special person to everyone and always found a way to uplift people and unravel problems with a tender and insightful touch. She was a full time wife, daughter, mother, sister, friend, disciple, employee, and public servant, somehow doing them all with a spiritual energy and brightness that drew people to her for her warmth, compassion, understanding, and patience---until the time of her final earthly breath.

She will not like this list but what she did is important to us all for what she did for her community and the way she did it so we too may follow her ways and witness and celebrate and learn what can be done by the Lord through willing servants. Her sons graduated from the Tuscaloosa City School system and earned degrees from Princeton, the University of North Carolina, and Wharton School at the University of Pennsylvania (Ben) and Vanderbilt, the University of Virginia, and the University of Alabama School of Law (Dan). She graduated from the public schools in Union Springs and earned a BS in Education with a certificate in Special Education from Auburn University. She taught in the public schools of Union Springs, Tuscaloosa City, state of Washington, and the Partlow State School. She worked in various positions in the development office of the University of Alabama and retired as its Director of Corporate and Foundation Relations. She served on the Tuscaloosa City Board of Education for 15 years, two years as Vice-Chair and was selected as Outstanding School Board Member by the Alabama Association of School Boards. For the last 12 years of her life, she served on the Board of Directors of the DCH Health System. She was a member of the board and Community Vice President of the Junior League of Tuscaloosa; served on the Rise Advisory Board; was a director and chair of the West Alabama Food Bank; a director and chair of Operation Warm-up; a director and secretary of the Central Branch of the YMCA; a representative on the State Textbook Committee; one of the founders and a board member of The Bigger C Encouragers; a member of the boards of directors of Adopt-A-School, Girl Scouts, Cancer Society, Heart Association, Diabetes Association, Meals on Wheels, Community Soup Bowl, Leukemia Society and others and a volunteer with Habitat for Humanity and the Community Soup Bowl of Tuscaloosa. She was a member of Kappa Delta sorority at Auburn and served as an Advisor and an alumnus associate for the KD chapter at the University of Alabama and was selected by the national organization to the Order of the Pearl, which recognizes alumnae who have made outstanding contributions to society outside Kappa Delta service. But equally important to her was her role as a PTA member (and various offices in it) and a Den Mother. After her death, the Community Foundation of West Alabama recognized her in 2013 as a Pillar of West Alabama for her significant contributions to improving life in the community. For that honor and her service to the community, in 2013, she was also recognized in separate resolutions of the Alabama State Senate and the Alabama House of Representatives. She served many roles and positions in the First United Methodist Church of Tuscaloosa and its UMW but those activities were manifestations of her deep connection with all of God's people, especially as she learned, worshiped, and served, not only in that congregation but in all places that offer the grace, love, and blessings of Christ. And while doing all of these things, for 19 years, she was living off and on with three different cancers and their harsh and debilitating treatments and conditions. But as she said, "I didn't fight cancer; I lived with it." To her, cancer was simply a part of her life and not its ruler.

So, there you have it. Certainly not brief but much shorter without the deleted stories and material. I regret and apologize for those people and events omitted. It was a fun and painful process. I thank God for the life and loves he has given me.

Clarence Glenn Powell

# BENJAMIN CALDWELL POWELL
## "BEN"
## 1966–

Jimmy, Here's our info. -Ben (BCP)

Your full name and nick name: Benjamin Caldwell Powell, "Ben"

Your date of birth: 8/29/1966

Your addresses, both email and USPS ( to send cc's of the book):
benjamin.c.powell@gmail.com
PO Box 1631
Blowing Rock, NC 28605

Your phone numbers, good but not required: 828-719-8487

The same for your male children and their male children (spouses and female children info):

Spouse:
Virginia Cherry Powell, "Virginia"
virginia.c.powell@gmail.com
PO Box 1631
Blowing Rock, NC 28605
828-719-8497

Children
Nathaniel Glenn Powell, "Nathan" - 8/12/1997
nathaniel.glenn.powell@gmail.com
PO Box 1631
Blowing Rock, NC 28605
828-719-8155

Kathryn Drake Powell, "Drake" - 10/7/1999
k.drake.powell@gmail.com
PO Box 1631
Blowing Rock, NC 28605
828-719-9955

Genevieve Moore Powell, "Genevieve" - 5/12/2006
genevieve.m.powell@gmail.com
PO Box 1631
Blowing Rock, NC 28605

Oliver Pugh Powell, "Oliver" - 10/10/2008
oliver.p.powell@gmail.com
PO Box 1631
Blowing Rock, NC 28605

Ben was born at Madigan General Hospital, Fort Lewis, in Tacoma, Washington on August 29th, 1966. After a brief stint on base, he moved with his parents, Caroline and Glenn, to Tuscaloosa, Alabama. Ben grew up in Tuscaloosa, attending Verner Elementary School, Eastwood Middle School, Central High School West, and Central High School East. He was recognized as the top Latin, Math, and Science student in his class and was co-valedictorian of the Class of 1984. He was one of five students from Alabama to join Princeton University's class of 1988. At Princeton, Benjamin majored in Chemistry, was a co-winner of the William Frost Memorial Prize in Chemistry, was inducted into Phi Beta Kappa, and graduated magna cum laude. His undergraduate thesis examined tropospheric ozone formation and placed in the New Jersey Environmental Expo. He was also awarded a special direct fellowship from the German Academic Exchange Service for one year of non-degree study in Germany, which he employed to study environmental science at the Universitaet Dortmund. He returned from Germany and joined Milliken & Company, working first as a shift supervisor in Georgia and later as an alliance manager in Detroit. He left Milliken in 1992 to earn an MBA from the Kenan-Flagler School at the University of North Carolina - Chapel Hill (1994). Through a blind date arranged by family, he met Virginia Cherry in July 1993, become engaged to her in December 1993, and married her in August 1994. Virginia and Ben moved to Bangkok, Thailand, where Ben attempted to start an environmental market search company and Virginia was the marketing director for Jim Thompson Thai Silk. They returned to the US and soon moved to Khorat, Thailand, where Ben work as a management consultant and Virginia taught English in a public girls school and at a business she co-founded. They left Thailand in 1997 so that Ben could earn a PhD in Management from the Wharton School at the University of Pennsylvania. Their first two children, Nathan and Drake, were born in Philadelphia. Ben then worked for six years at the Culverhouse College of Business at the University of Alabama, starting in 2001. Virginia was a community leader and was elected to the Tuscaloosa City School Board. Their third child, Genevieve, was born in Tuscaloosa in 2006. In 2007, Ben and Virginia moved to Blowing Rock, North Carolina, and Ben joined the faculty at Appalachian State University. Their fourth child, Oliver, was born the following year - in 2008. Ben, Virginia, and their children currently reside in Blowing Rock, NC, where Virginia works as a realtor and serves on the Blowing Rock Town Council.

# DANIEL CHAPPELL POWELL
## "Dan"
## 1969–

your full name and nick name
*Daniel Chappell Powell 'Dan"*

your date of birth
*01/10/1969*

your addresses, both email and USPS ( to send cc's of the book)
*3521 Windy Ridge, Tuscaloosa, Al., 35406*
*llewopnad@gmail.com*

your phone numbers, good but not required
*205-210-4099*

the same for your male children and their male children (spouses and female children info)
*Wife- Nicole Palardy Powell 09/29/71*
*Son- Peter Benjamin Powell 4/22/05*
*Daughter-Mary Caroline Powell 10/29/08*

---

I am Daniel Chappell Powell ("Dan") born January 10, 1969 in Tuscaloosa Alabama to Glenn and Caroline Powell. My only sibling is a brother, Ben Powell.

My parents were loving and generous with their time and my brother has been a great friend to me over the years.

I was a Cum Laude graduate of Vanderbilt University where I received a B.A. in religious studies with a concentration in philosophy.

I also graduated from the University of Virginia where I received an M.A. in ethics.

After college I taught in inner-city schools in Los Angeles, California, and Houston, Texas, with the Teach for America Program.

After Teach for America, I returned to Tuscaloosa to serve as Associate Director for the Center for Communication and Educational Technology at the University of Alabama before attending the University of Alabama School of Law.

Since graduating from law school, I practiced law for about one year (with the law firm of Phelps, Jenkins, Gibson & Fowler in Tuscaloosa, Alabama) focusing mainly on education law and medical malpractice. I hated practicing law.

So I returned the University of Alabama School of Law in 1998 as a practitioner in the Law School's Elder Law Clinic and as a Lecturer in the Legal Writing.

In 2003, I was promoted to Associate Dean of the Law School, directing online graduate programs in taxation and business transactions as well as the Continuing Legal Education department.

While in Law School, I met my lovely wife-to-be, Nicole Palardy Powell, working out at the student recreation center.

She was a PHD student in Clinical Child Psychology and the only woman in the recreation center reading a *Time* magazine instead of *Cosmopolitan*.

I asked to borrow the magazine so I could get her name off the mailing label.

For our second date, we traveled across the northeast together gathering data for her dissertation that dealt with helping adolescents cope with Type I diabetes.

We visited summer camps where I got a chance to meet many children with Type 1 diabetes.

Ironically, about a year later, I contracted a virus while practicing law that acted as a trigger for the disease.

Nicole diagnosed me while we were still dating.

We married a couple of year later and had two precious children.

Peter loves math and computers and took college classes in the 8th grade, and Mary loves animals and has better social skills that most adults I know.

My main interests have been spending time with my lovely wife Nicole and Peter and Mary.

My hobbies have included serving as the childrens' boy and girl scout leaders, coaching their soccer teams and being their friend.

I am an Eagle scout who enjoys outdoors and high adventure trips, service work with organizations such as Big Brothers and Big Sisters and Habitat for Humanity, playing tournament level racquetball and soccer (until I got to old for it). My life challenges included learning to live with type 1 diabetes at 30 years old and dealing with the loss of my sweet mother who passed in October of 2011.

But overall I have had a blessed life and any adversity has been handled through faith. I hope my remaining years will be in the service of others and the good Lord above.

Daniel Powell
Associate Dean for Graduate Law Programs
Director of Continuing Legal Education
The University of Alabama School of Law

Box 870382
Tuscaloosa, AL 35487
Phone 205-348-2648
www.alabamallm.com
www.clealabama.com

# BENJAMIN PHILIP POWELL
## "Ben"
## 1945–

Benjamin Philip Powell, MD (1945 -    )

I was born on August 4, 1945 and was the third son born to James Blackmon Powell and Anne Glenn Caldwell Powell. I was named after my Grandfather - aka Pop - and I was raised in Union Springs, Alabama.

I was blessed to have good parents, good brothers, a great church and a large extended family. I had a horse named Major and a pointer name Spot - and lots of opportunity to hunt and fish and camp out.

I attended The University of the South - 1963-1967- on an academic scholarship. Served as president of my fraternity and President of my senior class. Graduated cum laude and Phi Beta Kappa.

I attended medical school 1967-1971 at the University of Alabama/Birmingham.

NOTE the single most important event of my life: married Jeanne Hanby Forsyth on June 29, 1968 in Birmingham. (We recently celebrated our 50th wedding anniversary.)

Attended University of Utah for internship and residency 1971-1974. Served as chief resident in anesthesiology. Then entered private practice in Salt Lake at St. Marks Hospital.

Elizabeth Powell French born on 11/27/72; Benjamin Groves Powell born on 12/27/74; and Anne Powell Rogers born on 7/17/78. All Three born in Salt Lake City.

Served in Army Reserve Medical Corp there 1972-1978 - rank- Major at discharge.

Moved to Asheville, NC in 1979. Private practice at St. Joseph's Hospital and Memorial Mission Hospital. "Retired" 2004 - having served as Chief of Staff at St. Joe's and as president of my anesthesia group during that time span.

In 2005, started working in a general medical/bariatric clinic – only 1-3 days per week and with no night call. I enjoy the slower pace and enjoy the time spent with each patient.

Jeanne and I are blessed with good health. We are involved with Community and our Trinity Episcopal Church - BUT our major joy in life right now centers on our 9 awesome Grandchildren - 4 in Asheville and 5 in Charlotte.


One story that is worth repeating: I was born on August 4, 1945 and the A bomb was dropped on Aug 6. I was the only son born in hospital (St. Margaret's/Montgomery) - likely because my Dad Jim was in Okinawa. We found a type written letter from POP in Union Springs to my Mom in Montgomery stating: "I don't know what happened with this bomb, but I think it will help us end this war. From now on, we will call this boy BEN PHIL THE BOMB. Love, POP."

## 421 Vanderbilt Road, Asheville, NC 28803
## bppno1@aol.com
## 828 274 3300 home, 828 777 5930 cell

**ANTIQUE TRAY PRESENTED ARCHIVES**

The silver tray being received by Dr. Peter A. Brannon, director of the Alabama Archives and History Department, was presented to Mrs. E. Powell of Union Springs in 1856 by the Chunne Nuggee Horticulture Society, near Union Springs, as an award in a horticulture competition. Making the presentation at a ceremony last week at the Archives Building is 11-year-old Ben Powell, great-great-great-great-grandson of the original owner. Looking on at the presentation is Mrs. R. L. Lawrence, president of the Union Springs Horticulture Society.

Ben and Jeanne (dating), Jimmy
Birmingham, (circa 1965)

# BENJAMIN GROVES POWELL
## "B.G."
## 1972–

From: **Ben Powell** benjamingpowell@yahoo.com
Subject: Powell Legacy - BG Powell Family
Date: August 6, 2019 at 12:28 PM
To: James Powell jamesandmarypowell@gmail.com

Uncle Jim,

Benjamin Groves Powell
"B.G."
Born: December 27, 1974 (Salt Lake City, UT)
Wife: Lindsay Moniotte Powell (Married July 14, 2001)
Father: Benjamin Philip Powell
Mother: Jeanne Forsyth Powell
Resides: Charlotte, NC

Children:
Charles Richmond Powell (12/23/03), Age 15.
Caroline Caldwell Powell (06/14/05), Age 14.
Benjamin Moniotte Powell (01/16/07), Age 12.
Henry Groves Powell (12/17/08), Age 10.
Anne Crawford Powell (05/16/12) Age 7.

Bio: Attended UNC- Chapel Hill and graduated with a degree in international business in 1997. Married Lindsay in 2001 after moving to Baton Rouge, LA. and started a career in Sales. All five children were born in Baton Rouge and the family recently moved to Charlotte, NC. B.G. is an avid golfer, enjoys hiking, and taking trips to Disney World.

**Charles Richmond Powell**
"Charlie"

Born December 23, 2003 (Baton Rouge)
Father: Benjamin Groves Powell
Mother: Lindsay Moniotte Powell
Resides in Charlotte, NC
Attends Woodberry Forest School (9th).
Interests- Soccer, basketball, LSU football, summer at Camp Highlander, traveling, music, meeting new people.

**Benjamin Moniotte Powell**
"Ben"

Born January 16, 2007 (Baton Rouge)
Father: Benjamin Groves Powell
Mother: Lindsay Moniotte Powell
Resides in Charlotte, NC
Attends Holy Trinity Catholic Middle School (6th)
Interests- Competitive league soccer, basketball, watching Chelsea football club, summer at Camp Highlander, drawing, spending time with his family.

**Henry Groves Powell**
"Henry"

Born December 17, 2008 (Baton Rouge)
Father: Benjamin Groves Powell
Mother: Lindsay Moniotte Powell
Resides in Charlotte, NC
Attends St. Gabriel Catholic School (5th)
Interests- Spending time with friends and family, acting in school theater, flag football, riding his bike, summer at Camp Highlander.

B.G., Henry, Caroline, Charles, Anne, Benjamin, Lindsay, Wheezy

Every May when the temperatures here rise and the humidity gets worse, I think of Jim and the nights I spent in Union Springs towards the end of his days. We would watch Braves games on the highest volume setting and he would fall asleep in his La-Z-Boy after a couple of 'Jimmies' and a few handfuls of Goldfish. I would turn the volume down to maybe a jackhammer setting and sit there in the heat and humidity… Jim would usually get up around the end of the game to find the Braves had pulled out another one…good times.

Ben Powell
324 Ridgewood Avenue
Charlotte, NC 28209
benjamingpowell@yahoo.com
225 610 4651

# The Lineage
## of Floyd Berkeley Powell

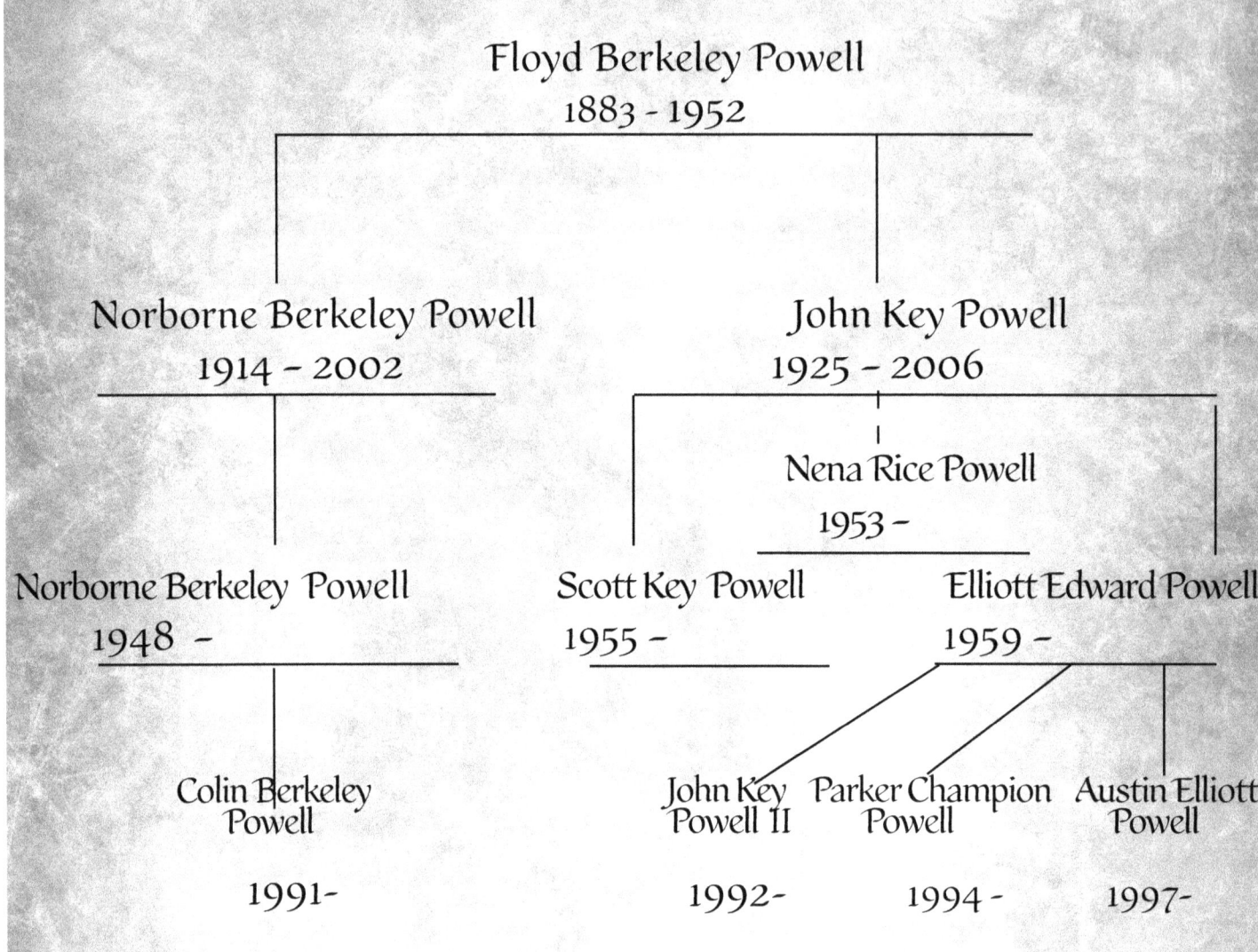

# FLOYD BERKELEY POWELL
## "Uncle Toy"
## 1883–1952

Likely photographed at University of Alabama.

Editor's note: I knew Floyd Berkeley Powell, "Uncle Toy," the brother of my Grandfather "Pop," because of his visits to Union Springs from his home in Tuskegee. He was usually dressed in a three-piece, double-breasted suit, proper, with an ever-present cigar. My early memories are that he had a family in Texas but had two "boom and bust" careers in oil in Texas and returned to his childhood home of Tuskegee. Grandson Berkeley has provided other information.

Floyd is the author of the "1925 Wesleyan Alumni" article earlier in this book.

Father with Sons   circa 1950.

Norborne     Floyd     Key

Brothers   Union Springs circa late 1940s.

Ben     Floyd

Family circa early 1950s

Glennie, Floyd, Julia (sister of "Mom"), "Pop," Key, Jim

# NORBORNE BERKELEY POWELL
## "Norborne"
## 1914–2002

NORBORNE BERKELEY POWELL, SR., M.D. died peacefully August 14th at the age of 88. He was born on July 24, 1914 in Montgomery, Alabama to Floyd Berkeley Powell and Eloise Sadler Powell. He grew up in Dallas, where he became an Eagle Scout. He attended the University of Alabama and joined the Sigma Nu fraternity. He received his medical degree from Baylor University College of Medicine in Dallas in 1938 and served his internship at Duke Hospital, where he met and married pathology resident, Dr. Elizabeth Ballis. Dr. Powell completed a Urology residency at Charity Hospital in New Orleans before moving to Houston in 1943 to enter private practice with Dr. Herbert Hayes. In 1947, he began solo private practice and became the second occupant of the newly completed Hermann Professional Bldg. Long admired for his clinical acumen, meticulous surgical technique, and warm bedside manner, he rose to the rank of Clinical Professor of Urology at Baylor College of Medicine in Houston. He published over 30 medical articles, including some of the seminal work with Dr. John McGovern on food allergies as a cause of bladder disease. Dr. Powell was a Charter Member of the Houston Surgical Society, as well as a member of the Harris County Medical Society, the Houston Urological Society, the Texas Medical Association, the American Urological Association, the American College of Surgeons, the International College of Surgeons, and both the Canadian and the Mexican Urological Associations. When he retired from medicine in 1986, he had practiced for almost 50 years. Dr. Powell was an extrovert who cherished his friends, loved his family, and cared deeply about his patients. He joined the River Oaks Country Club in 1952 and rapidly became an avid golfer, which served as the source of many new friendships. He was part of the longest-lived golf foursome at that Club, which also included Henry King, Raymond Elledge, and Dr. James Greenwood. He was its last surviving member. A man of many interests, Dr. Powell was also a voracious reader, especially in history and historical fiction. He traveled extensively in Europe, North & South America, and the Far East. A lifelong photographer, he documented these trips and his family with many treasured color and black & white photographs. He was a founding member of St. Phillip Presbyterian Church, where he had also served in the past as a deacon. He retired to Asheville, North Carolina and enjoyed the Smoky Mountains for 11 years before returning to Houston in 2000 because of failing health. He is survived by his wife of 64 years, Elizabeth B. Powell, MD; his son Dr. N. Berkeley Powell, Jr. and his wife Kimberly, their children Claire Campbell Powell and Colin Berkeley Powell; his daughter Barbara Key Powell of Vienna, Virginia; his brother John Key Powell of Columbia, South Carolina and his wife, Penny; and his first cousin, Gen. Thomas Sadler (USAF, Retired) of Charlotte, North Carolina and his wife, Ken.

# Norborne's Eulogy by His Son, Berkeley

We are here to remember and to affirm a wonderful life. He did have a great life: he had just turned 88 when he died and for 86½ years he was active, productive, and in remarkably good health. If we mourn, it is not his death we mourn but our own loss of his good company. I offer a very personal recollection of some of what he has meant to me.

Some of my earliest memories are of his reading bedtime stories to Barbara and me. After the usual run of Grimm's Fairy Tales and Mother Goose, he rapidly moved on to Bullfinch's mythology, Mark Twain, and Treasure Island. He read with gusto, taking the various parts by changing his voice. Especially the Tom Sawyer and Huckleberry Finn would break him up and get him laughing so hard that he would have to stop for the evening. After all excitement, it was sometimes hard to get to sleep.

He encouraged us to develop our talents and our character:

He transmitted his own love of music.
He paid for four years of art lessons.
He encouraged me to swim competitively for seven years.
He encouraged me to join the Cub Scouts and the Boy Scouts and to persevere in becoming an Eagle Scout, as he had been.
He bribed me to start reading good literature.
He took me to the Rice Stadium parking lot and taught me how to drive a stick shift, with all of the damage to the clutch and gears.
He stressed the importance of a well-rounded education: As a child of the Depression he had rushed through the University of Alabama getting 3 years of pre-medical credits in 2 years before the money ran out. He encouraged me to major outside of the sciences – to get a liberal education - and was pleased with my English major.
He seduced me into considering a medical career.
He encouraged me to travel during the summers I was in college and medical school. As a result, I spent summers studying or working in Austria, Boston, Montreal, and San Francisco.
He sweated bullets to pay for a first-class education for me: and then did it all over again in grad school for both Barbara and me. By doing so, he left me debt-free when I finished my training.
Character:

I remember his energy, his optimism, his good nature, and his sense of humor.

He led by example:

He married very well.
He showed us the hallmarks of a happy & rich marriage that was a marvelous partnership.
He brought with him the legacy of a wonderful extended family.
His good name smoothed my entry into medical practice in Houston.
His compassion & expertise peppered Houston with former patients who still remember him with great affection - decades after he touched their lives.
He wasn't perfect: He had terrible hay fever and some true food allergies. He was a rather finicky eater and all of the family suspected that some of his "food allergies" were actually things he would rather not eat. It made menu planning a nightmare.

At one point, he even professed to be allergic to several cheaper brands of Scotch whiskey, but had found that he can tolerate the better brands without any difficulty whatsoever. In a true spirit of scientific endeavor, he would from time to time check the better Scotches to be sure that they were still safe.

He came from the family of great storytellers. He had a marvelous sense of humor: he always said he would rather have a lucky surgeon than a good one. He was both. He loved music; he loved to dance; he loved people and he loved a good joke. He was an extrovert. I know he would have loved to have been here for this party, although I'm sure he would have been embarrassed by the praise.

When I think about him, it is amazing how much of what I am is because of what he did for me. When I miss him, I look at my hands, I realize that they are his hands. When I laugh, I can hear his laugh. When I miss him, I know I can find him in my heart and in your hearts.

> Editor's note: My Aunt Senie vividly reported her memory that Norborne, Berkeley's dad, had to live a year with Mom and Pop in Union Springs during Senie's senior year. "He almost ruined it for me, tagging after me on dates, dances and other activity." I recall her telling that story every time Floyd or Norborne names were mentioned.

# NORBORNE BERKELEY POWELL
## "Berkeley"
## 1948–

Dear Cousins,

Every year about this time, Kimberly's Nordic ancestry rears it's head. One morning she will walk into the room in a white gown and a holly wreath crown on her head, complete with four candles. She will hand me a mug of the traditional yuletide *gloog*, a potent Norwegian specialty, with which I will toast her good fortune and drain the mug of it's hot concoction.

Half a day later, I usually wake up to find myself in a cheap motel in Katy, Texas - with HBO, a case of whisky, and a bus ticket (for January 3rd) back to Houston. And you know: Those have been some of the best Christmases I've ever had. Traditions <u>are</u> important.

Oh, and we've moved half a mile - to downsize. All phone numbers are the same. New address after 22 yrs is now:

**2719 Essex Terrace, Houston, TX 77027.**

We also have a new granddaughter. Her name is Lee Chandler Powell and she turns 6 months old today, Dec 21st. She is Colin's daughter and she is lovely. I have scheduled her in January for a liposuction of her hands, forearms and cheeks, so don't worry about those plumpy parts.

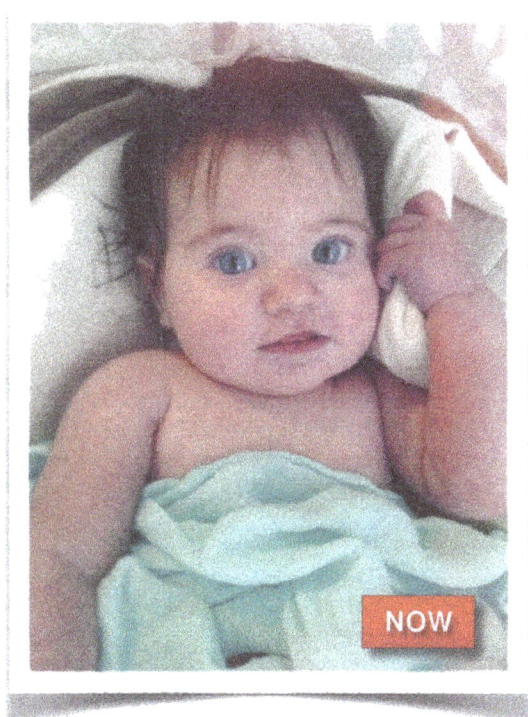

Kim, Colin, & day-old Lee

For the best picture of what we've been up to, please visit my travel foto website to see the trips. The most recent galleries are Mediterranean, South America, The West (specifically *Tetons* and *Yellowstone*), Texas Hill Country 3, and New York. Go to: powell-fotos.smugmug.com

All of us wish you and yours the very best in the coming year. Every year is a gift.

Much Love, *Berkeley & Kimberly*

Xmas 2013
dr.powell@mac.com
713 598 0004

From: **Berkeley Powell** dr.powell@mac.com
Subject: Berkeley Powell Family. -Fotos & Brief Bio
Date: August 7, 2019 at 2:58 PM
To: Powell Jim jamesandmarypowell@gmail.com

Dear Jim,

Here are some fotos of me and my family. Thank you for continuing to rattle my cage. I have also included two fotos of Toren Anderson and her son Aidan. Toren is RHP's daughter, Julia Powell Anderson's granddaughter. **If you like, you can use this letter as my bio.**

Kimberly and I are in the highlands of Mexico in San Miguel de Allende for the 2 months of July and August, both avoiding the stultifying Houston summer, and also taking intensive Spanish in this lovely 400 year old colonial Spanish town.

I did make a stab at autobiography in the late 1980's. The book, entitled "Up from the Swamp", was privately published as a single leather bound copy consisting of 260 blank pages. This was because I am a very private person and I have a lot to be ashamed of.
Since I have been unable to produce an accounting of myself, I offer in addition to these family fotos, the several thousand photographs on my travel photo website as some measure of my whereabouts and interests. Please see:

  Powell-Fotos.smugmug.com

I will say that my interests in art and science coalesced in my choice of plastic surgery as a career. I met some remarkable & gifted people both in the profession and as patients. I thoroughly enjoyed my practice. Along the way, I served as president of both the Houston Society of Plastic Surgeons and The Texas Society of Plastic Surgeons.

My pared-down medical website will remain active until May, 2020, and includes some before & after pictures of historical interest at:

  dr-powell.com

I retired because they demolished my office building. The economics of building out a new office and continuing practice into my 70s didn't work for me. Still, I was sobered by the spector of going from indespensible to irrelevant just by walking out of that office for the last time. Therefore, I focused my other interests of travel and photography into a small business as a landscape & art photographer. So rather than retire, I rebranded myself.

All of you reading this know that it takes a special kind of woman to marry a Powell. After 42 years of marriage, I realize how unreasonably lucky I have been to be with the only woman on the planet who could have put up with me for this long. She also shares my wanderlust and my sense of humor. Our goal is to do as much exploration as our health and temperament will allow. And then we will do something else.

Best regards to you all,

Berkeley Powell
dr.powell@mac.com
Please visit my Travel Foto Website:
  **powell-fotos.smugmug.com**

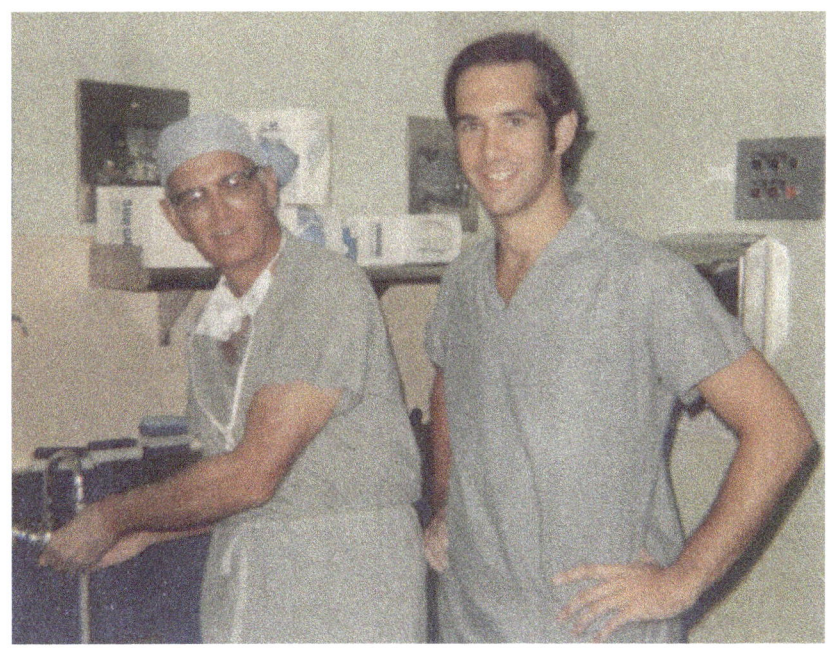

1967: My urologist father, 53, and me, 19, as a scrub tech.

1979: Kimberly, 31, and me, two years into the marriage as I was finishing my training.

2009: Claire and Kimberly, celebrating Claire's 21st birthday.

2018: Berkeley, 70, Kimberly and Colin, 27, at my retirement party after 38 years in medical practice.

2006: Colin 15, Berkeley, Kimberly and Claire, 18, in Switzerland.

2018: January, Kimberly and Berkeley on Mount Cook, New Zealand.

2013: In Dallas with Aidan Thomas Hornaday and his mother, Toren Anderson. Richard Holmes Powell's great-granddaughter and great-great-grandson.

# JOHN KEY POWELL
# "Key"
# 1925–2006

J. Key Powell died on May 24, 2006. Key was born on December 14, 1925 in Dallas, Texas and was the son of Floyd Berkeley Powell and Eloise Sadler Powell. In 1939, he moved to Tuskegee, Alabama. After completing high school, in 1943, he briefly attended Emory University. In December of 1943, he enlisted in the Army Air Corps as an aviation cadet. He was honorably discharged in November 1945, and immediately enrolled in January 1946 at the University of Alabama. He transferred to Southern Methodist University in 1947 for an additional year of undergraduate work and started Law School at SMU. He later transferred to law school at the University of Alabama.

He began his life insurance sales and management career in 1949 and elected early retirement from the John Hancock Companies in December of 1985. He served as General Agent for the State of South Carolina from 1959 until 1985. After his formal retirement, he formed Creative Giving Concepts - a company dedicated to helping others in the field of charitable giving and estate planning. Until his death, he still encouraged and instructed others on how to give.

Key served as President of several organizations including: the Hub City Kiwanis Club of Lubbock, Texas; the Columbia Rotary Club, and recently also was named 2006 Rotarian of the year; The John Hancock General Agents Association; University Associates at USC; and, the Columbia General Agents and Managers Association. He then served on the National Board of Directors of the General Agents and Managers Conference. He also served as the early Chairman for two terms of the Central Carolina Community Foundation; Chairman of the Advisory Board of the Center for Cancer Treatment and Research of Richland Memorial Hospital; two terms as Chairman of the local Salvation Army Advisory Board. He was a long time member of their William Booth Society; And in 1999, the Advisory Board of the Salvation Army designated him a Life Member. He was a member of the Alexis de Tocqueville Society of the United Way, a Ruling Elder of the First Presbyterian Church, a Chartered Life Underwriter (CLU), a Life Member of the Million Dollar Round Table, and a member of Sigma Alpha Epsilon social fraternity. He was a member of Forest Lake Club and the Palmetto Club; And just recently, Key was presented with the Order of the Palmetto by Governor Mark Sanford, and Senator Joel Lourie.

Key accepted Jesus Christ as his Lord and Savior on Monday, September 13, 1976 at a prayer group - Columbia Alive. He still attended the Columbia Alive meetings until his death. Columbia Alive is a dedicated group of men - both black and white - that meant so much to him in his walk with His Lord and Savior, Jesus Christ.

Key is survived by his wife of 55 years, Ann Penniman "Penny" Powell. Penny and Key had a daughter and son-in-law - Nena Ann Powell Rice and Marion Mullow Rice of Columbia; a son, Scott Key Powell of Pawleys Island; and, a son and daughter-in-law - Elliott Edward Powell and Elizabeth Champion Powell of Columbia; a granddaughter - Jessica Marie Powell of Ft. Collins, Colorado; and three grandsons - John Key Powell II, Parker Champion Powell, and Austin Elliott Powell all of Columbia. A nephew - Norborne Berkeley Powell, Jr., MD, a niece - Barbara Key Powell. A brother - Norborne Berkeley Powell, MD - predeceased him. In lieu of flowers, the family suggests donations to the local Salvation Army, or a charity of your choice.

# Session Resolution
First Presbyterian Church of Columbia, South Carolina
In Memory of
John Key Powell
December 14, 1925 – May 24, 2006

WHEREAS, Key was a devoted family man, born December 14, 1925, in Dallas, Texas, the oldest child of the late Floyd Berkeley Powell and Eloise Sadler Powell. He completed high school in Tuskegee, Alabama, and later attended Emory University, Southern Methodist University and the University of Alabama School of Law. Key and Ann Penniman "Penny" Powell were married in 1951 and became life partners and soul mates. In addition to their children, Nena Ann Powell Rice, Scott Key Powell and Elliott Edward Powell, Key is survived by his beloved grandchildren, Jessica Marie Powell, John Key Powell, II, Parker Champion Powell and Austin Elliott Powell.

WHEREAS, Key was a successful businessman and financial advisor, serving as an insurance agent for the John Hancock Company for 36 years, including 26 years as general agent for South Carolina. Key was a chartered life underwriter, a financial advisor for Renaissance Financial Services, a life member of the Million Dollar Round Table and founder of Creative Giving Concepts, dedicated to helping others in the field of charitable giving and estate planning. He was recently presented with the Order of the Palmetto, South Carolina's highest civilian honor, by Governor Mark Sanford for his lifetime of achievement and extensive contributions to his community.

WHEREAS, Key was an active philanthropist, establishing a scholarship at the University of South Carolina, the donor of two charitable trusts benefiting various religious and healthcare organizations, a Paul Harris Fellow of the Columbia Rotary Club, a member of the Alexis De Tocqueville Society of the United Way, a member of the William Booth Society of the Salvation Army, and a generous financial supporter of many other eleemosynary organizations.

WHEREAS, Key actively served his nation and community, enlisting in the Army Air Corp as an aviation cadet in December 1943, serving as president of the Hub City Kiwanis Club of Lubbock, Texas, the Columbia Rotary Club, University Associates at the University of South Carolina, chairman for two terms of the Central Carolina Community Foundation, chairman of the advisory board of the Center for Cancer Treatment and Research of Richland Memorial Hospital, two terms as chairman of the local Salvation Army Advisory Board, and a member of Sigma Alpha Epsilon Fraternity, Forest Lake Club and the Palmetto Club.

WHEREAS, Key was a man of abiding faith in the Lord Jesus Christ, having been born again on September 13, 1976, at a prayer group called Columbia Alive. Key remained active in Columbia Alive with a dedicated group of black and white men who meant so much to him in his walk with his Lord and Savior Jesus Christ. Key served with distinction as a ruling elder at First Presbyterian Church and was active at Christ Church of Columbia and in Bible studies and prayer groups throughout the community. Key demonstrated a bold witness, a joyful attitude and a hopeful outlook on life, centered in his abiding faith. He was "all in" for his Savior, putting his time, his money, his good name, and his considerable network of friends and acquaintances at the disposal of the Savior.

WHEREAS, John Key Powell departed this life on May 24, 2006, at age 81, a faithful husband of 55 years, a devoted father, a beloved community leader, a dedicated church officer, an humble servant of the living God, a giant of a man who lived large and taught us to do the same.

WHEREAS, the Session, for and on behalf of the congregation of the First Presbyterian Church of Columbia, South Carolina, desires to honor the memory of a faithful man whose legacy is a life well spent.

NOW, THEREFORE, be it resolved that the Session of the First Presbyterian Church of Columbia, South Carolina, in meeting duly assembled this 18th day of September, 2006, hereby recognizes John Key Powell for his dedication to his family, community, and, above all, for his shining example of living joyfully and unreservedly as a disciple of the Lord Jesus Christ.

BE IT FURTHER RESOLVED that this Resolution be entered by the Clerk into the minutes of the Session and a copy of the Resolution provided to his wife and family.

LANNEAU W. LAMBERT, Clerk of Session

Columbia, South Carolina

John Key Powell II and John Key Powell, CLU

# Ann Penniman Powell
# "Penny"
# 1928-2015
# wife of Key

Ann "Penny" Penniman Powell

Ann (Penny) was born December 21, 1928 and died ……….. Ann was born in Dallas, Texas and was the daughter of the late Edward Thomas Penniman and late Theodora Elliott Penniman Landrum. She attended Highland Park High School in Dallas and spent her first year in college at Edgewood Park Junior College for Women in Briarcliff Manor near New York City. She returned to Dallas and graduated from Southern Methodist University in 1950 and married the late John Key Powell on July 14. They moved to Tuscaloosa, Alabama where she taught $2^{nd}$ grade in the mountains of Alabama. After their daughter was born in 1953, they moved to Lubbock, Texas and Boston with Key's business career in life insurance before moving to Columbia in 1959. She was a full time housewife, raised three children, and was a great support and inspiration to her late husband John Key Powell. She built three beautiful homes in Columbia that her family and friends enjoyed so much. She loved to collect antiques and art from her extensive travel around the world. She had a unique style in design with the ethnic folk art she collected and appreciated. She was a member of First Presbyterian Church serving on several committees, a Garden Club, the Columbia Junior League, Sewing Club, Palmetto Club, Forest Lake Club, and was a multiple Paul Harris Fellow supporting the Rotary Club of Columbia.

Ann was completely devoted to her late husband Key and traveled with him on his numerous business ventures and around the world. She loved to garden, cook, entertain their numerous friends, and dedicated her life to the needs of her loving husband, children, and grandchildren.

Ann (Penny) is survived by her daughter, Nena Ann Powell Rice of Columbia, Scott Key Powell of Laramie, Wyoming, and Elliott Edward Powell and wife Betsy Champion Powell; grandchildren, Jessica Marie Powell Ericson and husband Steve from Severens, Colorado, John Key Powell II, Parker Champion Powell, and Austin Elliott Powell of Columbia; a nephew Berkeley Key Powell and wife Kimberly and son Colin and daughter Claire of Houston, and a niece Barbara Key Powell of Dover, Delaware. She is predeceased by her husband of 56 years, the Late John Key Powell.

# NENA RICE POWELL
## "Nena"
## 1953–

Editor's note: Nena is given the honor of being the only female in the Appendix of Powell males. She earned this by her interest, her timely and informative responses and her energetic steadfastness to help bring this effort to an accurate fruition.

## VITAE

### NENA POWELL RICE

**PERSONAL INFORMATION**

Address:
3530 Monroe Street
Columbia, South Carolina 29205
(803) 331-3431 Cell

University of South Carolina
South Carolina Institute of Archaeology and Anthropology
1321 Pendleton Street
Columbia, South Carolina 29208
(803) 576-6573 (Office phone is still active)-but use cell phone

Place and Date of Birth: Tuscaloosa, Alabama; September 8, 1953
Marital Status: Single

**EDUCATION**

MA — University of Denver, Denver, Colorado
Anthropology, 1990

BA — Southern Methodist University, Dallas, Texas
Anthropology, 1975

AA — Sullins College, Bristol, Virginia
Liberal Arts, 1973
Rollins College, Madrid, SPAIN
Spanish, Summer 1972

**AWARDS AND HONORS**

Lifetime Achievement Award, Archaeological Society of South Carolina, 2018
- Twenty Years Exemplary Service, Archaeological Society of South Carolina, 1985-2005
- Distinguished Service Award, Bachman Group of Sierra Club, 1994
- Silent Footprinter, Sierra Club South Carolina Chapter, 1994
- Outstanding Service, Archaeological Society of South Carolina, 1985-1990
- University of South Carolina Office Employee of the Year, 1990
- Certificate of Appreciation, Archaeological Society of South Carolina, 1985-1989
- Director's Special Award for Employee Excellence, South Carolina Institute of Archaeology and Anthropology, University of South Carolina, 1988

**MEMBERSHIPS**

- Society for American Archaeology
- Society for Historical Archaeology
- Southeastern Archaeological Conference
- Archaeological Society of South Carolina—Treasurer, Newsletter Editor, Membership

## MEMBERSHIPS (CONT.)

- Council for Professional Archaeologists of South Carolina
- Explorers Club of New York (Fellow Non-Resident-since 1987)-Chair (2007-2008), Program Chair (1998-2018), Membership Chair (1993-2001), Secretary, Vice Chair (2005-2006)
- Sierra Club—South Carolina Chapter Secretary; Vice-Chair, Program Chair; Appalachian Regional Conservation Committee, South Carolina Delegate to San Francisco Headquarters, Council Delegate for the South Carolina Chapter

## RESEARCH INTERESTS

Prehistory of Puebloan Cultures
Enthnohistory of the New World
Prehistoric Architecture
Southwestern Ceramic Analysis
Prehistoric Social/Political/Economic Organization
Ethnobotony (Southwest, Arctic, Southeast)
World Migration Theory

Alaska Archaeology
Lithic Analysis
Indigenous Societies
Environmental Archaeology
Museology
Public Outreach and Education
World Cultures

## MANAGEMENT AND ADMINISTRATIVE EXPERIENCE

1992 - present  South Carolina Institute of Archaeology and Anthropology
University of South Carolina Director of Development and Outreach and Assistant to the Director and State Archaeologist; Statewide Coordinator for the First through Twenty-Seventh South Carolina Archaeology Month, Secretary (in perpetuity) to the Archaeological Research Trust Board, Fund raising, acting librarian, events, conferences, fieldwork, promotions, media, tours (international and stateside), public education outreach; and Editor of *Legacy* magazine.

1988 - 2002  South Carolina Institute of Archaeology and Anthropology
University of South Carolina
Assistant to Associate Director for Research
Assists Associate Director for Research in the daily operation of the Research Division in the administration of proposal preparation, travel authorizations, correspondence, and purchase requisitions. Assists researchers in the Division in laboratory, analytical, and general research activities. Research Librarian responsible for acquisitions, cataloging, and overseeing usage of 29,000 volume library. Supports public and professional education in giving programs, organizing conferences, and coordinating Archaeological Society activities concerning SCIAA research and South Carolina archaeology. Assists Research Division archaeologists in conducting archaeological excavations and surveys.

## ADMINISTRATIVE EXPERIENCE (CONT.)

1985 - 1988	South Carolina Institute of Archaeology and Anthropology, University of South Carolina, Columbia, South Carolina
Assistant Information Management Director
Assisted Head of Information Management in maintenance of the state site files, archaeological site base maps, related reference maps, and the curation facility. Assisted in maintenance of the research library (14,000 volumes), National Register of Historic Places files, and other information files. Supported the Deputy State Archaeologist in the Project Notification Review and Compliance duties and in maintenance of the Archaeological Project Reports and correspondence files. Supported public and professional education in giving programs concerning SCIAA's functions and

South Carolina archaeology. Field supervisor of various archaeological projects throughout the state. Write-up of final reports.

1981 - 1983	Flatirons Surveying Company, Boulder, Colorado
Assistant Director, Archaeological Division; Administrative Asst.
Project coordinator for archaeological survey projects in Colorado, New Mexico, Wyoming, Utah, and Montana; update antiquity permit applications; proposal preparation; directed personnel; clerical and bookkeeping responsibilities, accounts, and payroll.

1980	University of Denver, Denver, Colorado
Assistant Director, Archaeological Field School
Project and logistic coordinator, assistance in proposal preparation, devised sampling strategy, directed students, instruction in survey and recording methods.

1977	New Mexico State University, Las Cruces, New Mexico
Project Supervisor
Managed feasibility studies of development impact on cultural resources throughout New Mexico.

1975	National Science Foundation Grant
Research Anthropologist
Assistance in the administration of multi-disciplinary grant; served as ethnohistorian and research anthropologist.

1975	Assistant to Program Chairman for the 40th Annual Society for American Archaeology meetings in Dallas, Texas. Accepted and edited over 1,000 abstracts for inclusion in program; organized symposiums; organized meeting rooms, visual equipment and in charge of registration; local arrangements.

REPORT WRITING AND EDITING EXPERIENCE

| | |
|---|---|
| 1985 - Present | South Carolina Institute of Archaeology and Anthropology<br>University of South Carolina<br>Columbia, South Carolina |
| 1983 - 1985 | University of Alaska Museum<br>Fairbanks, Alaska |
| 1981 - 1983 | Flatirons Surveying Company<br>Boulder, Colorado |
| 1980 | Powers Elevation Company<br>Denver, Colorado |
| 1980 | University of Denver<br>Department of Anthropology<br>Denver, Colorado |
| 1979 | School of American Research<br>Santa Fe, New Mexico |
| 1977 - 1978 | New Mexico State University<br>Division of Cultural Resource Management<br>Las Cruces, New Mexico |
| 1976 - 1977 | Bureau of Land Management<br>State Office<br>Santa Fe, New Mexico |
| 1976 | Museum of New Mexico<br>Laboratory of Anthropology<br>Santa Fe, New Mexico |
| 1975 | National Science Foundation Grant<br>Taos, New Mexico |
| 1974 - 1975 | Southern Methodist University<br>Archaeological Research Program<br>Dallas, Texas |

FIELD, LABORATORY, AND OTHER ARCHAEOLOGICAL EXPERIENCE

April 1985 - Present. South Carolina Institute of Archaeology and Anthropology, Office of the State Archaeologist. Assists SCIAA staff in archaeological surveys, testing, and excavation projects throughout South Carolina.

# FIELD, LABORATORY, AND OTHER ARCHAEOLOGICAL EXPERIENCE (CONT.)

| | |
|---|---|
| 1983 - 1985 | June 1983 – February 1985. University of Alaska Museum. Field supervisor of reconnaissance survey and systematic testing of sites in the Upper Susitna River Valley, Susitna Hydroelectric Project. Conducted accessioning and storage of artifacts, radiocarbon preparation, lithic analysis of over one million artifacts, artifact plate preparation, coding and data entry, writing and editing of draft and final report. |
| 1981 - 1983 | October 1981 – June 1983. Flatirons Surveying Company. Field supervisor of numerous archaeological surveys in five Western states: Colorado, Wyoming, Montana, Utah, and New Mexico. Documentation and preparation of Surface Use and Operations Plan (NTL-6) reports in coordination with federal environmental requirements. Also served on land surveying crew as rod and chainperson. |
| 1981 | July - September. University of Alaska, Department of Anthropology. Field crew member of an archaeological survey of the proposed gas pipeline on the North Slope of Alaska for Fluor-Northwest. Surveyed 156 miles from Happy Valley (20 miles south of Prudhoe Bay) to the Brooks Range at Pump Station 4. |
| 1980 | September - November. University of Denver, Department of Anthropology. Graduate teaching assistant for the Introduction of Cultural Anthropology. 140 students enrolled. |
| 1980 | June - September. University of Denver Archaeological Field School. Assistant director of field school. Conducted instruction of 11 students in surveying, ecological sampling, and recording techniques in the San Luis Valley, south-central Colorado. |
| 1980 | April - May. University of Denver Grant. Field supervisor of excavation of the oldest house in Denver at Four Mile Historic Park, Denver, Colorado. |
| 1980 | March - May. Denver Art Museum. Native American Arts Department. Worked with the collections in storage, inventoried all Native American paintings and worked on the Native American cradleboard exhibit. |
| 1980 | January - May. University of Denver. Graduate research assistant. Compiled research data on the San Luis Valley in preparation for the field school. |
| 1979 | June - September. School of American Research. Field supervisor of an intensive archaeological survey of 1,600 acres in the Red Mesa Valley near Prewitt, New Mexico for Plains Electric Company. |
| 1979 | April - June. School of American Research. Field supervisor of the Abiquiu Reservoir Project. Conducted mapping, recording, and sampling of archaeological sites that were to be inundated by floodwaters in the Abiquiu Reservoir near Abiquiu, New Mexico. |

# FIELD, LABORATORY, AND OTHER ARCHAEOLOGICAL EXPERIENCE (CONT.)

| | |
|---|---|
| 1978 - 1979 | December 1978 – January 1979. Preservation Systems, Inc. Restoration of the Tully House, oldest house in Santa Fe, for the Santa Fe Historic Foundation. |
| 1978 | May - November. New Mexico State University. Field supervisor of several archaeological surveys near Vado, Radium Springs, Jal, Cloudcroft, Placitas, Meadowvista, Jemez Springs, and Mount Taylor, New Mexico. |
| 1977 - 1978 | July 1977 – November 1978. New Mexico State University. Field supervisor of excavation of 12 archaeological sites for the Navajo Indian Irrigation Project, Block II, Farmington, New Mexico. (5 months in the field, 6 months write-up). |
| 1977 | April - July. New Mexico State University. Field supervisor of two archaeological surveys near Cuba and between Taos and Ojo Caliente, New Mexico. |
| 1977 | March - April. School of American Research. Field archaeologist on an archaeological survey of 13 sections of land on San Mateo Mesa near San Mateo, New Mexico for Houston Oil Company. |
| 1976 - 1977 | June 1976— January 1977. Bureau of Land Management. Field supervisor of five Navajo laborers and two archaeologists in the stabilization of two prehistoric Anasazi pueblo ceremonial centers and one historic homestead located in northwest New Mexico. Nine other archaeological sites were mapped in preparation for stabilization the following year. Prepared a stabilization workbook for each outlining the process, including a site report and analysis of the artifacts. Supervised mapping and drafted all maps. |
| 1976 | January - June. Museum of New Mexico, Laboratory of Anthropology. Co-crew leader of an archaeological survey of seven sections of land between Gallup and Grants, New Mexico. Conducted the analysis of ceramics and assisted in the final write-up reporting 105 archaeological sites. Field supervisor of two additional archaeological surveys near San Mateo, New Mexico. |
| 1975 | November - December. School of American Research. Field archaeologist of the excavation of a large archaic campsite near Abiqui, New Mexico. |
| 1975 | September - November. Grant. Research anthropologist studying Mexican-American immigration studies in border towns under the direction of Dr. Fernando Camara, Sub-director del Instituto Nacional, Mexico. The study focused on psychological, sociological, anthropological, and political implications. |

## ARCHAEOLOGICAL FIELD/LAB EXPERIENCE (CONT.)

1975
June - August. National Science Foundation Grant. Research Anthropologist. Assisted in writing a student-oriented grant proposal on the impact of tourism in Taos, New Mexico. The culture change study included multi-disciplinary input from economists, anthropologists, sociologists, psychologists, and art historians. Compiled bibliographic research on the ethnohistory of Taos through time. Assisted other members of the research team in gathering data on the economic structure of every business enterprise in Taos and administered psychological and sociological questionnaires among all cultural factions in the Taos area. Responsible for writing the introduction and ethnohistoric section of the final report.

1974 - 1975
March 1974, and July 1974 - May 1975. Southern Methodist University. Field and research archaeologist on the Los Esteros Project, Santa Rosa, New Mexico. Conducted the archaeological survey of the reservoir and research on tipi rings.

1974
June. Southern Methodist University. Research archaeologist. Conducted a literature search of Gregg and Rusk Counties, East Texas, in preparation for two large-scale archaeological projects.

1974
May - June. Southern Methodist University. Field archaeologist on the Tennessee Colony Reservoir Project, East Texas.

1974
January - March. Southern Methodist University. Field archaeologist on the Nambe Falls Reservoir Project on the Nambe Indian Reservation, north-central New Mexico. Conducted an excavation of a 50-room pueblo, pithouse, and field house. Project photographer. Conducted analysis of all flotation samples.

## PUBLICATIONS

1996-2017   Editor of 45 issues of *Legacy*, the magazine of the SC Institute of Archaeology and Anthropology, University of South Carolina, Columbia, South Carolina.

1992-1996   Editor of 10 issues of *PastWatch*, the magazine of the Archaeological Research Trust, SC Institute of Archaeology and Anthropology, University of South Carolina, Columbia, South Carolina.

1990   An Unusually Large Biface from the Phil Neeley Site, 38BM85, Bamberg County, South Carolina, Junior Author with Albert C. Goodyear, Kenneth E. Sassaman, Tommy Charles, and Chester B. DePratter. *South Carolina Antiquities*, Volume 22, Numbers 1 & 2, pp.1-16, Archaeological Society of South Carolina, Columbia, South Carolina.

1990   Tipi Rings and Nomadism in the High Plains. Unpublished Masters Thesis, University of Denver, Denver, Colorado.

PUBLICATIONS (CONT.)

1990    Management Summary of Archaeological Investigations of The Wedge Plantation (Area G), near McClellanville, Charleston County, South Carolina. Unpublished manuscript on file at the South Carolina Institute of Archaeology and Anthropology, University of South Carolina, Columbia, South Carolina.

1987    Management Summary of Archaeological Investigations of The Wedge Plantation (Area F), Near McClellanville, Charleston County, South Carolina. Unpublished manuscript on file at the South Carolina Institute of Archaeology and Anthropology, University of South Carolina, Columbia, South Carolina.

1986    Emergency Salvage Excavation of Impending Impact on General William Moultrie's Plantation Site on Windsor Hill (38CH230), Charleston County, South Carolina. Unpublished manuscript on file at the South Carolina Institute of Archaeology and Anthropology, University of South Carolina, Columbia, South Carolina.

1985    Archaeological Investigation of the Susitna River Valley, Interior of Alaska, Contributor. University of Alaska Museum, Fairbanks, Alaska.

1980    Excavation of the Bee House at Four Mile Historic Park: Phase I. Manuscript on file at the University of Denver, Denver, Colorado.

1980    Prehistory and History of the Ojo Amarillo: Archaeological Investigations of Block II. David T. Kirkpatrick, Editor, Volumes 1-V. New Mexico State University, *Report No. 276*, Las Cruces, New Mexico.

1979    Archaeological Investigations Coincident with Proposed Transmission Line Corridors at the Prewitt Power Plant. School of American Research, Santa Fe, New Mexico.

1978    An Archaeological Clearance Survey of Two and One-Half Sections of Land on La Jara Mesa, West of Mount Taylor, West-Central New Mexico. New Mexico State University, *Report No. 263*, Las Cruces, New Mexico.

1978    An Archaeological Clearance Survey of Eight Proposed Pipelines for the El Paso Natural Gas Company. New Mexico State University, Report No. 242, Las Cruces, New Mexico.

1978    An Archaeological Clearance Survey of Nine Proposed Drill Locations in the Jemez Mountains, New Mexico. New Mexico State University, *Report No. 240*, Las Cruces, New Mexico.

1978    An Archaeological Clearance Survey of a Proposed Underground Telephone Line West of Cloudcroft, New Mexico. New Mexico State University, *Report No. 238*, Las Cruces, New Mexico.

1978    An Archaeological Clearance Survey of Two Proposed City Parks Located in Placitas and Meadowvista, New Mexico. New Mexico State University, *Report No. 235*, Las Cruces, New Mexico.

1978    An Archaeological Clearance Survey of a Proposed Seismic Cable Line near Radium Springs, New Mexico. New Mexico State University, *Report No. 229*, Las Cruces, New Mexico.

PUBLICATIONS (CONT.)

1978 An Archaeological Clearance survey of a Proposed Underground Telephone Line near Vado, New Mexico. New Mexico State University, *Report No. 221*, Las Cruces, New Mexico.

1977 An Archaeological Clearance Investigation of Seventy-Nine Drill Locations Eight Miles South of Cuba, New Mexico. New Mexico State University, *Report No. 133*, Las Cruces, New Mexico.

1977 An Archaeological Clearance Survey of a Proposed Powerline from Taos to Ojo Caliente, New Mexico. New Mexico State University, *Report No. 125*, Las Cruces, New Mexico.

1976 A Cultural Resource Investigation of Two Proposed Drill Locations on Mount Taylor near San Mateo, New Mexico for Gulf Petroleum Corporation, Minerals Division. Laboratory of Anthropology, Museum of New Mexico, Santa Fe, New Mexico.

1976 A Cultural Resource Investigation of Two Proposed Drill Locations North of San Mateo, New Mexico for Continental Oil Company. Laboratory of Anthropology, Museum of New Mexico, Santa Fe, New Mexico.

1975 An Archaeological Resource Investigation of Several Tract Between Gallup and Grants, New Mexico. Paul Grigg, Senior Author. Laboratory of Anthropology, Museum of New Mexico, Santa Fe, New Mexico.

1974 An Evaluation of the Recorded History and Prehistory of Gregg and Rusk Counties, East Texas. Manuscript on file at the Archaeological Research Program, Southern Methodist University, Dallas, Texas.

REFERENCES

Dr. Albert C. Goodyear, III
Associate Director for Research
SC Institute of Archaeology and Anthropology
1321 Pendleton Street
Columbia, South Carolina 29208

Dr. Charles Cobb
Florida Museum of Natural History
Museum Road, Dickinson Hall
P. O. Box 117800
Gainesville, FL 32611-7800

Dr. Stephen Loring, Archaeologist
Smithsonian Institution
National Museum of Natural History
Anthropology Department
Washington, DC

Dr. David Anderson, Archaeologist
Department of Anthropology
Knoxville, TN

## Inside...

**DIRECTOR'S NOTE**

**RESEARCH**
Broad River Archaeological Field School—Season 2
South Carolina Archaeology Book
Excavations at White Pond
King Phillip IV Painting
Gerald Lee Thomas Artifact Collection Donation—Tribute of James L. Michie
Update of SCIAA Research Library Cataloging Project
Please Support Stanley South Student Research Endowment Fund
New Books—*Early Human Life on the Southeastern Coastal Plain* and *Prehistoric Chipped Stone Tools of South Carolina*

**SAVANNAH RIVER RESEARCH**
New Documentary Film—*Mart to Art: A Repurposed Life*

**MARITIME RESEARCH**
Welcome to Ryan Bradley
Charleston Field Office Moves to new home at Warren Lasch Conservation Center

**ARCHAEOLOGICAL RESEARCH TRUST**
Donors

**ANNOUNCEMENTS**
Nena Powell Rice Receives Lifetime Achievement Award from ASSC

---

Thank you for your generous support of the Archaeological Research Trust (ART) Endowment Fund and the printing of *Legacy*. Please send donations in the enclosed envelope to Nena Powell Rice USC/SCIAA, 1321 Pendleton Street, Columbia, SC 29208, indicating whether you want to continue receiving *Legacy* and include your email address. All contributions are appreciated. Please visit our website at: http://www.artsandsciences.sc.edu/sciaa to download past issues, and let the Editor know if you wish to receive *Legacy* by email.

Thank You! Nena Powell Rice, Editor, (803) 331-3431 Cell, (nrice@sc.edu).

---

# UNIVERSITY OF SOUTH CAROLINA
### College of Arts and Sciences

VOL. 22, NO. 1, JULY 2018

# Legacy
South Carolina Institute of Archaeology and Anthropology

## Nena Powell Rice Retires in June 2018

Nena Powell Rice officially retired June 29, 2018, and she has offered to continue to volunteer editing *Legacy*, serving as Secretary of the Archaeological Research Trust (ART) Board, assisting with the poster and programming for South Carolina Archaeology Month, continue the maintenance of the SCIAA Research Library, and assist with the 6th Annual Arkhaios Archaeology Film Festival (p. 3).

Nena began her 33+-year career at SCIAA on April 21, 1985. Even though she plans to stay in touch with colleagues at SCIAA and the archaeological community of South Carolina, she is looking forward to more travel, kayaking, birding, hiking, and camping on scientific adventures still to be explored! As she always says, "I would rather be in my tent without a battery charger."

Figure 1: Nena Powell Rice being congratulated by President Harris Pastides and First Lady Patricia Moore-Pastides at her 30-Year Pin Ceremony in April 2018. (Photo courtesy of USC Photographer)

*Legacy*
*Magazine of the South Carolina Institute of Archaeology and Anthropology*
*University of South Carolina*
*SC Institute of Archaeology and Antrhopology*
*1321 Pendleton Street*
*Columbia, SC 29208 USA*

# Nena Powell Rice Receives Lifetime Achievement Award

On February 17, 2018, the Archaeological Society of South Carolina, Inc. presented Nena Powell Rice with the Lifetime Achievement Award. The Award was presented in recognition of her support for South Carolina archaeology through the Society over the past 30 years. Nena was the Treasurer for over 26 years, worked to set up the Trust Fund, helped organize the annual conference program and banquet each year, was one of the founders of the Archaeology Field Day dating back to 1988, and related public outreach efforts in her position at the South Carolina Institute of Archaeology and Anthropology to the work of the Archaeological Society of South Carolina wherever possible. Her decades of commitment to the cultural and natural heritage of South Carolina was sustained, heartfelt, and greatly appreciated by her archaeological colleagues in South Carolina.

Nena Powell Rice with Lifetime Achievement Award. (Photo by Susan Davis)

> What is the connection tho Francis Scott Key.. Etta Key Sadler was your great great grandmother? Please explain the tree... and thanks for all the info,   Jim
>
>> On Oct 2, 2018, at 11:13 AM, RICE, NENA <RICEN@mailbox.sc.edu> wrote:
>>
>> Etta is our family connection to Francis Scott Key! Nena
>>
>> Sent from my iPhone

On 10/8/18, 2:12 PM, "RICE, NENA" <RICEN@mailbox.sc.edu> wrote:

Hi Jim,

All I know is that Etta Key Sadler (married to Clarence Milton Sadler), my portraits, was Dad and Norborne's grandmother (grandparents). Etta's mother was Virginia Coleman Key. I have her wedding ring (married in 1853-etched on the inside), that Etta also wore, and passed to me through Eloise Sadler Powell, our grandmother. So, Etta was my great grandmother. I do not know Virginia's husband's parents' name, but Virginia's husband must be related to Francis Scott Key, as I always heard he was our fifth great uncle. He was alive during the War of 1812, so he would have been of the right age to be her husband's relation.

I hope that is helpful. I used to have the whole tree going back, that Floyd, our grandfather married to Eloise (we called her Bamama), worked on back in the day. The papers I had, I gave to Scott to scan (years ago), but I never got the real papers back. I am a keeper of papers, and when I get back scans, they are filed. But I cannot find them anywhere now. Maybe Scott still has them??

Thanks, Jim
803-331-3431 Cell (Only Phone)
nrice@sc.edu

# SCOTT KEY POWELL
## "Scott"
## 1955–

From: sp sp80549@yahoo.com Subject: Re: The Powell Tradition
Date: November 3, 2019 at 11:37 AM
To: James Powell jamesandmarypowel@gmail.com

Jim, try this. I am using an old copy of MS Word and not easiest to copy and paste. Hopefully it does. I made a couple of small edits.
Scott Key Powell 5933 Lake View Dr.
Fort Collins, CO, 80526
970.342.0027
sp80549@yahoo.com

Dear Powell, et al,

There is a reason I've been hard to keep track of, which I will explain, or try to diagram shortly.
I am the middle child of John Key Powell and Ann Penniman. Older sister Nena 53' and younger brother Elliott 59'.

The summer of '55, Elvis first met Buddy Holly in his garage in Lubbock, TX. Just across town I dropped in on September 28.
At 1, we moved to Boston for Hancock training. In 59, moved to Columbia, SC.
Normal 'To Kill a Mockingbird' childhood, on a lake, with homemade boats and a lot of undeveloped woods, next to Ft Jackson. Fridays after school we would disappear until church, ugh, and then again until Bonanza came on. No shoes, no boundaries.

At 15, desegregation sent me to Pottstown, Pa for 4 years of Dead Poet's Society Episcopal prep school. The Hill School.
15?, '70 till '74. Just got drivers license at 15. Puberty.
And now, for the next 4 years, no cars, no girls, coat and tie to the bathroom, POTTSTOWN! The heroin capital and home of Mrs Smith's Pies and Kiwi shoe polish. On the SureKill River, 30 miles west of Philly.

No girls age 15-19!
Please never do this to another human being. Now at least they are co-ed. I think the Trump offspring attended The Hill.
(Couldn't get into Andover)
Summers I would work for my second father, Burwell Manning, who was a farmer and developer. Only time off was if it rained, so we usually clocked 100+ hours a week at $1.10 an hour my first summer. Driving tractors, hanging with old black men who take you raccoon hunting and carp fishing. Miss a day to go to the beach, fired. Late 2x? Fired. He taught me a great work ethic and a love for manual labor and birds of prey. And I spent many summers working for BO. He also has the best dove field in the state and I had a key!

Anyway, after The Hill, I enrolled in The USC, met a girl first week, stayed in bed for 5 weeks, dropped out and moved to the beach with Dad's blessing.
Not.
Anyway, 4 years at Pawley's Island, running the only bar, got me up to speed on women in the late '70s. In '78, I entered Embry Riddle Aeronautical University, in Prescott, AZ.

The main campus in Daytona was full and no flying for 2 years so I became part of the first class of the Prescott campus for ERAU.
First thing I did in Prescott was go to the courthouse where Tom Laughlin kicked some Posner butt in 'Billy Jack.' Still my favorite movie.

There were 320 of us new pilots. (14 girls). What is it with me, school and girls?
We had 25 new Grumman Tigers, and we all soloed in 2 weeks. You flew and rode observer one day and had Air Science classes every other day. Got my Private SEL cert on October 28. We could rent the new Tigers for $22/hour wet, with fuel, and go anywhere. The day after I got my ticket, I flew to Santa Fe to visit my Indiana Jones sister who was surveying Taos.

The Grand Canyon was 20 minutes away by air and on my first date with my future wife, Kelly, we rented a small Cessna 150, 2 feet of snow on the ground, flew to the canyon, beautiful blanketed in white, flew over it, (10,000 ft so if you lose only engine you can glide to North or South Rims), and then landed in GC City, took the free shuttle to the park, had lunch at the El Tovar Lodge, walked the rim . . . years later we would spend a hellish 4 days hiking the bottom of the canyon in July . . . and then back to the plane, with quick detour over San Francisco Peaks and Sunset crater, in Flagstaff, before my successful controlled crash back in Prescott. All landings are controlled crashes.

Growing pains . . .

320 of us took over a quiet weekend airport and increased operations from 2 to 3 K a year, to over 60,000 take offs and landings.
Over worked flight instructors.
There are never more than 6 planes flying in the pattern at any given time.
The day I soloed, there were 16 doing touch and goes, and that became the norm until we had two non fatal accidents, one mid air, and all of the instructors quit.

As the oldest and prettiest, I had been elected student body President.
For the next month I flew from Sky Harbor to Daytona, not in a Tiger, but on Eastern, to explain to Pres Hunt what everybody wanted.
ERAU then went international to find 35 new instructors and my second CFI was Rafael Baere, of the Israeli air force. He was a blast until the school closed down but before he left, I got 2.7 hours in my log book with him in an aerobatic Belanca Super Decathlon. Anything you can do in a plane, upside down, we did twice; parachute required. Better that Six Flags.
As ERAU tried to regroup the squadron, most of the 320 headed to Flight Safety or other schools to finish their ratings.

I had applied for and was hired to tend bar for two guys opening their first restaurant in Prescott. I continued there after leaving flight school and became manager. The place was super successful , no thanks to my management but The Two Squires knew the business.

One Thursday as I was getting the bar ready for dinner, the Secret Service came in and told us that Richard Nixon had a grandmother who lived in Prescott when he was a child, that he was there visiting, and that he and Bebe Rebozo wanted to dine with us Friday night.
This was about 5 years after his resignation.
Sure enough they came in. The SS watched me crack the seal on a new bottle and pour two Dewar's

and waters and watched Mark cut and cook his New York Strip. He still was more of a curiosity then and no one carried cell phones, so I don't have photo evidence. Sorry.

After a year and a half they sold 2 Squires and went their own ways. Mark Shugrue, one of the 2, and our chef, Richard Raymond, and I began a move to Sedona.
Mark had signed a 50 mile no compete clause and Sedona is about 60 miles away.
Richard and I were offered a percentage of the new restaurant and for the next year we converted an old church into 'Shugrues.'
I was flying back and forth from Prescott, to Sedona to Phoenix restaurant supply non stop.

We were breakfast, lunch and dinner, 7 days a week and took the town by storm. You had to have reservations for any meal.
22 hour days.
Kelly had come with me but worked at another restaurant and bar, Dude's Far Western. Owned by a retired Jane Russell. Yes, the. One night I went to pick up Kelly after we closed and she's sitting talking to Red Skelton. Another . . . Dick van Dyke.
Y'all'll get a kick out of this. One summer Jane and her husband, John Peoples, invited their staff plus one, to Lake POWELL for the weekend, camping and skiing. Couldn't turn that one down. Oh to have had a smart phone.

Sedona is the sight of 100s of movies. You've all seen Red Rock Crossing if you know who John Wayne is. So we had tons of actors in town and waiting in line without reservations to eat all the time. Mac Davis cussed me out one day because it was 2 hour wait for and egg and coffee. I offered him a seat at the bar and a free Bloody Mary?

Anyway, after the longest year of my life, and hardest job, I sold my interest and did a hellish hike at the bottom of the Canyon with some SC friends and then left Arizona. Mark became hugely successful. He opened 10 restaurants in Sedona and Lake Havasu. And we have remained friends.

Kelly Moore, the youngest of 8 siblings from Denver and I married at the Chapel on the DU campus in '82. She has an amazing family. I went from 2 siblings, 2 cousins, 1 uncle, no grandfathers, 2 distant grandmothers . . . to now having 75 immediate family at gatherings. And I love being adopted by this group even though Kelly and I are no longer married.
All of the Ex's are always at family events, of which there are many.

Meanwhile, back at the ranch, we married and moved to Columbia, where I entered the insurance business, not knowing why?
I did know that dad had left school but he had a new Cadillac every 2 years, 3 country clubs, an ok house and played a lot of golf and took a lot of vacations.

After a year in sales I was sent to Hancock's home office in Boston, as dad had done back in '57, to be groomed for management, which completed the oval of life. Akunamatata.

What a great, big city and year. 10 young couples and lots to do, see and eat.
So many restaurant stories. Durgin Park, Legal Seafood, Anthony's Pier 4, $3 lobsters from Quincy Market. Charlie's clam chowder.

Two of the 10 candidates returned home after a year. I, and Steven Hornsby from Newport News, VA. The rest were hired by other banks and financial institutions in Boston. (They should have made us sign a non-compete clause)
I completed Xerox's courses to all my CLU, ChFC degrees and courses and various other management schools.
Let Hancock train them, and we'll steal them.

So after Boston in '84, I became sales manager in Dad's old agency in Columbia.
He had just semi-retired. I had a great year, hired a young single mom who was an accountant, one 7 y/o son, who was smart, hungry and talented and had tons of clients with money problems.
I led and shadowed her for a year and she became the number one producer for the nation her first year. I believe she is still very successful.
I briefly went to work with dad's new financial services operation.

Kelly and I had our only child, a girl, Jessica Marie Powell, February 20, 1988. All that day I sat next to Henry McMaster in the waiting room, now SC governor, as his wife Peggy was in labor next door with his first son Henry.

December 1989, Kelly, Jess and I moved to Fort Collins, CO.
Although divorced a year later, we have remained good coparents and friends, even taking vacations and family holidays together.
Neither has remarried which isn't relevant.

I did not begin again in the insurance business. I was OK at it but never got motivated by the money. I was happier driving tractors for Burwell.
I became very involved with injured birds of prey and the local search and rescue team, while deciding what I wanted to be when I grew up.
Both a big part of my life, but for a different chapter in my book.

I was hired by the Colorado Div of Wildlife for a survey of Peregrine falcons the spring of '91. Slowly recovering from the effects of DDT, banned in '75, they were making a comeback and I like getting paid to find and watch birds.
Travel to different known sites and surveys of suspected nest sites, we would live in tents for 10 days, take side trips to hidden hot springs to rinse off every few days, and then return home to turn in notes and get ready to go back in 4 days.
Best summer of my life. Long hard locations, they love isolated, hard to reach cliffs between 7,000 and 11,000 feet ASL. I really got to know Colorado that year.

After that job, I was hired by a professor from Colorado State (CSU) to move to Everglades Park and help him survey and trap Snail Kites, a very rare raptor that had never been banded as an adult which was our goal.
After 3 months, living in the Park, piloting our airboat, so cool but unfortunately before cheap cameras, we lost funding and I returned to Columbia for a month to refuel and then get back to CO to see my now almost 4 y/o daughter.

I remained very involved with the Raptor Program and began managing apartments to provide a free place to live and an income, and freedom to go search for lost mushroom pickers or hunters at 2:00

am up in the mountains. Or drive to Steamboat Springs to retrieve a Golden Eagle that had been hit by a car.

Fast forward to the year 2005, the year before dad died.
I made a move . . . because of another chapter in the book . . . back to the Salt Life.
Those 4 years at Pawley's, after The Hill had infected me with Pluff Mud and I missed the water.
I began a home maintenance business, I was putting up Purple Martin bird houses along the Grand Strand and had just begun as a part time kayak guide for Black River Adventures.
Most importantly, dad and I had a very healing year together and got to spend time that repaired a lot of damage. All was good.

I should have knocked on wood.

Then Mom called and said "your father didn't eat his fried chicken wings last night. And I think something is wrong.
Every Monday for 60 years that was the menu.
I made the 135 mile trek from the beach to the midlands and met his doctor the next day. "Liver cancer"
"Oh, shoot, now years of chemo."
We'll be back tomorrow for test results.
"Key, it is in the artery. 0% survival rate. No chemo. You'll be dead in 5 weeks."

So I went to the beach, ended my 3 jobs, packed up my truck and headed back, for the umpteenth time, to Columbia SC. 5 weeks and 3 days later I learned about morphine and end of days.
 I stayed with Key's widow for about a year.

Back in Colorado, I missed my child and I could not stay in the place I had first left back in 1970 at 15.
So as I headed west on I-26 toward Asheville and points west . . . I got a call from fate.

A friend was looking for someone to come manage Harrietta, a 1,000 acre, 1700's, historic, rice plantation on the South Santee River in North Charleston county. Little town named McClellanville. Ground Zero for hurricane Hugo in '89.
A quaint little drinking village with a fishing problem.
Amazing property. Jane Fonda and Ted Turner have a plantation just across the river from us.
Harrietta was the sister property to Hampton Plantation farther upstream from us on the S. Santee.
Home to Archibald Rutledge.
It was an amazing 5 years and I'll always remember bathing in 100% deet.

Here is a link to my You Tube channel and a video of part of my life in the Lowcountry. (removed)
So now Jess is engaged and I miss her . . . so I find myself heading west on I-26 again.

Detour to Laramie, WY, for a long year and a half, I finally made it back to FOGO. (Fort Collins, CO)

The end is near . . .

Jessie is married to a good man. Steven Ericson. On Kelly's, my ex-wife's birthday, May 10, 2017, my child had a little girl, Nora Marie Ericson. So we only have to remember one birthday.

And I am constantly being chased away with a broom because I am semi-retired and live 4 miles away. They had to put me on a schedule.
Then, this year, on the day before her wedding anniversary in August she gives me a grandson. Declan Ericson.

I bought a boat this summer as I live 100 yds from Horsetooth reservoir.
I also have a couple of well-managed rental homes and room to play, and build tree houses and swings.
I am 64, and lucky to have made it this far I guess. I quit smoking for the last time years ago but it is never soon enough. I find out Monday about my roller coaster prostate numbers, I meet a cardiologist Friday for the first time, and my body has a long To Do list of rust and remorse.

I do remember that reunion weekend, so long ago at Litchfield. How strange it was to be in a room with so many Powells, and know none of them?
I've always wondered about my lineage to Francis Scott Key and Ancestry dot com? Would love any info should anyone have to time to dig that deep hole. I am good at writing jingles and love fire works . . . so maybe I am related.

If anyone ever gets west of the Mississippi, and north of the Rio Grande, you are welcome to give us a shout out.
Or as my only 1st cousin would say      "I can give you the names of several nice hotels in the area."


Quiz?
Take out our family tree and figure out who that cousin is.

**Editor's note: Your first cousin, Berkeley.**

Key and Penny with President Reagan

See other family photos at: youtube.com/watch?v=UsuRnGUcTHM
and at: youtube Harrietta Plantation, south santee river, south carolina

# ELLIOTT EDWARD POWELL
## "Elliott"
## 1959–

From: **Elliott Powell** eep@1stsun.com
Subject: THE POWELL BOOK
Date: June 5, 2018 at 4:39 PM
To: Mary Powell powell710@bellsouth.net
Cc: **dan powell** llewopnad@gmail.com, **ben and virginia powell** benjamin.c.powell@gmail.com, **jimbo** jbp3@bellsouth.net, **Glenn Powell** cgpowell2@gmail.com, **nena powell rice** RICEN@mailbox.sc.edu, **Ben P. Powell** bppno1@aol.com, **Jake Powell** wahoojj@gmail.com, **Berkeley Powell** dr.powell@mac.com, **Richard Powell III** richard.powell@jacksonthornton.com, **Ross Powell** rrpdmd@outlook.com

**...Sorry I didn't get this to you sooner Mary.** Thank you for putting this together. In looking through my parent's records< I found a tremendous amount of family heritage information, photos and letters. I'm not sure what might be relevant, but I thought I would share that with you, if you are interested?

your full name and nick name
**Elliott Edward Powell - "Elliott"**
your date of birth
**12/23/1959**
your addresses, both email and USPS (to send cc's of the book)
**Home: 7 Brampton Circle Columbia, SC 29206**
**Office: 2711 Middleburg Dr., Suite 311 Columbia, SC 29204**
eep@1stsun.com
your phone numbers, good but not required
**Cell- 803 622-1714**
the same for your male children and their male children (spouse's info)
Wife- **Elizabeth Heath Champion Powell – "Betsy"  12/12/1956**
Son- **John Key Powell, II**
    *Born in Columbia, SC  04/12/1992 (not married yet)
    *Player on two state high school football championship teams
    *Graduate of College of Charleston
    *Lived and worked for a year for the Kruger Family as a professional Hunter in South Africa
    *Currently Works for Southland Fishery and lives in Columbia, SC
    *jkeypowell@gmail.com Cell- 803 760-8590
Son- **Parker Champion Powell**
    *Born in Columbia, SC  06/23/1994 (not married yet)
    *Player on two high school state championship golf teams
    *Graduate of the University of South Carolina
    *Worked his way through school at Forest Lake Club -Golf Course (avid golfer)
    *parkerpowell@gmail.com Cell- 803 760-2774
Son- **Austin Elliott Powell**
    *Born in Columbia, SC  10/24/1997 (not married yet)
    *six-year starter on his high school tennis team played in three state championships (winning one)
    *Rising Junior at Wofford College –Spartanburg, SC
    * Junior Fall semester will be spent studying abroad in Europe (prestigious economics program)
    * austinpowell769@gmail.com Cell- 803 807-7165

your father and grandfather with their full names, birth and death dates
**Father- John Key Powell, CLU December 14, 1925 to May 24, 2006**
**Grandfather- Floyd Berkeley Powell Died 1952** (Refer to Berkeley Key Powell for actual)

a brief bio of you: who, what, where, and why and other interests

**Elliott Powell is a native of Columbia, SC** and with the exception of his college years at the College of Charleston and two years working in Arizona, he has lived in South Carolina's state capital all of his life. He was married July 14, 1990 to Elizabeth "Betsy" Champion Powell of Spartanburg, SC and has three sons. His father J. Key Powell. CLU (December 14, 1925 – May 24, 2006) introduced him to the concept of outsourcing human resources through a service formerly known as Employee Leasing (now Professional En ployment/ PEO), and Elliott then played a pioneering role in bringing the industry to South Carolina and the nation, starting in the late 1980s.

His family attends First Presbyterian Church (the largest Associate Reformed Presbyterian church in America), where he served as chair of the diaconate, and now serves as an elder. A Rotarian with perfect attendance since June of 1990, he has served multiple terms on the board of the Columbia Rotary Club (over 100 years old and largest civic club in SC) where he is also a three time Paul Harris Fellow. He helped establish the Gills Creek Watershed Association, and after serving for many years as the organization's board president, he was elected to emeritus board status.

From his father's example of giving back to his neighbors and the community, Mr. Powell has served two terms as president of the Lake Katharine Homeowners Association. He is a long-time member of the Salvation Army of the Midlands board of directors. He is a past chairman of the board of Crime Stoppers of the Midlands, and served two terms on the board of Sistercare, Inc. (a local battered women's shelter). He is a member of the University Associates… (longtime Gamecock and supporter of the University of South Carolina), where his father started the business scholarship program. He is also a member of Forest Lake Club in Columbia.

His company, First Sun Employee Leasing, Inc. dba First Sun HR & Benefit Solutions (established in 1986), was the first company to offer PEO services in South Carolina. His company working with (Alliance Employee Leasing Group) went on to be listed as #15 in Inc. 500: America's fastest-growing private companies (Oct 1992).

When taking time away from work, Elliott enjoys spending time at his North Litchfield Beach home (The KeyHole – in the family since 1974) on the coast of SC. He loves scuba diving, photography, boating, golf, art, coaching kid sports, and traveling the world. His relationship with The Lord, wife and three sons is where he finds his greatest joy!

FINAL INTERESTING FACT: Elliott and his wife Betsy share the same marriage anniversary as both sets of parents… Key & Penny Powell and Frank & Betty Champion all married on July 14.

Parker, John Key, Austin, Betsy & Elliott

and Ace Ventura

# Postlogue and Acknowledgments

When this effort was undertaken, I did not comprehend the immensity of time and effort it would require. The assumption that reaching out to living family members would evoke the same feelings of enthusiasm from them that I felt for compiling and writing this history of Powells was at times tested. But the journey has been well worth these efforts by all.

I have learned much about my ancestral background in terms of "real people," not just fleeting, foggy childhood memories of "old people telling me stuff." Children and the young spend little time considering their pasts because their pasts and futures are NOW ... THE MOMENT.

I wish I had listened more and more attentively and could remember better.

This journey has aptly exposed the frailties, imperfections and failures of people and their families. Throughout our history, early deaths from now preventable causes, wars and their drafts, economic cycles, estrangements, divorces, significant generational disagreements, family separations and challenges not noted have threatened to fracture the supporting structure of FAMILY. I have consciously omitted dwelling on these, instead emphasizing the strengths and successes of FAMILY. Granted, the past's togetherness—whether geographic, of necessity, or by choice—is lost to the technologies that have so changed society and our lives by offering instant and constant nonpersonal gratification and access to information and socialization.

If this effort offers and effects any renewal of FAMILY and its traditions for us, the living Powells, and for our future generations, then the effort has been successful.

A final thanks to all who have contributed their time and remembrances, both past and current. Catherine Mitchell, proof reader and copyeditor, reviewed the completed book and offered helpful suggestions.

There are not enough "THANK YOUS" to express my debt of gratitude for my publisher, Dr. Micki Cabaniss, and her contributions as my professional advisor. As she led me through the process, through months of work meetings, she has become a friend. Though there were "bumps, trials and tribulations," she steadfastly reassured me of the worthiness of the project, always reminding me of the end goal. Thank you, Micki.